Textual Revisions

Textual Revisions:
Reading Literature
and Film

edited by
Brian Baker

Chester Academic Press

First published 2009
by Chester Academic Press
University of Chester
Parkgate Road
Chester CH1 4BJ
(http://www.chester.ac.uk/academicpress/)

Printed and bound in the UK by the
LIS Print Unit
University of Chester
Cover designed by the
LIS Graphics Team
University of Chester

Editorial material
©Brian Baker, 2009
The individual contributions © the respective authors, 2009

All Rights Reserved
No part of this publication may be reproduced, stored in a retrieval system or transmitted in any form or by any means without the prior permission of the copyright owner, other than as permitted by current UK copyright legislation or under the terms and conditions of a recognised copyright licensing scheme

A catalogue record for this book is available from the British Library

ISBN 978-1-905929-75-7

CONTENTS

Introduction *Brian Baker*	1
Part 1: Adapting the Nineteenth-Century Novel	33
The Materialisation of the 'Austen World': Film Adaptations of Jane Austen's Novels *Deborah Wynne*	38
'The Amazing Cinematograph' : Cinema and Illusion in Francis Ford Coppola's *Bram Stoker's 'Dracula'* *Paul Foster*	58
Part 2: Adapting the Twentieth-Century Novel	85
Modernist Writing, the Cinematic Image and Time *Deniz Baker*	88
From Image to Frame: the Filming of *The French Lieutenant's Woman* *William Stephenson*	116
Part 3: Adapting Drama	141
'The rain it raineth in every frame': a Defence of Trevor Nunn's *Twelfth Night* (1996) *Graham Atkin*	145
The Film of Harold Pinter's *The Caretaker* *Ashley Chantler*	169

Textual Revisions

Part 4: Adaptation and Genre	197
'Can You See?': Spielberg's Screen Adaptation of Philip K. Dick's 'The Minority Report' *Brian Baker*	203
'Refracted Light': Peter Jackson's *The Lord of the Rings* *Chris Walsh*	234
Contributors	259

INTRODUCTION

Brian Baker

The history of the connection between writing and what we might call the visual arts is a long one. Before the age of the printing press, the book itself assumed the status of an artistic artefact, reproduced by hand; and of course, in the illuminations of manuscripts produced in the scriptoria of monasteries, the interconnection of writing and the visual is evident. Closer to our own time, the novel, for a long time, was a literary form that was illustrated: we can think of the famous literary productions of Charles Dickens and Hablot Knight Browne as 'Boz' (writer) and 'Phiz' (illustrator) in the nineteenth century, for instance. It is only in the last one hundred years or so that book illustration has been relegated to the realm of children's literature. It is probably no coincidence that, in Anglophone culture, the phenomenon of the 'graphic novel' (no matter the sophistication of particular texts) is also popularly identified with children's comic books.

There is also a long history of the literary use of visual elements, from the use of 'white space' on the page in poetry, to the typographic effects, squiggles and black printed pages of Laurence Sterne's *The Life and Opinions of Tristram Shandy* (1759); from the crude pen drawings of Kurt Vonnegut's *Breakfast of Champions* (1973), to the use of illustrations and photography in W.G. Sebald's *Austerlitz* (2001). The concept of the literary text as itself a visual object has sometimes been suppressed, but not for long; and the rise of cinema, the interaction of writers with film, and the subject of this collection of essays, the screen adaptation of literary texts, brings this connection to the fore.

Textual Revisions

Part One: Key issues

No matter how much academic critics would like to sideline the issue – and much effort has been expended doing so – there is little point denying that in the popular discourses about film, in reviews and in the everyday round of people talking to each other about the movies, the issue of *faithfulness* is the main evaluative criteria by which a screen adaptation is judged to be successful. This is inevitable and, in a sense, only right and proper. For a film production company to invest millions of dollars into a movie, some of the risk involved is defrayed if the idea behind the film is 'pre-sold' (has recognisable prior existence in popular culture, such as in the case of a 'big screen' version of a TV series, a 'remake', or a film sequel), or if the film is an adaptation of a well-known novel (or play, or comic book). If the *economic* cost is defrayed, however, the *critical* cost is more likely to remain a gamble, for the screen adaptation is always judged *twice*: once as a film in its own right, and once against the film-watcher's own experience of the novel or play that has been adapted. All of us must have had the experience of watching a screen adaptation and, even if liking the film, leaving the cinema feeling disappointed because the rendering of the literary text has not matched up to our experience of the source text. 'It wasn't very faithful,' is then the complaint. Of course, this is not at all fair to the adapted text. It is a form of double jeopardy: the film is 'tried' twice. However, if film production companies want audiences to recognise the film's title and draw us through the cinema's doors, it is hardly *un*fair of us to presume to bring our knowledge of that prior text to bear in an evaluation of the 'success' (or otherwise) of the film.

Introduction

It does mean, however, that the evaluation of the screen adaptation, in a popular sense, is doubly subjectivised, and therefore probably doubly unreliable. While I think that faithfulness (or 'fidelity' in the language of screen adaptation studies) is the *first* criterion by which we evaluate an adaptation, it must not be the only or final one. In fact, the very idea of faithfulness can be questioned and broken down. What is it, for instance, are we asking the screen adaptation to be faithful *to*?

There are a number of answers to this question. The primary answer is probably the 'story' or narrative. Inevitably, in a two-hour film, the kind of story information that can be presented is far less than in a 300-page novel. (Kenneth Branagh's full-text film version of *Hamlet* (1996) ran for over four hours; a 'full text' adaptation of a nineteenth-century novel might well run into double figures in terms of running time.) There must, therefore, be a process of *compression* and *selection* with regard to narrative in adaptations of novels. Often, this means that sub-plots are lost; or characters are discarded, or their narrative functions elided (two friends of the main character in a novel, for instance, become one in the film version). If major changes to the main narrative trajectory (what in Hollywood would be called 'story arc') are made, the screen adaptation runs a severe risk of being derided for lack of faithfulness. This is particularly so for the *endings* of stories, what we would call narrative resolutions. Sometimes, however, the compression effect might help to simplify, clarify and energise a novel's cluttered construction. I feel that this is certainly true of Curtis Hanson's 1997 adaptation of James Ellroy's crime novel *LA Confidential*, for instance. Alternatively, the film narrative might be 'too faithful' and, in attempting to render the complexities of novelistic prose and novelistic narrative on screen, seem confused or lacking clear direction.

Narrative and character are, I believe, the two most crucial elements bearing upon fidelity; but we might also note the use of dialogue (taken from the novel or created by the screenwriter); the location, setting or period in which the narrative takes place; or, most difficult of all to define, the idea of faithfulness to the 'spirit' or 'essence' of a text. The idea of the text's 'spirit' is usually a kind of cumulative effect produced upon the reader of a novel, often then read back onto authorial intention; it is an overall impression or assessment of what the text is 'about', what it 'says'. This is the least translatable, or definable, of any evaluative criteria of adaptation as a process or as a screen text; but it is surely the experience of every viewer of an adaptation (who has read the source text) as to whether the screen version 'feels right'.

Again, the subjectivism inherent in this approach is deeply troublesome, if not entirely disabling, in thinking of fidelity issues as a critical tool for writing on adaptations, and it is little wonder therefore that academic writers in this field have determined to set it aside. While I agree with this necessity, I also think it is right to acknowledge the power this discourse holds over our experience of the adapted film. Sarah Cardwell, for instance (see below), would have the critic bracket off the source text entirely, and treat adaptations as a film genre or mode, rather than in comparison with a literary 'original'. While I sympathise with this rhetorical gesture, I do not think it is entirely helpful or necessary, and most importantly, I do not think it is true to the experience of watching this particular kind of film. For certain, some viewers would treat adaptations as a kind of genre, and perhaps be drawn to watch other televisual adaptations of Jane Austen, for instance, having seen the famous 1995 BBC dramatization of *Pride and*

Introduction

Prejudice; and clearly, any screen adaptation is available to be viewed by someone with no prior knowledge of the literary text. It is also important to note that screen adaptations do not work in a cultural vacuum; the film or television version dramatises the literary text in intertextual relation to other, prior adaptations of the same or similar texts.

Most theorists of adaptation do not go so far as Cardwell. In fact, the attempts of Geoffrey Wagner or J. Dudley Andrew to formalise the different ways in which the literary text can be adapted to the screen renders into a more objective, critical and academic discourse the kinds of response we experience when watching an adapted film in the cinema or on television. (For more on these theorists, see below.) Some of the initial questions we might ask about the process of adaptation might be as follows:

1. Is the literary text compressed or expanded on screen?
2. How does the screen version treat character, narrative, or setting?
3. What kind of visual strategies are used to convey subtext, symbol, theme, metaphor or other literary/linguistic figures?
4. What kind of visual strategies are used to create the 'world' of the film, and how does this compare to novelistic 'description'?
5. Do different modes/genres/forms of source text (drama or novel; science fiction, romance or crime story) require different modes of adaptation?
6. How does the film treat time and space, in comparison with the source text?
7. Does the screen adaptation 'read' the source text in a particular way, attempting to reveal something about it or argue something about it? Does it go beyond a

'neutral' dramatisation? Is 'neutrality' possible? Is 'fidelity' possible?

All of these questions have been approached by theorists and critics of adaptation, and some of these questions inform the writing of the essays that are collected in this volume. However, what most critics avoid is the biggest pitfall in terms of the discourse of fidelity: the implicit assumption that the literary 'original' is *better* than the screen adaptation because it is *literature*, and because it precedes the film (it is *original*). From this starting point, with its implicit (or explicit) value judgements about novel or play and film, little work of critical value can be done.

A correlative of the issues of *what* and *how* a literary text is adapted is the question of authorship: *whose text* is this? It is a difficult question to answer, not least because of the collaborative/industrial manner of most film production, but also because the question of authorship is itself contested within the field of film studies. Since the rise of the theory of the *auteur* (see Brian Baker's essay), the film *director* has been presumed to be the locus of film meaning, inscribing his signature on the material. (The masculine pronoun 'his' is entirely deliberate: a major problem with *auteurism* is the comparative historical paucity of female directors, of women *auteurs*. In the history of Hollywood cinema, the privileging of the director is often ahistorical and works to downplay the importance of women screenwriters, who were fundamental to the Hollywood studio system in the 1930s and 1940s.) How can one person, one *man*, be the creator of meaning in a film? Even if one sees the director as the central organising force, particularly for the narrative and visual texture of a film (and this was not always so: the *producer* was key in the 1930s and 1940s), the input of the screenwriter(s), director of photography, set designer,

Introduction

composer of the musical score, and especially the actors, all effect the way in which a film makes meaning.

This is also not to assume that authorship is unproblematic in literary studies. W. K. Wimsatt and Monroe Beardsley's 'The Intentional Fallacy', first published in 1946, is a landmark theoretical work in its determination to focus upon the creative (literary) text itself, rather than presuming what the author of that text 'intended'.[1] Wimsatt and Beardsley argued that the critic must concern herself or himself with the text itself, the 'internal evidence' present in the literary work, rather than having recourse to 'external' information to analyse the poem (biographical details, letters, context and so forth). The disconnection between historical 'author' and the literary work or text was further cemented in Roland Barthes' famous essay 'The Death of the Author', which argued that a text is a sign-system, 'a multi-dimensional space in which are married and contested several writings, none of which is original: the text is a fabric of quotations, resulting from a thousand sources of culture.'[2] Barthes' famous dictum, which closes the essay, 'the birth of the reader must be requited by the death of the Author', is a call to decentre the 'author' from the production of textual meaning and thereby undo presumptions of the author's priority and literal 'authority', as well as suggesting that the text itself is not an 'original' artwork fabricated from the author's consciousness, but a product of language and

---

[1] W. K. Wimsatt and Monroe C. Beardsley, 'The Intentional Fallacy', in *20th Century Literary Criticism: A Reader*, ed. by David Lodge (London: Longman, 1972), pp. 334-344.

[2] Roland Barthes, 'The Death of the Author', in *The Rustle of Language*, trans. by Richard Howard (Oxford: Basil Blackwell, 1986), pp. 49-55 (p. 53).

(thereby) of other texts.³ The French post-structuralist theorist, philosopher and historian Michel Foucault proposes that the author is a 'function' of discourse:

> ... we could say that in a civilization like our own there are a certain number of discourses that are endowed with the "author function", while others are deprived of it. A private letter may well have a signer – it does not have an author; a contract may well have a guarantor – it does not have an author. An anonymous text posted on a wall probably has a letter – but not an author. The author function is therefore characteristic of the mode of existence, circulation, and functioning of certain discourses within a society.⁴

The 'author function' is 'the regulator of the fictive, a role quite characteristic of our era of industrial and bourgeois society'.⁵ The author is then bound up with the social, economic and cultural organisation of society since (Foucault argues) the eighteenth century, with individualism, with property rights, with copyright, and with systems of power and control that are challenged by 'the fictive'. To dethrone the 'author', and assert the primacy of 'writing', is therefore not only a critical gesture, it is a political one.

Even if we agree with Wimsatt and Monroe, Barthes and Foucault in asserting that the concept of the 'author' is really part of the apparatus of the text itself, there is no access to authorial 'intention', and the sovereignty of the

---

³ Barthes, 'The Death of the Author ', pp. 49-55 (p. 55).

⁴ Michel Foucault, 'What is an Author?', in *The Foucault Reader*, ed. by Paul Rabinow (London: Penguin, 1991), pp. 101-120 (pp. 107-8).

⁵ Foucault, pp. 101-120 (p. 119).

Introduction

author over the meanings produced by the text has been set to one side (allowing us to read the text 'against the grain'), that is not to say that there are no 'authors' (i.e. a person or persons writing a novel, a poem or a play) or, in the case of screen adaptation, that the process of adaptation is a kind of mechanical or institutional system devoid of human agency. However, Giddings, Selby and Wensley (in their introduction to the collection *Screening the Novel*) attempt to rethink the role of the author in the literary field as well as the cinematic:

> Philip Simpson provides a necessary corrective to the romantic ideal of the novelist in sole control of his creative and aesthetic endeavours while the film and television-maker is engaged in factory-line, product-driven labour. As he points out, early novelists were paid for each page produced, and Dickens's episodic serials meant strict editing for length, and the shape determined externally.[6]

The literary author is always already inscribed into systems of production and consumption that parallel those found, in different forms perhaps, in the cinema. Screenwriters such as Andrew Davies in British film and TV are themselves recognisable 'authors' of a particular mode of adaptation, but how does one ascribe authorial priority in Davies's adaptation of an Austen novel? As Whelehan and Cartmell write, 'The film of the novel

---

[6] Robert Giddings, Keith Selby and Chris Wensley, 'The Literature/Screen Debate: An Overview', in *Screening the Novel: The Theory and Practice of Literary Dramatization*, ed. by Robert Giddings, Keith Selby and Chris Wensley (Basingstoke: Macmillan, 1990), pp. 1-27 (p. 3).

necessarily displaces the author; she is merely one authority among many *auteurs*'; meaning is itself produced by many viewers/readers/consumers.[7]

What has become clear is that a technique employed by film-makers in the last twenty years or so is to use the authorial name, particularly of 'classic' texts, as an authenticating gesture or 'signature' on the film text. (Foucault's 'author function' is a particularly appropriate critical tool here.) Thus, Francis Coppola's film of *Dracula* (discussed by Paul Foster in this collection) is titled *Bram Stoker's Dracula*; similarly, there have been films of *William Shakespeare's Romeo + Juliet* (directed by Baz Luhrmann, 1996), and *Mary Shelley's Frankenstein* (directed by Kenneth Branagh, 1994), among others. This use of the authorial 'signature', Erica Sheen has argued, is problematic: 'The adaptation – particularly the kind of adaptation that flaunts the signature of its own authorial origins – pays lip service to the intellectual, but subsumes it into the general circulation of mass communication'.[8] This bears upon the issue of fidelity, of course; the title of *Bram Stoker's Dracula* seems to suggest that this is the true, 'authentic' version (deeply ironic in this case, as Foster's essay outlines, and also in the case of Luhrmann's exuberant, 'pop' *Romeo + Juliet*). For Coppola's film, it also suggests a 'return to the novel' and a distancing from the productive history of Dracula films, from Browning's Universal *Dracula* (1932) to

---

[7] Imelda Whelehan and Deborah Cartmell, 'Introduction - Pulping Fictions: Consuming Culture across the Literature/Media Divide', in *Pulping Fictions*, ed. by Deborah Cartmell, I.Q. Hunter, Heidi Kaye and Imelda Whelehan (London: Pluto, 1996), pp. 1-10 (p. 3-4).

[8] Erica Sheen, 'Introduction', in *The Classic Novel: From Page to Screen*, ed. by Robert Giddings and Erica Sheen (Manchester: Manchester University Press, 2000), pp. 1-13 (p. 7).

Introduction

the series of films made by Hammer Studios in Britain in the 1960s – although, of course, Coppola's adaptation is always refracted through this generic history even as it marks its difference from it. Screen adaptation is *never* a simple translation from one text to another; Barthes' suggestion that the text is a 'fabric of quotations' pertains to film as much as literary texts. Particularly in genre film, adaptation always occurs through the lens of other, prior films.

The final issue I would like to consider before moving on to the *critical* history of screen adaptations is the importance of narrative and narration in literature and film. Erica Sheen quotes Suzanne Speidel in asserting the Hollywood belief in the translatability of narrative or story from medium to medium, from literary text to film: 'In Suzanne Speidel's words, "the central assumption behind Hollywood screenplay strategy is the independence of any story from its chosen mode of discourse"'.[9] They are not alone. Academic critics and theorists of screen adaptation, such as Seymour Chatman, Brian McFarlane and Robert Stam (see below) all focus upon narrative as a means by which the literary and filmic texts can be compared. These critics draw upon the literary field of 'narratology', a development of structuralism and formalism in literary studies (Chatman and Stam draw upon the work of Gerard Genette; MacFarlane on that of Barthes).[10] Narratological approaches focus on how narrative is structured, on how the underlying chronology of events is 'told' to us, in what order and by what means (what kind of narrator, for

---

[9] Sheen, pp. 1-13 (p. 9).

[10] See Gerard Genette, *Narrative Discourse: An Essay on Method*, trans. by Jane E. Lewin (Ithaca, NY: Cornell University Press, 1980); Roland Barthes, *S/Z*, trans. by Richard Miller (London: Cape, 1975).

instance); and also might consider character actions, or setting as narrative 'functions' through which a reader makes meaning of a text. Clearly, there are marked formal differences between literary and film narrative (a film *shows* a place where a novel *describes* a scene), but this mode of critical analysis attempts to draw out the specific characteristics of filmic narrative and novelistic narrative through comparative analysis, rather than simply asserting a fundamental similarity.

Other considerations with regard to narrative are narration and point of view. The following questions might be asked of how narration works in film:

1. How does the film present or express the narrative event of the novel?
2. Are there some things which cannot be expressed in a similar way (directly *transferred*), therefore have to be *adapted*?
3. Is the film's story 'told' or 'presented'?
4. Does the film use 'first-person narration'? Is this represented through subjective camera/point-of-view, or oral narration or voice-over?
5. Does the film use 'omniscient' narration? Is this presented through 'showing' rather than 'telling'? What is the role of *mise-en-scène*? What is the role of editing? What role does actor performance/style/costume play? Is the camera outside or inside the 'world' of the film? Is there a narrator, and is this narrator inside or outside the 'world' of the text?
6. Is there 'restricted narration'? Does the film limit our knowledge of events to the point of view of one character (or more)? Do the characters reflect upon the narrative 'action'?

Introduction

Is it possible, for instance, in the screen adaptation of an autobiography, for the film to narrate in the 'first person'? Even if the film uses voice-over, the narrative world almost always contains the subject of the autobiography *as a character* within the diegesis or 'story-world'; we do not 'see though their eyes' (literally or visually) for the entirety of the film. (The adaptation of the Raymond Chandler crime story *Lady in the Lake* (1947) attempted to do just that, with other characters talking directly to camera. This not very successful experiment indicates why this technique is used sparingly in film narrative.) Often, of course, it is a matter of a film attempting to find similar, or analogous, means to convey narrative information to the viewer, rather than directly transferring a textual element from a novel or a play. This is particularly the case, as Deniz Baker and William Stephenson explore, in adaptations of more formally experimental novels. Putting it most crudely, perhaps it is the difference between a *linguistic* and a primarily *visual* medium that must be negotiated in any screen adaptation; and ultimately, that is what criticism in this field must seek to grapple with.

Part Two: A critical history

The history of critical writing about the relationship between film and literature really goes back to the mid-twentieth century. The Russian film-maker and film critic Sergei Eisenstein (director, most famously, of *The Battleship Potemkin*) wrote about the connection between the novels of Charles Dickens and the filmic narrative of D. W. Griffith in his book *Film Form* (1949).[11] The first major book

---

[11] Sergei Eisenstein, *Film Form: Essays in Film Theory*, trans. by Jay Leyda (New York: Harcourt, 1949). For more detail on this, please see the short introduction to the section 'Adapting Nineteenth Century Fiction'.

on screen adaptations was, however, George Bluestone's *Novels into Film*.[12] Surprisingly, the main thrust of Bluestone's argument was that the determining specificities of each medium – literature and film – meant that the two cannot really be compared. Indeed, he states: 'Just as the cinema exhibits a stubborn antipathy to novels, the novel here emerges as a medium antithetical to film.'[13] In adaptation, he argues, 'changes are inevitable the moment one abandons the linguistic for the visual medium.'[14] He suggests that although the two media involve 'ways of seeing', literature's reliance upon a 'mental' image and film's use of a 'visual' image construct a fundamental incompatibility between them. However, it is important to stress that literary texts were, and continue to be, a primary source for narrative material in Hollywood and other national cinemas, as Bluestone himself acknowledges: 'the moment the film went from the animation of stills to telling a story, it was inevitable that fiction would become the ore to be minted by story departments.'[15] Someone, somewhere (in Hollywood), continues to believe that there *is* a fundamental compatibility.

But in what, then, could that compatibility or 'translatability' exist? For an important strand of film/literature criticism and theory, it is in the concept of

---

[12] George Bluestone, *Novels into Film* (Berkeley: University of California Press, 1957).

[13] Bluestone, p. 23.

[14] Bluestone, p. 4.

[15] Bluestone, p. 2.

Introduction

narrative itself. Bluestone, when he speaks of 'story departments', implicitly acknowledges this. Seymour Chatman, in his article 'What Novels Can Do That Films Can't (and Vice Versa)' writes after the development of what came to be known as 'narratology' in the study of literary texts, a development of structuralism, Russian formalism and semiotics (the study of sign-systems) which came to focus upon the means by which narratives are constructed in texts, from the organisation of time to an analysis of novelistic description. The most important revelation of narratology, Chatman suggests, is the 'double time structuring' of all texts: the textual manner in which story events are narrated (the *récit*, in Gerard Genette's terms) and the underlying chronology that we, as readers, must decode from the narration (the *histoire*).[16] While acknowledging that 'close study of film and novel versions of the same narrative reveal with great clarity the peculiar powers of the two media', Chatman still suggests that 'any narrative can be actualised by any medium which can communicate the two time orders. Narratologists immediately observed an important consequence of this property of narrative texts, namely, the translatability of a given narrative from one medium to another'.[17] This identification of a narrative 'deep structure' means that, while his article spends much time in close analysis of the *differences* between the way film and literary texts construct narrative, Chatman's work relies upon an assumption of fundamental compatibility resting on a shared reliance on

---

[16] Seymour Chatman, 'What Novels Can Do That Films Can't (and Vice Versa)', *Critical Inquiry*, 8 (1980). Reprinted in *Film Theory and Criticism: Introductory Readings*, ed. by Leo Braudy and Marshall Cohen, 5th edn (New York: Oxford University Press, 1999), pp. 435-451 (p. 435).

[17] Chatman, pp. 435-451 (p. 436).

narrative. This emphasis on narrative is also fundamental to the method of Brian McFarlane in *Novel to Film* (1996). McFarlane sidelines many of the common issues of 'the discourse of adaptations' (such as the fidelity issue, or authorship) in favour a structuralist approach much indebted to the work of Roland Barthes. McFarlane argues that the 'cardinal functions' or 'kernels' of literary narrative can be transferred to the film form, and his book then proceeds to analyse five adaptations in great detail to work through this theoretical model.[18]

Sarah Cardwell, in her own book on television adaptations of the classic novel, *Adaptations Revisited* (2002), praises McFarlane's text as offering 'one of the most advanced and coherent examples of comparative theory', although she ultimately rejects the comparative model entirely and asks for adaptations to be considered more as a filmic or televisual mode or genre *in themselves*.[19] Cardwell's praise is partly produced by the quality of McFarlane's work, and his willingness to bring in intertextual and contextual material to read the adapted text, but one feels that she is most sympathetic towards the doubts 'McFarlane himself has expressed ... concerning the flexibility and scope of the approach he propounds.'[20] She places McFarlane in a critical tradition which also includes J. Dudley Andrew, who also employs the critical language

---

[18] Brian McFarlane, *Novel to Film: An Introduction to the Theory of Adaptation* (Oxford; Oxford University Press, 1996), pp. 13-15.

[19] Sarah Cardwell, *Adaptations Revisited: Television and the Classic Novel* (Manchester: Manchester University Press, 2002), p. 67. For a detailed overview of a wide range of texts that analyse adaptation, see the entirety of Part I of Cardwell's text.

[20] Cardwell, p. 64.

Introduction

of poststructuralism in his writing on adaptation. Both Andrew, and Geoffrey Wagner in *The Novel and the Cinema* (1979), offer short taxonomies of modes of screen adaptation. Wagner's modes are *transposition, commentary,* and *analogy*. The first, *transposition*, 'has been the dominant and most pervasive method used by Hollywood throughout its history. In the *transposition* mode, 'a novel is directly given on the screen, with the minimum of apparent interference.'[21] It is also, according to Wagner, the least satisfactory of adaptive modes. The second category, *commentary*, 'is where an original is taken and either purposely or inadvertently altered in some respect. It could also be called a re-emphasis or re-structure.'[22] The final mode, *analogy*, 'must represent a fairly considerable departure for the sake of making *another* work of art .... an analogy ... cannot be a violation of a literary original since the director has not attempted (or has only minimally attempted) to reproduce the original.'[23]

Dudley Andrew's modes or categories also take a three-part scheme. In the first, *borrowing*, 'the artist employs, more or less extensively, the material, idea, or form of an earlier, generally successful text'; in the second, *intersecting*, the original text is 'intentionally left unassimilated in adaptation':

> ... all such works fear or refuse to adapt. Instead they present the otherness and distinctiveness of the original text, initiating a

---

[21] Geoffrey Wagner, *The Novel and the Cinema* (Rutherford: Fairleigh Dickinson University Press, 1979), p. 222.

[22] Wagner, p. 223.

[23] Wagner, p. 227.

dialectical interplay between the aesthetic forms of one period with the cinematic forms of our own period.[24]

The *intersecting* adaptation is a 'refraction of the original' and 'insists that the analyst attend to the *specificity* of the original within the *specificity* of the cinema.'[25] The final category, *fidelity or transformation*, consists of 'matching equivalents' in different media; the 'imagery functions equivalently in films and novels.'[26] This taxonomy is certainly of use in conceptualising modes of screen adaptation, but it is Andrew's more general appreciation of the form which is most illuminating. He suggests that, because all human experience of the world is filtered through the lenses of ideology, there is no direct access to reality, only to 'some prior whole lodged unquestioned in the personal or public system of experience.' Similarly, all representation corresponds to a pre-existing 'prior whole': 'every representational film *adapts* a prior conception'.[27] Adaptation, then, is not only a particular process or filmic mode; it reveals the way all representation works. All representational art *is* adaptation.

Morris Beja, in *Film and Literature: An Introduction* (1979), suggests not that the process of adaptation is reliant upon something that is somehow outside of both texts (Andrews's 'prior whole'), but that the reception of the

---

[24] Dudley Andrew, 'Adaptation', in *Film Theory and Criticism: Introductory Readings*, ed. by Leo Braudy and Marshall Cohen, 5th edn (New York: Oxford University Press, 1999), pp. 452-460 (p. 454).

[25] Andrew, pp. 452-460 (p. 455).

[26] Andrew, pp. 452-460 (p. 456; p. 457).

[27] Andrew, pp. 452-460 (p. 453).

Introduction

adapted text is 'affected not only by whether we know the original but also by our perception and evaluation of it'.[28] The frames of interpretation of the adapted text therefore include cultural and other vectors which surround its 'evaluation', unconsciously or consciously. This leads Beja to make the judgement that a film adapted from a mediocre book is often better than one made from a 'masterpiece'. He goes on to suggest that:

> … what a film takes from a book matters; but so does what it brings to a book. When it brings dedication and talent (or, if we are truly fortunate, genius), the result can be what André Bazin calls "the novel so to speak multiplied by the cinema". The resulting film is then not a betrayal and not a copy, not an illustration and not a departure. It is a work of art that relates to the book from which it derives yet is also independent, an artistic achievement that is in some mysterious way the "same" as the book but also something other: perhaps something less but perhaps something more as well.[29]

The insistence that the adapted text is not a 'copy' but an independent artwork that deserves consideration on its own merits leads logically to Sarah Cardwell's stance that the comparative approach is flawed, and the 'source' text should be bracketed off entirely in an analysis of adaptation (as a film mode or genre). The detailed consideration of the film text in terms of the theoretical

---

[28] Morris Beja, *Film and Literature: An Introduction* (London: Longman, 1979), p. 87.

[29] Beja, p. 88.

discourses of film studies (rather than treating the screen adaptation as a form of visual literature) is something that Cardwell also advocates, while lamenting the comparative paucity of such approaches hitherto. Perhaps it is the development of the academic study of film adaptation within departments of English, rather than Film Studies, which has perpetuated this seeming lack.

From the mid-1990s to the early 2000s, a number of edited collections of essays considering screen adaptations were published, each of which generally contained insightful introductions sketching an overview of the subject (*Screening the Novel*'s introduction refers exactly to that) and adding key ideas to the debate, while the essays contained therein expanded the type of texts considered and also testified to a growing plurality of critical approaches.[30] *Screening the Novel*, the earliest collection in this tranche, makes an interesting distinction in the very first footnote of the introduction, which bears upon the use of 'dramatization' in the subtitle of the text. The authors draw upon the distinction made at the time in BBC television programmes based on literary texts:

---

[30] See Robert Giddings, Keith Selby and Chris Wensley, *Screening the Novel: The Theory and Practice of Literary Dramatization* (Basingstoke: Macmillan, 1990); *Cinema and Fiction: New Modes of Adapting, 1950-1990*, ed. by John Orr and Colin Nicholson (Edinburgh: Edinburgh University Press, 1992); *Adaptations: From Text to Screen, Screen to Text*, ed. by Deborah Cartmell and Imelda Whelehan (London: Routledge, 1999); *Classics in Film and Fiction*, ed. by Deborah Cartmell, I. Q. Hunter, Heidi Kaye and Imelda Whelehan (London: Pluto, 2000); *Film and Literature: Points of Intersection*, ed. by Phoebe Davison (Lampeter : Edwin Mellen Press, 1997); *Film/Literature/Heritage: A 'Sight and Sound Reader'*, ed. by Ginette Vincendeau (London: BFI, 2001); *Writing and Cinema*, ed. by Jonathan Bignell (Harlow: Pearson Longman, 1999).

Introduction

> An "adaptation" is the preparation of a television version of a work which is already in dramatic form, for example a stage play. A "dramatization" is the preparation of a television drama from a work which was not previously in dramatic form, for example a prose narrative.[31]

This terminology is not followed up explicitly by any of the later writers on adaptation, but attests to the writers' attempt to engage with critical and productive discourses outside the range of literature specialists. The collections edited in whole or in part by Cartmell and Whelehan shift the focus again, away from literary study towards concepts derived from cultural studies. The editors therefore are interested in the relationship between the adaptive process of a literary 'classic' and the idea of 'cultural capital', that canon-formation and cultural assumptions form a frame (just as Andrew and Beja proposed) through which the screen adaptation is produced and consumed. The entrenchment of hierarchies of value in the analyses of adaptations of Shakespeare, for instance, are considered in order to broaden the kind of critical perspectives that can be brought to bear on the study of screen adaptations, and even to use the study of adaptation to produce analyses of the contemporary cultural and socio-political organisation of Britain, the United States or elsewhere. In Cartmell and Whelehan's hands, the study of adaptation becomes a means by which a path through 'English' into 'Cultural Studies' may be forged.

Perhaps the critical monograph on screen adaptations which has the most depth and breadth is Kamilla Elliott's

---

[31] Giddings, Selby and Wensley, *Screening the Novel*, pp. 1-27 (p. 24, n. 1).

Rethinking the Novel/Film Debate (2003).[32] Elliott does indeed 'rethink' the debate, extending the consideration of the relationship between narrative forms to explore formal inheritances and interchanges, cultural interchanges, and relevant disciplinary boundaries that bear upon the relationship between film and literature, such as the connection between poetry and painting, or between the nineteenth-century novel and illustration. This broadening out of the frame of reference places the connection between film and literature in a critical discourse that exceeds simple considerations of 'adaptation'; screen adaptation becomes only one example of a long cultural history of the relationships between language-based cultural forms and visual forms. Drawing upon Eisenstein's investigation of the connection between the novels of Charles Dickens and the cinema of D. W. Griffith that I mentioned earlier, Elliott considers the critical model of the 'Cinematic Victorian Novel', but argues that 'the assertion that film derived its visuality primarily from nineteenth-century novels is at best dubious' and instead proposes a much closer connection with the theatre, and in particular the editing technique of montage which, Elliott argues, 'brings film closer to theater in an effort to restore the theatrical vivacity that film technologies fail to capture with static cameras and single shot scenes.'[33] Just as Cartmell and Whelehan suggested that the production and consumption of screen adaptations is indivisible from ideas of cultural capital, Elliott argues that it is the early (and ongoing) history of film-makers using the prestige or cultural capital of novels by writers such as Dickens which has informed

---

[32] Kamilla Elliott, *Rethinking the Novel/Film Debate* (Cambridge: Cambridge University Press, 2003).

[33] Elliott, p. 122; p. 123.

Introduction

the critical history of adaptations and the critical judgements made about them.

I would like to end this short survey of the critical field by turning to the work of Robert Stam. With Alessandra Raengo, he edited *Literature and Film: A Guide to the Theory and Practice of Film Adaptation* (2005), a heavyweight collection of essays, and *A Companion to Literature and Film* (2004). He also wrote, on his own this time, *Literature Through Film: Realism, Magic, and Art* (2004).[34] Stam brings an interesting sensibility to the field. A scholar who straddles the discursive and critical boundary between literary and film studies, Stam's earlier work was heavily informed by the writings of the Russian critic Mikhail Bakhtin, and in particular his concepts of dialogism, heteroglossia and carnival, all of which Bakhtin identified with novelistic discourse. Stam's critical work proposes a revision of the study of film discourse along these lines. In a very long and detailed introduction to *Literature and Film: A Guide to the Theory and Practice of Film Adaptation*, Stam revisits the major adaptation theorists and critical issues, and suggests that studies of screen adaptation have tended to reinscribe hierarchies of value, privileging literature over film. He suggests that there are eight reasons for this:

1. Anteriority equates with seniority (literature is the older form);
2. Dichotomous thinking leads to a sense of literature and film in conflict with each other;
3. 'Iconophobia' (a prejudice against the visual arts);

---

[34] *Literature and Film: A Guide to the Theory and Practice of Film Adaptation*, ed. by Robert Stam and Alessandra Raengo (Oxford: Blackwell, 2005); *A Companion to Literature and Film*, ed. by Robert Stam and Alessandra Raengo (Oxford: Blackwell, 2004). Robert Stam, *Literature Through Film: Realism, Magic, and Art* (Oxford: Blackwell, 2004).

4. 'Logophilia' (a corresponding inclination towards linguistic forms);
5. Anti-corporeality: the 'seen' is 'obscene';
6. A myth of facility: films are easy to make and (particularly) to consume;
7. Class prejudice;
8. 'Parasitism': that film 'preys' upon the original literary text.

All of these are probably true in varying degrees. To counteract these critical tendencies, Stam proposes narratology as the way forward. He suggests three main areas: the first is a concentration on narrative, a 'comparative narratology', drawing heavily on Gerard Genette's narratological terminology.[35] (We have seen this style of adaptations analysis before, of course, particularly in the article by Seymour Chatman.) Another is to focus upon narrators; a third is to analyse the construction of point of view and 'focalisation'. This formalism should not be a critical straitjacket, however, argues Stam; rather, considerations of context, ideology, gender, race, or censorship – in fact the typical literary studies/cultural studies/film studies critical toolbox – should also be deployed to explore the complexities and specificities of adapted texts.

Textual revisions

It is clear that the study of screen adaptations is burgeoning, both as a subject of study offered in university

---

[35] Robert Stam, 'Introduction: The Theory and Practice of Adaptation', in *Literature and Film: A Guide to the Theory and Practice of Film Adaptation*, ed. by Robert Stam and Alessandra Raengo (Oxford: Blackwell, 2005), pp. 1-52 (pp. 31-45).

Introduction

English departments and as a legitimate field of critical enquiry. In Britain, the Association of Literature on Screen Studies was founded in 2006, and a journal, *Adaptation*, began publication in 2008. As yet, no dominant methodological or critical paradigm has emerged, and the field is pluralist and contested. This small collection takes account of that pluralism and, though written by members of English departments, is informed by a wide range of theoretical and critical discourses. This collection is divided into four sections, each of which contains two essays. They are each prefaced by a short introductory section which will outline in a little more detail the specific issues concerning each area, and will also introduce each essay. The first, on 'Adapting Nineteenth-Century Fiction', comprises essays by Deborah Wynne on adaptations of Jane Austen and Paul Foster on Coppola's screen version of *Dracula*; the second, 'Adapting Twentieth-Century Fiction', consists of Deniz Baker's analysis of the connection between modernism and film, and William Stephenson's analysis of John Fowles's *The French Lieutenant's Woman* to investigate the connections between postmodernist literary texts and film. In the third section, 'Adapting Drama', Graham Atkin offers a 'defence' of Trevor Nunn's film of *Twelfth Night*, and Ashley Chantler considers the film of Harold Pinter's *The Caretaker*. Finally, the fourth section, 'Adaptation and Genre', comprises Brian Baker's analysis of *Minority Report* and the connection between science fiction and film, while Chris Walsh's essay considers Peter Jackson's three *Lord of the Rings* films with the Tolkien source texts.

It remains for me to thank my contributors for their efforts in producing such insightful original essays for this volume, and for their patience. I must also thank Peter Williams of the Chester Academic Press for his forbearance and commitment to the project, and gratefully acknowledge the part he has played in bringing *Textual Revisions* finally to fruition. Lastly, I would like to acknowledge Alison Platt and the late Professor Ian MacKillop, who were to have contributed to this volume before the latter's untimely death.

Bibliography

Andrew, Dudley, 'Adaptation', in *Film Theory and Criticism: Introductory Readings*, ed. by Leo Braudy and Marshall Cohen, 5th edn (New York: Oxford University Press, 1999), pp. 452-460

Barthes, Roland, 'The Death of the Author', in *The Rustle of Language*, trans. by Richard Howard (Oxford: Basil Blackwell, 1986), pp. 49-55

Barthes, Roland, *S/Z*, trans. by Richard Miller (London: Cape, 1975

Beja, Morris, *Film and Literature: An Introduction* (London: Longman, 1979)

Bignell, Jonathan, ed., *Writing and Cinema* (Harlow: Pearson Longman, 1999)

Bluestone, George, *Novels into Film* (Berkeley: University of California Press, 1957)

Introduction

Cardwell, Sarah, *Adaptations Revisited: Television and the Classic Novel* (Manchester: Manchester University Press, 2002)

Cartmell, Deborah, and Imelda Whelehan, eds., *Adaptations: From Text to Screen, Screen to Text* (London: Routledge, 1999)

Cartmell, Deborah, I. Q. Hunter, Heidi Kaye, and Imelda Whelehan, eds., *Classics in Film and Fiction* (London: Pluto, 2000)

Chatman, Seymour, 'What Novels Can Do That Films Can't (and Vice Versa)', *Critical Inquiry*, 8 (1980). Reprinted in *Film Theory and Criticism: Introductory Readings*, ed. by Leo Braudy and Marshall Cohen. 5th edn (New York: Oxford University Press, 1999), pp. 435-451

Davison, Phoebe, ed., *Film and Literature: Points of Intersection* (Lampeter: Edwin Mellen Press, 1997)

Eisenstein, Sergei, *Film Form: Essays in Film Theory*, trans. by Jay Leyda (New York: Harcourt, 1949)

Elliott, Kamilla, *Rethinking the Novel/Film Debate* (Cambridge: Cambridge University Press, 2003)

Textual Revisions

Foucault, Michel, 'What is an Author?', in *The Foucault Reader*, ed. by Paul Rabinow (London: Penguin, 1991), pp. 101-120

Genette, Gerard, *Narrative Discourse: An Essay on Method*, trans. by Jane E. Lewin (Ithaca NY: Cornell University Press, 1980)

Giddings, Robert, Keith Selby and Chris Wensley, *Screening the Novel: The Theory and Practice of Literary Dramatization* (Basingstoke : Macmillan, 1990)

McFarlane, Brian, *Novel to Film: An Introduction to the Theory of Adaptation* (Oxford; Oxford University Press, 1996)

Orr, John, and Colin Nicholson, eds., *Cinema and Fiction: New Modes of Adapting 1950-1990* (Edinburgh: Edinburgh University Press, 1992)

Sheen, Erica, 'Introduction', in *The Classic Novel: From Page to Screen*, ed. by Robert Giddings and Erica Sheen (Manchester: Manchester University Press, 2000), pp. 1-13

Stam, Robert, *Literature Through Film: Realism, Magic, and Art* (Oxford: Blackwell, 2004)

Introduction

Stam, Robert, and Alessandra Raengo, eds., *A Companion to Literature and Film* (Oxford: Blackwell, 2004)

Stam, Robert, and Alessandra Raengo, eds., *Literature and Film: A Guide to the Theory and Practice of Film Adaptation* (Oxford: Blackwell, 2005)

Vincendeau, Ginette, ed., *Film/Literature/Heritage: A Sight and Sound Reader* (London: BFI, 2001)

Wagner, Geoffrey, *The Novel and the Cinema* (Rutherford, NJ: Fairleigh Dickinson University Press, 1979)

Whelehan, Imelda, and Deborah Cartmell, 'Introduction - Pulping Fictions: Consuming Culture across the Literature/Media Divide', In *Pulping Fictions*, ed. by Deborah Cartmell, I. Q. Hunter, Heidi Kaye, and Imelda Whelehan (London: Pluto, 1996), pp. 1-10

Wimsatt, W. K. and Monroe C. Beardsley, 'The Intentional Fallacy', in *20th Century Literary Criticism: A Reader*, ed. by David Lodge (London: Longman, 1972), pp. 334-344

Part 1

Adapting the Nineteenth-Century Novel

ADAPTING THE NINETEENTH-CENTURY NOVEL

Until recently, it was the critical orthodoxy amongst scholars of screen adaptations that the closest proximity of film to a literary form was to the nineteenth-century novel, particularly the 'realist' Victorian novel. Indeed, the Soviet film-maker Sergei Eisenstein wrote a famous passage in his *Film Form* (1949) that made explicit comparison between the 'cinematic' writings of Charles Dickens and the cinematic narrative of D. W. Griffith:

> Let us look at how montage came to Griffith – or Griffith came to montage.
>
> Griffith came to it through the device of parallel action. But it was none other than Dickens who gave Griffith the idea of parallel action! … there was the same fascination for Dickens' novels as there is now for film. … And perhaps the secret is that what links Dickens to cinema is the astonishingly plastic quality of his novels. Their astonishing visual and optical quality.[1]

The proximity of film to novel, it was thought, can be seen in the shared use of narrative (unlike some forms of poetry, for instance), character, and the construction of an immersive 'world' for the reader/viewer of the text to believe in. Roland Barthes, in 'The Reality Effect', noted

---

[1] Sergei Eisenstein, 'Dickens, Griffith and Ourselves [Dickens, Griffith and Film Today]', in *Film Theory and Criticism: Introductory Readings*, ed. by Leo Braudy and Marshall Cohen, 5th edn (New York: Oxford University Press, 1999), pp. 426-434 (p. 426; p. 427).

how realist discourse built in redundancy of descriptive detail, in order to convince us of the concreteness of the scene being described.² The depiction of the details of a room, for instance, has no meaning – metaphorical, symbolic, thematic – other than to present the room in itself, to convince us of its materiality. The narratively redundant description of a chair does not signify a chair; it signifies 'the real'. In cinema, the construction of the 'real' is problematic, as Jill Nelmes argues:

> The concept of the "real" is problematic in cinema .... The concept is generally used in two different ways. First, the extent to which a film attempts to mimic reality so that a fictional film can appear indistinguishable from documentary. Second, the film can establish its own world, and can by consistently using the same conventions establish the credibility of this world.³

In both literary realism and in Hollywood continuity narrative, there seems to be a shared set of assumptions or techniques to suppress any sense of self-consciousness or self-reflexivity in the text, to prevent the reader/viewer from coming to a realisation that they *are* engaging with a text rather than the 'real' itself. Both literary realism and the Hollywood continuity system, it could be argued, aim for maximal 'transparency'. Philippe Harmon's list of major features of realist discourse is as follows:

---

[2] Roland Barthes, 'The Reality Effect', in *The Rustle of Language*, trans. by Richard Howard (Oxford: Basil Blackwell, 1986), pp. 141-148.

[3] Jill Nelmes, *An Introduction to Film Studies* (London: Routledge, 1996), p. 90.

1. Readability and narrative coherence ensured by a maximisation of reader knowledge;
2. Psychological motivation is a key generator of narrative events;
3. The mode of description tends to erase the markers of authorship and readership;
4. The mode of narration tends to erase markers of 'storytelling';
5. Resistance of the 'heroic' mode with regard to its central character;
6. Avoidance of ambiguity at narrative and textual levels: no puns, linguistic slippage, unresolved narrative threads;
7. Blurring of the distinction between appearance and reality, outside and inside, particularly with regard to character;
8. The world is describable, knowable, an object.[4]

By comparison, the elements of Hollywood continuity style are these:

1. Individual characters and their personal actions and choices determine the narrative;
2. Motivation for action is as clear and as complete as possible;
3. Time is subordinate to these events of personal importance. The plot will order the story to present the character-driven causes and effects most clearly;
4. A strong tendency to avoid subjective effects, and to maintain the illusion of 'objective' reality;

---

[4] Philippe Harmon, 'Philippe Harmon on the Major Features of Realist Discourse', trans. by Lilian R. Furst and Seán Hand, in *Realism*, ed. by Lilian R. Furst (London: Longman, 1992), pp. 166-185.

5. Strong closure and resolution to a narrative. Avoidance (wherever possible) of 'loose ends'.

There seems, therefore, to be a strong connection between literary realism and the conventions of Hollywood continuity-style narrative. The shared emphases are particularly on maximal narrative clarity, particularly effected by character motivation and avoidance of self-consciousness and destabilisation of the illusion of a material 'real'. In this case, then, it is little wonder that critics have assumed a clear connection between the nineteenth-century 'realist' novel and film.[5] In a sense, the logic is circular, and what seems to be a developmental narrative (cinema is produced out of the forms of the nineteenth-century novel) can be read in reverse: the fact that cinema has drawn heavily on the nineteenth-century novel for narratives make it appear that there is a strong formal connection between cinema and the novel, but the connection is not causal or developmental. Film has also drawn heavily on the theatre. However, film-makers aware of the principle of fidelity may well be encouraged to mimic novelistic devices in cinematic form (like Eisenstein's example of 'parallel action' and 'cross-cutting') when adapting a novel. The question begged here is whether the mode or genre of literary source text has a determining effect on the mode of screen adaptation. Does a 'realist' novel, for instance, demand a 'realist' adaptation?

Here, Deborah Wynne's argument in her essay in this section is an interesting one. Wynne argues *against* fidelity in adaptations, suggesting instead that the freer the film version, the more effective it can be. Certainly, this

---

[5] See the 'Introduction' to this volume for details of Kamilla Elliott's counter-argument to this assumption.

argument avoids the trap that some adaptations of the nineteenth-century novel (particularly of Austen) fall into: at once an over-reverence for the source text, combined with a 'heritage'-style staging of an impossibly clean, pretty and ideal (ahistorical) past, reducing both film and literary text to commodities to be unthinkingly consumed. There, the codes of cinematic realism blend into romance or melodrama; but at the other end of the scale, a determinedly 'gritty' film dramatisation can fall into the equal (but opposite) cliché.

There is more to adaptations of the nineteenth century than simply 'realism', of course, as the two essays in this section attest. If a strictly 'realist' mode of adapting Austen may not be true to the acid narration and critical depictions of social life in her novels, how might one adapt Henry James's narratives (written at the other end of the century)? And, in novels written in the period leading up to and after 1895, the year of the Lumière brothers' first exhibition of their films, is there a more complicated relationship between writing and visual culture, or writing and cinema, at work? Paul Foster, in his essay, suggests a different approach to the film/literature relationship: not that film 'adapts' a literary original, but that by the end of the nineteenth century *both* literature and cinema are produced out of the same cultural, social and historical forces.

THE MATERIALISATION OF THE 'AUSTEN WORLD': FILM ADAPTATIONS OF JANE AUSTEN'S NOVELS

Deborah Wynne

The film adaptations of novels transform one sort of object, the book, with its black and white columns of print, into a very different sort of object, the film, with its visual effects and soundtrack, a transformation which, as Robert Stam suggests, 'grant[s] a kind of objective materiality' to the process of reading novels.[1] Indeed, the illusion of conferring materiality on the past is a major characteristic of the 'period drama' (or 'costume drama'), whose obsession with historical accuracy in its lavish displays of costume, domestic interiors, landscapes and objects is a contributory factor to the enormous popularity of the genre.[2] Among the most popular period dramas in recent decades are the film adaptations of Austen's work, such as Ang Lee and Emma Thompson's adaptation of *Sense and Sensibility* (1995) and the BBC television adaptation of *Pride and Prejudice* (1995), directed by Simon Langton, with a screenplay by Andrew Davies. However, while such film adaptations offer a visual abundance of detail, the novels

---

[1] Robert Stam, 'Introduction: The Theory and Practice of Adaptation', in *Literature and Film: A Guide to the Theory and Practice of Film Adaptation*, ed. by Robert Stam and Alessandra Raengo (Oxford: Blackwell, 2005), pp. 1-52 (p. 45).

[2] The popularity of the 1995 BBC series, *Pride and Prejudice*, for example, may have led to a massive increase in sales of Austen's novels, no doubt contributing to the high ratings of that particular novel in recent polls of readers. For the results of a recent BBC 'Big Read' poll, see 'www.bbc.co.uk/arts/bigread', where Austen's novel was voted into second place after Tolkien's *Lord of the Rings*.

The Materialisation of the 'Austen World'

themselves are remarkably frugal in descriptions of material things, for ironically, as Barbara Hardy has maintained, in the Austen novel, 'things are kept in their place'.[3] Everything in the *mise en scène* which makes the film adaptation appear an 'authentic' recreation of the past - the tea-cups, furniture, dresses and carriages - are rarely described by Austen, who tends to avoid extended descriptions of the appearances of people and things.[4] This chapter examines some of the issues surrounding recent attempts to create a filmic 'Austen world', considering some of the traditional, historically 'accurate' film adaptations of Austen's novels along with those which deliberately deviate from a realistic recreation of the lives of the middle classes and the gentry during the late eighteenth and early nineteenth centuries.

Film's power to suggest a fully-realised materiality is both part of its illusion (for the viewer has no access to that materiality except via the image transmitted to the eye) and its potential to achieve a totalising realism (for the eye seeing an apparently 'real' world is arguably more easy to convince than an eye scanning pages of words). With film, which relies heavily upon the visual field, 'things' tend to be always there and the scarcity of descriptions of things in Austen's novels simply could not be matched in a traditional film adaptation, for in the period drama objects

---

[3] Barbara Hardy, 'The Objects in *Mansfield Park*', in *Jane Austen: Bicentenary Essays*, ed. by John Halperin (Cambridge: Cambridge University Press, 1975), pp. 180-96 (p. 184).

[4] For a discussion of Austen's avoidance of 'visualty' in her work, see Nancy Armstrong, *Fiction in the Age of Photography: The Legacy of British Realism* (Cambridge, MA: Harvard University Press, 1999), p. 124. For a general evaluation of Austen's style, see D. A. Miller, *Jane Austen, or The Secret of Style* (Princeton, NJ: Princeton University Press, 2003).

are needed to add 'authentic' background detail. Additionally, the detailed recreation of the past is an important aspect in the marketing of a film, as any scrutiny of the Jane Austen fan website, 'The Republic of Pemberley', will testify, for many fans of the Austen costume drama indicate that the pleasure of looking at images of an elaborately reconstructed Regency 'world' is an indispensable part of the enjoyment of the genre.[5]

The visual pleasures offered by the modern film adaptation have been unashamedly emphasised in the 1995 BBC adaptation of *Pride and Prejudice*, for example, where, as each episode's opening credits roll, the camera sweeps over fold after fold of various rich textiles, revealing buttons, lace, the gloss of luxurious satins and silks in pastel shades, while the busily working needle and thread is a reminder of the role played by the costume designers and dressmakers employed on the production team. This is an unusual moment of self-referentiality in a traditional period drama, a 'performance' of costume-making which unashamedly proclaims the product on offer: a television 'costume drama' designed primarily for a female audience. However, while some film adaptations have striven for a high level of historical accuracy and claim to be 'faithful' to the original novels, others have forged alternative worlds for Austen's characters, often to radical effects. Both types of adaptation will be examined here in order to highlight a reading of novels and film adaptations which takes into account some of the problems and opportunities faced by film-makers attempting to adapt Austen's work. I have approached both novels and films with the view that all objects 'count'; that is, that

---

[5] 'The Republic of Pemberley' can be accessed at: http//www.pemberley.com

The Materialisation of the 'Austen World'

everything has meaning. When Austen troubles to describe a ring, a toothpick-case, a letter, she does so because such objects carry a considerable weight within the narrative.

While such singular emphasis is difficult to achieve within the crowded visual field of the film adaptation, it is important to remain aware that each frame is carefully constructed to create specific effects. Indeed, the rendering of objects in historically accurate Austen adaptations has prompted a number of recent critics to associate the costume drama with the 'heritage industry', promoting safe and visually satisfying images of the national past.[6] As Julianne Pidduck has suggested:

> The adaptations characteristically render Austen's interiors dense with rich furnishings, heavy oil paintings, expensive ornaments. This *mise en scène* orchestrates a sumptuous longed for experience of gracious nineteenth-century living, what has been called 'museum pleasures'.[7]

The conservative pleasures of the film adaptation can thus be aligned with English Heritage and the National Trust, promoting a safely distant past which is above all

---

[6] For comprehensive discussions of the links between 'heritage' and costume drama see Andrew Higson, *English Heritage, English Cinema: Costume Drama Since 1980* (Oxford: Oxford University Press, 2003) and Julianne Pidduck, *Contemporary Costume Film: Space, Place and the Past* (London: BFI Publishing 2004). See also Clara Tuite, *Romantic Austen: Sexual Politics and the Literary Canon* (Cambridge: Cambridge University Press, 2002), pp.12-13.

[7] Julianne Pidduck, 'Of Windows and Country Walks: Frames of Space and Movement in 1990s Austen Adaptations', in *The Postcolonial Jane Austen*, ed. by You-me Park and Rajeswari Sunder Rajan (London: Routledge, 2000), p. 120.

'comfortable'.[8] The oppressive social system in which Austen places her characters is always in danger of being minimised in the adaptations by representations of the apparent comfort of the material conditions of their lives. The Dashwood sisters and their mother in Emma Thompson and Ang Lee's adaptation of *Sense and Sensibility* may suffer the inconvenience of a slightly smoky fireplace (as they do of course in the novel), yet to many contemporary viewers their detached cottage set in idyllic countryside is more likely to resemble the country home of a stockbroker, an eminently desirable property, thus distorting the viewer's awareness of the women's dispossession.[9] This indicates one of the major problems of translating a text grounded in a specific historical moment to later audiences (which, of course, applies to readers of the text as well as viewers of adaptations); that is, how can plots based on outmoded mores and social structures be made intelligible to modern audiences? In the film adaptation, the recreation of the material world can play an important role in making a text from the past intelligible. However, this is not necessarily linked to the issue of how historically 'authentic' an adaptation claims to be, for historically 'faithful' recreations can fail to convey adequately the qualities of the social milieu of Austen's heroines, while 'unfaithful' adaptations which set out to flaunt their 'inauthenticity' can sometimes better convey the social experiences Austen represents.

---

[8] Pidduck, in 'Of Windows and Country Walks', goes on to say that, 'this panoply of detail at times evokes the claustrophobic weight of history, oppressive patriarchal laws of inheritance, the strict codes of comportment that Austen at once problematizes and upholds.' (p.120).

[9] *Sense and Sensibility* [Motion picture], dir. by Ang Lee, ad. by Emma Thompson (Columbia, 1995).

The Materialisation of the 'Austen World'

Some of the most successful adaptations of Austen's novels understand the compromises involved in attempting to reconstruct a historically accurate 'world' and consequently refuse to compromise. Both Amy Heckerling with *Clueless* (1996) and Patricia Rozema with *Mansfield Park* (1999) choose to abandon historical accuracy altogether. Aware of the problems of attempting 'completeness' (the goal towards which traditional adaptations tended to work), both film-makers present a 'fragment' of Austen.[10] Historically 'accurate' adaptations can raise questions which are difficult to answer in an entertaining way and it could be tedious to many film viewers to be presented with explanations as to why the Dashwood sisters and Bennet sisters face disinheritance, or the reasons for Emma Woodhouse's financial security, or why Fanny Price feels under so many obligations, or the debates surrounding Sir Thomas Bertram as a possible slave-owner. The abandonment of historical accuracy frees the film-maker to explore other aspects of a novel, selecting an alternative focus, such as money and moral corruption or the absurdity of social rules and fashions. Instead of slavishly recreating period detail, film-makers then become free to use objects in different ways and to different effects.

An example of avoiding the potential pitfalls of adapting an Austen novel to the letter can be taken from *Sense and Sensibility*, where Emma Thompson, in her screenplay, chooses to reject an object which plays an important role in the novel, substituting instead another, less problematic object which serves a different purpose and adds a comic effect missing from the original. The object in the novel is Edward Ferrars's ring, which in the film becomes a handkerchief, a much less socially and

---

[10] Amy Heckerling and Patricia Rozema both directed and wrote the screenplays for their film adaptations of Austen.

symbolically complex object. In the novel, the ring Edward wears functions as an engagement ring, although this meaning is a secret one and is 'unreadable' by both Elinor and Marianne. The passage in which the ring first becomes evident to Marianne and Elinor (and the reader) is worth quoting in full:

> ...Marianne remained thoughtfully silent, till a new object suddenly engaged her attention. She was sitting by Edward, and in taking his tea from Mrs Dashwood, his hand passed so directly before her, as to make a ring, with a plait of hair in the centre, very conspicuous on one of his fingers.
>
> 'I never saw you wear a ring before, Edward,' she cried. 'Is that Fanny's hair? I remember her promising to give you some. But I should have thought her hair had been darker.'
>
> Marianne spoke inconsiderately what she really felt – but when she saw how much she had pained Edward, her own vexation at her want of thought could not be surpassed by his. He coloured very deeply, and giving a momentary glance at Elinor, replied, 'Yes; it is my sister's hair. The setting always casts a different shade on it you know.'
>
> Elinor had met his eye, and looked conscious likewise. That the hair was her own, she instantaneously felt as well satisfied as Marianne; the only difference in their conclusions was, that what Marianne considered as a free gift from her sister, Elinor was conscious must have been procured by some theft or contrivance unknown to herself. She was not in a humour, however, to regard it as an affront, and affecting to take no notice of what passed, by instantly talking of something else, she internally resolved henceforward to catch every opportunity of eyeing the hair and of

The Materialisation of the 'Austen World'

satisfying herself, beyond all doubt, that it was exactly the shade of her own.[11]

This passage, for a number of reasons, may present difficulties for a modern film audience. Firstly, it is misleading. Elinor believes at this point that Edward is capable of the secret theft of a lock of her hair, a romantic action which suggests that he possesses a hitherto unknown depth of passion and sense of adventure. The passage also serves to feminise Edward as he displays at the tea table a fancy piece of jewellery bestowed on him by a woman to serve as an indicator of her possession of him. The discovery of the ring makes him 'colour very deeply'; his blush is perhaps also the result of the lie that he tells when he states that the hair belonged to his sister. A few chapters later the mystery is explained when Lucy Steele informs Elinor:

> 'I gave him a lock of my hair set in a ring when he was at Longstaple last, and that was some comfort to him, he said, but not equal to a picture. Perhaps you might notice the ring when you saw him?'
>
> 'I did,' said Elinor, with a composure of voice, under which was concealed an emotion and distress beyond any thing she had ever felt before. She was mortified, shocked and confounded. (pp. 155-6)

---

[11] Jane Austen, *Sense and Sensibility*, ed. by Tony Tanner (Harmondsworth: Penguin, 1967), chap. 18, p. 123. Further page references will be cited in the text.

Textual Revisions

The mortification and shock arise not only from the knowledge of Edward's engagement to Lucy, but also from the shattering of the romantic image of him as a young man capable of secretly performing a 'rape of the lock' on the unsuspecting Elinor. Added to this is the knowledge we gain that Edward is deceitful in lying about the hair and in not making his engagement to Lucy known to Elinor.

This ring, like virtually all items of jewellery mentioned by Austen, serves an important function in the narrative, just as rings acted as powerful social signals in eighteenth-century society. D. A. Miller, in a perceptive discussion of *Sense and Sensibility*, has highlighted the 'semiotic function' of jewellery in Austen as 'the sign – and even some part of the substance – of everyone's required socialization', going on to describe what he sees as the 'ornaments and trinkets that flood the represented social field' of the Austen novel.[12] Yet there is scarcely a 'flood' (as there is in many Victorian novels, where objects such as jewels, ornaments and trinkets can sometimes appear in danger of overwhelming the narrative), for Austen places her objects with particular care. Elinor's misreading of Edward's ring, because of the unfortunate coincidence of her hair resembling the colour of Lucy's, is a particularly humiliating episode because it does double work in the narrative as an indication of Edward's timidity and as a 'hands off' sign placed on him by Lucy.

This is just one indication of the importance of jewellery in Austen's novels, yet it is virtually untranslatable as far as a film adaptation is concerned. Firstly, the visual field in a costume drama is already crowded with jewellery which is worn by most characters as an 'authentic' costume accessory. Secondly, attempting

---

[12] Miller, pp. 11-12

to emphasise a ring containing a lock of hair on a man's hand (with a close-up, for example) may seem slightly bizarre (or at least, difficult to interpret) to modern viewers. However, it is Elinor's belief (which she keeps to herself in the novel) that Edward is romantic and daring enough to steal a lock of her hair, and this could only be conveyed ponderously through conversation, flashback or voice-over. The work of the ring as a token of betrothal would need to be further emphasised. In a film this small detail, if a film-maker chose to represent it, has the potential for over-emphasis, whereas in the novel it works unobtrusively to convey powerful suggestions about Edward's timidity and cowardice and Elinor's desire for a romantic figure.[13]

Emma Thompson wisely omits the ring from her screenplay of *Sense and Sensibility*, for its symbolic weight is perhaps too great in the already crowded *mise en scène* of the period drama. Thompson finds an alternative object, however, to indicate to Elinor Lucy's bond with Edward. Both women possess one of Edward's handkerchiefs, on which his initials are prominently embroidered. We see Edward bestowing this gift early in the film, when (in a scene created by Thompson) Elinor stands at the doorway in tears as she listens to Marianne playing her dead father's favourite music. The handkerchief is kept as a treasure by Elinor, and we later see her handling it when she is

---

[13] The difficulty of foregrounding objects in specific historical contexts may be one reason for Rozema's decision not to include Fanny Price's necklace in her version of *Mansfield Park*. The elaborate meanings and confusions which Austen represents in her depiction of the chains and cross Fanny wears at her first ball are complex indeed.

melancholy and alone.[14] Lucy's possession of an identical handkerchief, which she flaunts before Elinor in the film in a forced display of tears, instantly proclaims to the viewer that Edward has been consoling two weeping women, a gesture which does nothing to disturb his status as romantic hero. The handkerchief is a mildly comic alternative to the ring. It carries no social weight of a gesture of betrothal, is associated with 'feminine' tears, and its value is largely sentimental (unlike a ring which possesses a greater monetary value). The handkerchief, even an embroidered one, also verges on the ridiculous because of its association with bodily fluids. In the film this is an excellent visual substitute for the ring. However, it does not function, as the ring does in the novel, to indicate Edward's weak character and Elinor's false hope that he is, beneath his mild exterior, a dashing hero after all (she does not regard his secret theft of a lock of hair as 'an affront', but as a sign of his passion). This is not necessary in the film, for Edward is portrayed according to the conventions of the romantic hero, being more kind, sensitive and active than he is portrayed in the novel.

I have focused on what appears to be a minute detail in the novel in order to illustrate why film adaptations of Austen's novels may work better as films when avoiding a complete 'fidelity' of detail. Historical accuracy in a film is potentially in danger of leading to a dead end, of being an end in itself, overwhelming the narrative with 'detail', which is why an entirely 'faithful' film recreation of Austen would, arguably, be dull. This is why the most historically 'inaccurate' adaptations of Austen can often be most

---

[14] Elinor, in Thompson's characterisation, is here closely aligned to *Emma*'s foolishly sentimental Harriet Smith, who hoards 'treasures' belonging to Mr Elton.

satisfying as films, because the film-maker is left free to shift away from a concern with getting the background details 'right' to a concern with imaginatively using what is at work in Austen's texts. Indeed, disquiet and unease are often important features of an Austen novel, yet they tend to be marginalised by the lavish detailing of the period drama. The property-less heroines never quite seem so badly off when they are visually represented in smart frocks, eating well-cooked dinners in pleasant dining rooms before windows revealing expansive, well-kept grounds, all of which can militate against the sense of unease at work in the novels.

Much of the disquiet in *Emma* centres on Jane Fairfax, a character who, like the penniless Fanny Price in *Mansfield Park*, is a dispossessed heroine who faces the prospect of earning her own living. Emma Woodhouse, 'handsome, clever and rich', for example, is never depicted actually buying goods in the Highbury shop (her friend Harriet Smith, on the other hand, is 'tempted by every thing and … always very long at a purchase'), because her needs in terms of clothes, ornaments, cosmetics, books are 'automatically' met in the world of the novel's economy without the narrator having to mention them.[15] Yet film versions of *Emma* inevitably depict the heroine shopping in Highbury, despite the fact that the heiress in Austen's novel is above the delights of the local village shop's wares.[16] However, other female characters in the novel, Harriet Smith, Jane Fairfax and Miss Bates, are pointedly

---

[15] Jane Austen, *Emma*, ed. by Ronald Blythe (Harmondsworth: Penguin, 1966), p. 241. Further page references will be cited in the text.

[16] For example, Douglas McGrath's *Emma* (1996) depicts Emma shopping on a number of occasions, even carrying a basket for her purchases.

not rich and their precarious social positioning is repeatedly emphasised by Austen, who indicates their social fragility through the small things these women possess, from Harriet's 'most precious treasures' (p. 335) (the things once owned by Mr Elton that she hoards) to the petticoats, caps and workbags of Miss Bates. The extraordinary gift of a pianoforte sent to Jane is so singular because neither she nor her family could afford to buy one. Emma's ease as a woman of property is set against a background of women who lack adequate means and must cherish the little they possess. Yet all of the 'period' adaptations of *Emma* fail to signal the representational distinction which is so evident in Austen's narrative.[17] Similarly, the property-less Jane Fairfax, a potentially tragic figure, represents the only threat to the comedy of Austen's novel, for she signals the sexual and economic vulnerability of the unprotected young woman; however, despite her importance in the novel, she is not depicted in terms of a serious threat to the comedy in the period film adaptations. Jane exists in the novel on the very threshold of the world of Highbury and the analogy she makes to Mrs Elton between the position of the governess and that of the slave (p. 300) generates a disturbance which exposes the insecurity of the gentlewoman without money in eighteenth-century society.

Amy Heckerling in *Clueless* (1996), however, dispenses with Jane Fairfax altogether, along with the complexities of property ownership and inheritance which underpin Austen's plot, in order to focus on the comedy of errors engendered by Emma's mistaken attempts to control her small world. In this way she successfully modernises and

---

[17] Among the 'faithful' period adaptations are McGrath's and Diarmuid Lawrence's television production, *Emma* (1996).

simplifies *Emma* for film audiences, while still managing to be 'faithful' to Austen's comic vision. Austen refuses to discuss the details of Emma's material wealth and this property is translated into Cher's much more easily representable desire for consumer goods. Whereas in eighteenth-century society the only respectable identity was that of the property owner, in the late twentieth century the equivalent social identity belongs to the consumer. *Clueless* is a translation of class identity and property power into a contemporary story of gender identity and consumer power. Heckerling abandons all of the elements of disquieting female poverty in Austen's text in order to recreate the novel's satirical use of free indirect speech (via Cher's 'clueless' voice-overs) and to maintain a single focus on the lovable heroine's vanity and the absurdities of the enclosed world she inhabits. As David Monaghan has argued:

> ... despite Heckerling's description of *Clueless* as a "light" movie lacking any "real life" agenda ... there is more than clever but superficial humor in the interplay between film and source. Not only is Heckerling correct to label her film a comedy of manners but she shares Austen's awareness of the possibilities inherent within the genre for a subtle but unobtrusive exploration of important social/cultural issues.[18]

What Heckerling understands is that she can apply Austen's comedy to a wholly different society and culture, which is what makes *Clueless* one of the most radical and

---

[18] David Monaghan, '*Emma* and the Art of Adaptation', in *Jane Austen on Screen*, ed. by Gina Macdonald and Andrew Macdonald (Cambridge: Cambridge University Press, 2003), 197-227 (p. 214-15).

successful attempts to *adapt* a nineteenth-century novel into film.

Patricia Rozema's *Mansfield Park*, however, instead of rejecting Austen's complex subterranean disquiet, as Heckerling does in *Clueless*, with her refusal to find an equivalent for Jane Fairfax, actually foregrounds it. In his review of the film, Alastair Duckworth referred to Rozema's 'Brontification of Austen', a point also made by Jan Fergus in her comment that it is 'as if the Brontës had collaborated on the screenplay'.[19] Yet this is not so much an eccentric addition by Rozema, for the 'Brontës' (or, more particularly, the qualities we associate with the Brontës' novels) are already at work in Austen; not, of course, on the novels' sparkling comic surfaces, but as an undercurrent in her texts. In *Emma*, for example, Jane Fairfax can be read as a forerunner of Jane Eyre, the potential governess who lacks a distinct class identity and who is vulnerable to the attentions of a wealthy but unstable man. Recognising this tendency in Austen, Rozema draws our attention to the fact that *Mansfield Park* has its own woman in the attic (albeit, not a mad one), as Fanny Price inhabits the neglected East Room at the top of the house. In the film, this room is filled with lumber to emphasise Fanny Price's exclusion from the material wealth of Mansfield Park. Rozema's inversion of Austen's novel is not only signalled by her refusal to depict Fanny Price as silent and still (as Austen tends to do), but also in her depiction of the material world. She deliberately thwarts the viewer's expectations of the visual pleasures of the costume drama. For example, the heroine, for the most

---

[19] Alastair M. Duckworth, 'Film Review: *Mansfield Park*, directed and written by Patricia Rozema, 1999', *Eighteenth-Century Fiction*, 12, (2000), 565-71 (p. 567) and Jan Fergus, 'Two *Mansfield Parks*: Purist and Postmodern', in Macdonald and Macdonald, p. 71.

part, wears a gown resembling a long black gymslip with a masculine white shirt beneath, indicating both her poverty and her reluctance to enter the marriage market, while Mansfield Park itself is a semi-derelict mansion with peeling plaster on the interior walls, a visible signifier of the corrupt sources of Sir Thomas's wealth as a slave-owner and the onset of the decline of the landed gentry's social and political power.[20]

Perhaps the most radical use of objects in this film, however, is the extraordinary prominence given to pens and ink, without which Austen's novels would never have materialised. Rozema emphasises the textuality inherent in adapting a book, someone else's written words, into a film. The film's opening shots present slow-motion close-up shots of quill pens, black ink being poured and reams of paper. At first these close-up images are difficult to read, but as the camera gradually pulls back to reveal the materials of writing we enter a further realm of intertextual reference, for these shots offer an ironic rewriting of the pink lace and delicate buttons of the BBC *Pride and Prejudice* opening sequence, which emphasise the popular televisual 'materialisation' of the novel. In Rozema's film, the original writing process itself becomes the overriding theme, for Fanny Price is shown as a storyteller, a Jane Austen figure (rather than the quiet heroine of the novel), who moves from the poverty-stricken necessity of the oral tale in the opening shots as she tells her sister a story (which Rozema takes from Austen's own juvenilia), to the empowered position at the end of the film of the author about to publish her first work. Pens and sheaves of paper

---

[20] For a discussion of the recent debates surrounding Sir Thomas as a slave owner, see John Wiltshire, 'Decolonising *Mansfield Park*', *Essays in Criticism*, 53 (2003), 303-322.

feature regularly throughout the film, from Edmund providing Fanny with the materials to write a letter to her brother (also an episode in the novel) to an additional scene at Fanny's parents' home in Portsmouth, when her mother is disturbed at the cost of all the paper Fanny is 'wasting' as she writes. All of this stresses the precariousness of women's writing in the eighteenth century, a world where pens and ink cost a considerable amount of money and women who write are liable to be seen as wasting both money and time. However, Fanny's role as a writer, as well as a heroine, is confirmed in the film when, in her first embrace with Edmund as he declares his love, we see her inky fingers in a close-up, an indication that love and writing are not mutually exclusive qualities within the film's fantasy world.

The film adaptors of Austen's novels have a number of choices to make: to be 'faithful' to the whole novel or not, to be 'faithful' to a single aspect of the novel only, to aim for historical accuracy or use a contemporary setting, or, like Rozema, to be radically 'unfaithful' to the surface of the novel in order to portray its subtexts. Whatever decisions are taken, each *mise en scène* works towards the director's vision of the 'Austen world' and, as I have hoped to show, the disjunction between Austen's reticence about objects and the necessity for them in a film adaptation allows a space for radical experimentation.

Bibliography

Primary Works

Austen, Jane, *Emma*, ed. by Ronald Blythe (Harmondsworth: Penguin, 1966)

The Materialisation of the 'Austen World'

Austen, Jane, *Sense and Sensibility*, ed. by Tony Tanner (Harmondsworth: Penguin, 1967)

Clueless [Motion picture], dir./ad. by Amy Heckerling (Paramount, 1995)

Emma [Motion picture], dir./ad. by Douglas McGrath (Miramax, 1996)

Emma [Television series], dir. by Diarmuid Lawrence, ad. by Andrew Davies (Independent Television, 1996)

Mansfield Park [Motion picture], dir./ad. by Patricia Rozema (Miramax, 1999)

Pride and Prejudice [Television series], dir. by Simon Langton, ad. by Andrew Davies (BBC Television, 1995)

Sense and Sensibility [Motion picture], dir. by Ang Lee, ad. by Emma Thompson (Columbia, 1995)

Secondary Works

Armstrong, Nancy, *Fiction in the Age of Photography: The Legacy of British Realism* (Cambridge, MA: Harvard University Press, 1999)

Duckworth, Alastair M., 'Film Review: *Mansfield Park*, directed and written by Patricia Rozema, 1999'. *Eighteenth-Century Fiction*, 12 (2000), 565-71

Textual Revisions

Fergus, Jan, 'Two *Mansfield Parks*: Purist and Postmodern', in *Jane Austen on Screen*, ed. by Gina Macdonald and Andrew Macdonald (Cambridge: Cambridge University Press, 2003), pp. 69-89

Hardy, Barbara, 'The Objects in *Mansfield Park*', in *Jane Austen: Bicentenary Essays*, ed. by John Halperin (Cambridge: Cambridge University Press, 1975), pp. 180-96

Higson, Andrew, *English Heritage, English Cinema: Costume Drama Since 1980* (Oxford: Oxford University Press, 2003)

Miller, D. A., *Jane Austen, or The Secret of Style* (Princeton, NJ: Princeton University Press, 2003)

Monaghan, David, '*Emma* and the Art of Adaptation', in *Jane Austen on Screen*, ed. by Gina Macdonald and Andrew Macdonald (Cambridge: Cambridge University Press, 2003), pp. 197-227

Pidduck, Julianne, 'Of Windows and Country Walks: Frames of Space and Movement in 1990s Austen Adaptations', in *The Postcolonial Jane Austen*, ed. by You-me Park and Rajeswari Sunder Rajan. (London: Routledge, 2000), pp. 116-37

Pidduck, Julianne, *Contemporary Costume Film: Space, Place and the Past* (London: BFI Publishing, 2004)

Stam, Robert, 'Introduction: The Theory and Practice of Adaptation', in *Literature and Film: A Guide to the Theory and Practice of Film Adaptation*, ed. by Robert Stam and Alessandra Raengo (Oxford: Blackwell, 2005), pp. 1-52

Tuite, Clara, *Romantic Austen: Sexual Politics and the Literary Canon* (Cambridge: Cambridge University Press, 2002)

Wiltshire, John, 'Decolonising *Mansfield Park*', *Essays in Criticism*, 53 (2003), 303-22

'THE AMAZING CINEMATOGRAPH': CINEMA AND ILLUSION IN FRANCIS FORD COPPOLA'S *BRAM STOKER'S 'DRACULA'*

Paul Foster

In a key scene from Francis Ford Coppola's *Bram Stoker's 'Dracula'* (1992), Dracula visits the cinematograph upon his arrival in London, 1897, accompanied by Jonathan Harker's fiancée, Mina Murray. On show are erotic shorts, footage from the Jubilee Day procession that summer, as well as the Lumières' *Arrival of a Train at the Station* (1895). The vampire spectator is suitably impressed by this crowning development of nineteenth-century visual culture: 'Astonishing,' he tells his 'date' and intended victim, 'there are no limits to science.'[1] Up until now, the emphasis upon early cinema has been stylistic rather than thematic. In the introduction to *Bram Stoker's 'Dracula': The Film and the Legend* (1992), the official companion book to the film that includes James V. Hart's screenplay, Coppola explains how:

> We have tried for a unique, striking visual style that immediately says you are in the realm of magic. We explored the tradition of early cinema when magicians first brought cinema to the world – which was the period when Stoker wrote *Dracula*. So we have used

---

[1] *Bram Stoker's 'Dracula'*, dir. by Francis Ford Coppola, ad. by James V. Hart (Columbia Pictures, 1992).

'The Amazing Cinematograph'

many of those naïve effects, tricks done with the camera or with mirrors, to give the film almost a mythical soul.[2]

Coppola is referring to stage magicians like George Méliès, whose experience at the Théâtre Robert Houdin allowed him to exploit the illusionist potential of the new medium. *Dracula* (1897) readily lends itself to this kind of adaptation on account of the illusory quality of Stoker's vampire. Dracula is also a magician of sorts: he shifts shape and vanishes into thin air, orchestrates howling wolves and conjures armies of rats, and is endowed with hypnotic power. The novel is characterised by telling moments of perceptual drama. For example, on the way to the castle, Jonathan Harker sees blue flames in the forest which the coach driver (Dracula) stops to examine. 'Once there appeared a strange optical effect,' notes Jonathan:

> … when he stood between me and the flame he did not obstruct it, for I could see its ghostly flicker all the same. This startled me, but as the effect was momentary, I took it that my eyes deceived me straining through the darkness.[3]

The body is rendered transparent and insubstantial, contrary perhaps to the characterisation of the vampire in terms of its bodily needs, the emphasis on materiality. Jonathan explains it away prematurely as is his wont, but

---

[2] Francis Ford Coppola and James V. Hart, *Bram Stoker's 'Dracula': The Film and the Legend* (New York: Newmarket Press, 1992), p. 5. All further references will be given in the body of the text.

[3] Bram Stoker, *Dracula*, ed. by Maud Ellmann (Oxford: Oxford University Press, 1996), p. 13. All further references will be given in the body of the text.

the 'strange optical effect' provides the reader with an early indication of the supernatural status of the Count, his transgression of the boundary between life and death. The following essay will continue to look at the theme of illusion and the stylistic emphasis on early cinema in *Bram Stoker's 'Dracula'*, before it gives closer consideration to the depiction of Dracula in London and the cinematograph scene itself, and then concludes with some thoughts about the contemporaneous emergence of cinema and *fin-de-siècle* Gothic more generally.

It is possible to detect an allusion to the magic theatre at the beginning of *Bram Stoker's 'Dracula'*, in terms of the lantern Dracula is holding when he welcomes Jonathan to the castle, one which throws a grotesque shadow upon the wall behind and gives the lie to his warm words of welcome. 'The main feature of conjuring and magic theatre', according to Paul Hammond, 'was the exploitation of optical trickery to achieve spectacular imagery, with isolated illusions linked by melodramatic narrative'.[4] In many ways, this provides an accurate description of the castle scenes themselves. The vampire, of course, casts no reflection. At one point, Dracula's arm creeps up behind Jonathan as he shaves and rests upon his shoulder, visible to the viewer but invisible in the glass. Dracula rather prosaically throws the mirror – 'a foul bauble of man's vanity' – out of the window in the novel (Stoker, ed. Ellmann, p. 26). Coppola uses the opportunity for another trick, as well as for psychological comment on Jonathan himself. Having glided unnaturally behind Jonathan, Dracula spots the mirror over his guest's shoulder. As he shields himself from this tell-tale object, it shatters. Jonathan, bewildered by the absent reflection, is

---

[4] Paul Hammond, *Marvellous Méliès* (London: Gordon Fraser Gallery, 1974), p. 7.

'The Amazing Cinematograph'

looking into the mirror at the time; it is his image that splinters, symbolic of his crisis of subjectivity in Transylvania.

The mirror renders Dracula invisible but he also has the power to make himself unseen in the film. Upon his arrival in England, Dracula copulates in bestial form with Lucy Westenra in the garden at Hillingham. When they are overlooked by Mina, the reincarnation of his former wife, he commands her not to see him. Conversely, he orders her to meet his gaze, after he spots her on the crowded London streets. Having introduced himself, when she ignores his subsequent advances and leaves him standing on the pavement, he demonstrates his ability to vanish and rematerialize at will; disquietingly, he reappears in front of her. Interestingly, Abraham van Helsing pulls a similar trick in the garden at Hillingham before the men. The 'metaphysician philosopher' who Quincey Morris thinks 'sounds like a goddamn witch doctor' is also a magician of sorts and appears to possess preternatural powers of detection, something that is suggested by the way in which he waltzes with Mina upon their introduction, for she has recently waltzed with Dracula. Having looked directly into her eyes with his powerful gaze, he sniffs her as if to search for the scent of the vampire, whom he resembles even more than in the novel.[5] The way in which he tucks into bloody roast beef and downs dark coloured alcohol when dining with the Harkers emphasises the point. In the garden he is battling to remove the rationalist blinkers that prevent Dr Seward from identifying the cause of Lucy's dramatic loss of blood. 'You do not let your eyes see,' he chides, 'that which you cannot account for.' He illustrates

---

[5] Van Helsing is played by Anthony Hopkins, who was previously Hannibal Lecter in *The Silence of the Lambs* (1991). Hopkins brings something of that role to Van Helsing.

the shortcomings of this logic by vanishing: before his suggestions of 'astral bodies' and 'materialisation' can be scoffed at, he disappears as the men momentarily turn away, only to reappear behind an obelisk some metres distant.

'Transylvania is not England,' counsels Dracula at the end of the mirror scene. 'Our ways are not your ways. There shall be many strange things.' Moments later, Jonathan spots Dracula outside; he is sliding down the castle wall, head first. Jonathan opens the window in disbelief, though even his novelistic counterpart cannot doubt the evidence of his own senses on this occasion: 'I thought it was some trick of the moonlight, some weird effect of shadow; but I kept looking, and it could be no delusion' (Stoker, ed. Ellmann, p. 34). The way in which the vampire defies gravity provides another example of its illusory quality, and the sight of the upside-down count introduces a sequence of similar trick shots as Jonathan explores the topsy-turvy world of the castle. Upturned rats scurry along the beams above, drops drip upwards from a perfume bottle and one of the vampire brides even sticks to the ceiling when Dracula flings her off Jonathan. In *Dracula*, Jonathan assumes that he must be dreaming when he first sees the vampire women, 'for, though the moonlight was behind them, they threw no shadow on the floor' (Stoker, ed. Ellmann, p. 37). Coppola restores the shadow of the vampire, another key component of this illusory quality. For example, Dracula's shadow trails behind him; at the end of the mirror scene, it belatedly moves across the room after he has made his exit. On another occasion, Jonathan turns to where Dracula should still be standing according to his shadow, only he has vanished in order to reappear on the side opposite. Such stagy effects make the magic theatre rather than hell the spiritual home of the vampire, though as Iain Sinclair notes

'The Amazing Cinematograph'

in his review of the film, this was 'a world Stoker would have been happy to acknowledge, a world to which he would have been granted access through his long association with Henry Irving'.[6] Once in London, Dracula accosts Mina outside what appears to be the Lyceum; certainly, there is a sandwich-board man visible on the pavement advertising Irving as Hamlet.

Stoker does not mention Dracula visiting the cinematograph and strictly speaking, the reader ought not to imagine him so doing, if, as Clive Leatherdale points out, the novel is set in 1893.[7] Thomas Edison's Kinetoscope, a peepshow machine, premiered in October 1894, while Robert Paul's Theatrograph and the Cinématographe-Lumière were first exhibited in February 1896.[8] *Bram Stoker's 'Dracula'* makes the addition of the cinematograph plausible by shifting the setting to 1897, the year of the novel's publication. If the cinematograph is at odds with the titular claim of the film, it could be argued that its addition is in tune with the modern technological thrust of the novel: the emphasis on advances like the telegraph, the typewriter and the phonograph, which the film retains in a way that distinguishes it from previous adaptations. The problem with this argument is that these devices are used by the vampire hunters and facilitate Dracula's defeat, whereas the cinematograph is linked with

---

[6] Iain Sinclair, 'Invasion of the Blood', in *Film/Literature/Heritage: A 'Sight and Sound' Reader*, ed. by Ginette Vincendeau (London: British Film Institute, 2001), pp. 101-104 (p. 103).

[7] Bram Stoker, *Bram Stoker's 'Dracula' Unearthed*, ann. and ed. by Clive Leatherdale (Westcliff-on-Sea: Desert Island Books, 1998), p. 24.

[8] For a discussion of English early cinema, see John Barnes, *The Beginnings of the Cinema in England* (Newton Abbot: David & Charles, 1976).

the vampire, a curious association in one way given his primeval nature.

If we set aside the issue of the year, it is not far-fetched to imagine Stoker's count visiting the cinematograph, in the sense that it chimes with the vampire's paradoxical yearning to be modern. 'I long to go through the crowded streets of your mighty London,' he tells Jonathan, 'to be in the midst of the whirl and rush of humanity, to share its life, its change, its death, and all that makes it what it is' (p. 20). His speech echoes Charles Baudelaire's description of the *flâneur*, who 'set[s] up house in the heart of the multitude, amid the ebb and flow of movement, in the midst of the fugitive and the infinite'.[9] Of course, Dracula's reference to 'death' clearly hints that he is no 'lover of life' like Baudelaire's *flâneur* (Baudelaire, p. 9). He is a Gothicised *flâneur*.[10] Dracula thinks of London as an attractive hunting ground, its crowds a potential source of food and concealment. Yet there is an additional sense perhaps in which Dracula wants to translate himself into modernity by assuming the role of the *flâneur*. His passage from East to West is a temporal as well as a physical journey.

Coppola's Dracula also speaks of the desire 'to be in the midst of the whirl and rush of humanity'. He repeats the

---

[9] Charles Baudelaire, *The Painter of Modern Life and Other Essays*, trans. and ed. by Jonathan Mayne, 2nd edn, (London: Phaidon, 1995), p. 9. All further references will be given in the body of the text.

[10] For a discussion of Dracula as *flâneur*, see Gill Davies, 'London in *Dracula*; Dracula in London', *Literary London Interdisciplinary Studies in the Representation of London* (2004) <http://www.literarylondon.org/london/journal/march2004/davies.html> [accessed 30 April 2006]. Linda Dryden also discusses the Gothic *flâneur* in *The Modern Gothic and Literary Doubles: Stevenson, Wilde, and Wells* (Basingstoke: Palgrave Macmillan, 2003).

'The Amazing Cinematograph'

above speech almost *ad verbatim*, though he fulfils his wish in a different way, as we shall see. Carol Corbin and Robert Campbell suggest that it is his search for his reincarnated wife 'that takes him to the modern city of London', which is true in its way, though it is the very decision to go to London that has led to her discovery (when Dracula spots the photograph of Mina carried by Jonathan, the solicitor who has come to Transylvania to facilitate his move).[11] In other words, Dracula has chosen London because it *is* a modern city, with all that modernity entails. As Ben Singer observes,

> Modernity implied a phenomenal world – a specifically urban one – that was markedly quicker, more chaotic, fragmented, and disorientating than in previous phases of human culture. Amid the unprecedented turbulence of the big city's traffic, noise, billboards, street signs, jostling crowds, window displays, and advertisements, the individual faced a new intensity of sensory stimulation. The metropolis subjected the individual to a barrage of impressions, shocks, and jolts.[12]

Physically rejuvenated by the blood of the crew of the *Demeter*, Dracula strolls through London shortly after his arrival. If he is out searching for Mina, he also seems to be

---

[11] Carol Corbin and Robert A. Campbell, 'Postmodern Iconography and Perspective in Coppola's *Bram Stoker's 'Dracula'*', *Journal of Popular Film and Television*, 27 (1999), 40-48 (p. 42). All further references will be given in the body of the text.

[12] Ben Singer, 'Modernity, Hyperstimulus, and the Rise of Popular Sensationalism, in *Cinema and the Invention of Modern Life*, ed. by Leo Charney and Vanessa R. Schwartz (Berkeley: University of California Press, 1995), pp. 72-99 (pp. 72-73).

enjoying the 'sensory stimulation' of the street. Carriages drive by, a boy hurtles across the road, men and women crowd along the pavement – a snapshot of metropolitan experience. Amongst them we see road-sweeps, flower-sellers, even a street artist (the so-called painter of modern life, perhaps). A vendor holds aloft a copy of *The Standard*, which reminds the viewer that this is also the age of print media and new journalism. Significantly, when we first see Dracula, he is walking past a butcher's shop, red meat neatly arrayed in the window, a visual reminder of the vampire's atavism. Amusingly, he also walks past a dentist's sign.

The city was not just a question of sensory bombardment. In *Fashioning Gothic Bodies* (2004), Catherine Spooner explains:

> The accelerating commercial culture of the late nineteenth century increasingly became concerned with bodies on display: with women walking unchaperoned through the urban streets and department stores; with fashionably dressed dandies, swells and 'men about town'; with music-hall stars, celebrity actresses and freakshow exhibits. ... Men and women were increasingly displaying *themselves* with the myriad of new techniques of self-presentation afforded by commercial culture. Management of social surfaces took on new complexities as the choice of what to wear and how to wear it became ever more varied, to an ever-wider range of people.[13]

---

[13] Catherine Spooner, *Fashioning Gothic Bodies* (Manchester: Manchester University Press, 2004), p. 86. All further references will be given in the body of the text.

'The Amazing Cinematograph'

Stoker's Dracula speaks of his desire to blend into the crowd: 'I am content if I am like the rest,' he tells Jonathan, 'so that no man stops if he sees me' (Stoker, ed. Ellmann, p. 20). He realises his wish by loitering anonymously in Piccadilly. Coppola's Dracula, however, does not so much acquire the characteristics of the *flâneur* as those of the dandy. According to Deborah Parsons in *Streetwalking the Metropolis* (2000), 'An important difference between the "dandy" and the *flâneur* is that the latter observes whilst the former displays himself for observation. ... The dandy did not want to merge with the crowd but display his distinction from it'.[14] In fact, the *flâneur* is of the crowd but also separate from it, as his role of observer suggests, only he remains anonymous, unlike the eye-catching dandy. Dracula both maintains his aristocratic 'distinction' and modernises himself through his dress and the acquisition of the latest fashion accessories. He is stylishly suited, long hair flows from beneath his top hat, and in his gloved hands he carries a cane adorned with his crest. He clearly intends to make a powerful impression. The blue-tinted spectacles he sports even recall the peacocks at Hillingham, the upper-class address of his first female victim; specifically, the feather of the peacock that veils our view of Mina as she kisses Jonathan goodbye, with its blue-rimmed eyes. Corbin and Campbell suggest that Dracula's appearance marks him out negatively as a stranger, but this rather misses the point of his overt self-display, his assumption of a modern subjectivity that rests upon being seen in public and in a certain way (though one might well question the wisdom of such a choice). In fact, Dracula actually plays up to his foreignness by posing as a tourist,

---

[14] Deborah L. Parsons, *Streetwalking the Metropolis: Women, the City and Modernity* (Oxford: Oxford University Press, 2000), p. 20. All further references will be given in the body of the text.

another form of modern spectatorship, so that he can introduce himself to Mina, whom he rather fortuitously spots. Mina herself represents one of those 'bodies on display' identified by Spooner, for she is walking unchaperoned through the city, as Dracula flirtatiously and rather mischievously points out, given that he has imprisoned her fiancé: 'A woman so lovely and intelligent should not be walking the streets of London without her gentleman.' Dracula's request for directions to the cinematograph is met with the suggestion that, if he is looking for culture, he ought to visit a museum instead.

Carrol Fry and Robert Craig maintain that his incarnation as dandy 'represents Dracula's better nature', demonstrated by the self-control he exerts in not biting Mina, when she eventually escorts him to the cinematograph.[15] This is very different to the predator that ruthlessly feeds on Lucy and that characterises the vampire more generally in the novel. It is also noteworthy given the association of the dandy with monstrosity in late-nineteenth-century Gothic texts like Oscar Wilde's *The Picture of Dorian Gray* (1891). *Bram Stoker's 'Dracula'* seems to reverse this association. In her discussion of the model of subjectivity behind the Gothic dandy, Spooner notes how 'representations of the dandy seem to reproduce a Jekyll-and-Hyde dualism', but suggests we should be wary,

> ... of reiterating the surface-and-depth model of polished exterior concealing monstrous interior. Just as Jekyll himself guesses that man 'will ultimately be known for a mere polity of multifarious,

---

[15] Carrol L. Fry and John Robert Craig, '"Unfit for Earth, Undoomed for Heaven": The Genesis of Coppola's Byronic Dracula', *Literature/Film Quarterly*, 30 (2002), 271-78 (p. 275).

incongruous and independent denizens', a multiple and fragmented rather than merely doubled subject, dandies in Victorian Gothic resist simple dualisms. (p. 87)

Stoker's Dracula is the quintessential plural and disunified subject, and Coppola's costume designer, Eiko Ishioka, has spoken how she 'wanted to give Dracula an infinite variety of personality.... Is he a man or a beast? Devil or angel? Male or female? He is constantly changing, in a different mood each time, like a kaleidoscope' (Coppola and Hart, p. 38). Nonetheless, the scene in which Dracula receives Mina's note, informing him of her departure for Transylvania and of her imminent marriage to Jonathan, clearly suggests the emergence of an essential primitive self. Grief-stricken, his tears melt the handsome features of the dandy and restore the monstrous old face of Dracula; that night he takes a savage delight in condemning Lucy 'to living death – to eternal hunger for living blood.' The ending of the film undercuts this idea in turn. When Mina kisses the dying monster, it is the fifteenth-century prince whose face the dandy shares that is restored.

Spooner also identifies the 'hypnotic power' of nineteenth-century Gothic dandies like Lord Ruthven, Silas Ruthyn and Count Fosco, who anticipate the *fin-de-siècle* figure of George du Maurier's Svengali (pp. 96-97). As critics have noted, Stoker's Dracula has much in common with Svengali, not least in terms of the hypnotic power they exercise over young women, and both *Trilby* (1894) and *Dracula* can be read in terms of the late nineteenth-century debate on hypnotism and crime. Specifically, the sexual anxieties that surrounded the figure of the hypnotist: women were 'to beware the enchantment of strangers and, in particular, the dangers of sexual conquest through hypnosis by unknown men'.¹⁶ Coppola's Dracula retains this hypnotic power, demonstrated by the aforementioned ability to make himself un/seen. 'I couldn't control myself,' Lucy recalls when woken in the garden by Mina, 'I had to, it sort of pulled me and lured me and I had no control – his red eyes!' Lucy is hypnotised before being attacked, though this does not absolve her from complicity as it does in *Dracula*.¹⁷ 'Lucy is not a random victim attacked by mere accident,' Van Helsing tells Morris, 'she is the willing recruit, a breathless follower, a wanton follower, I daresay – a devoted disciple.'

Female conduct is beyond reproach in the novel because (sexual) agency is wholly displaced onto the hypnotic vampire in a way that it is not in the film, contrary to Lucy's protestation above. As Corbin and Campbell state, 'Stoker's women ... are all victims of the Count, taken in rape-like encounters over which they have no control' (p. 45). Another way of reading their powerlessness would be to see it in terms of the coding of female desire; that is to say, Stoker carefully justifies or rationalises the women's attraction to the taboo figure of the vampire by making him literally irresistible. Female desire is a less problematic issue for the late twentieth-century film-maker, with the result that the hypnotic power of the vampire becomes virtually ornamental in *Bram Stoker's 'Dracula'* because both Lucy and Mina are

---

¹⁶ Daniel Pick, *Svengali's Web: The Alien Enchanter in Modern Culture* (New Haven, CT: Yale University Press, 2000), p. 96.

¹⁷ According to Van Helsing, 'She was bitten by the vampire when she was in a trance, sleep-walking – ...and in trance could he best come to take more blood. In trance she died, and in trance she is Un-Dead, too. So it is that she differ from all other' (Stoker, ed. Ellmann, p. 201).

'The Amazing Cinematograph'

'willing'. Mina's initial encounter with Dracula appears to justify the warning 'to beware the enchantment of strangers', as he leads her into the back of the cinematograph and prepares to attack her. Similarly, when Dracula and Mina drink absinthe in the café together, 'the film's floating lights and tinkling music conjure a drug-induced seduction' (Corbin & Campbell, p. 48). Yet it is the benign quality of the vampire's magic that is demonstrated on this last occasion, as Dracula recalls his wife's suicide and turns Mina's subsequent tears into diamonds, another 'trick'. Finally, it is Mina who persuades Dracula to make her a vampire. While Lucy is pretty much an exaggerated version of Stoker's character, it goes without saying that the love theme distorts the original Mina. At one point, we even see the woman who was responsible for the collation of the papers in Stoker's *Dracula* tearing pages from her diary and throwing them into the sea.

Parsons discusses the role optics played in the developing commercial culture of the nineteenth century:

> The interest in optics itself became a commodity as entertainment became increasingly aligned with spectacle, resulting in leisure activities such as panoramas and dioramas, 'toys' such as the kaleidoscope and the stereoscope, the growth of the tourist industry and the development of large, spectacular department stores. (p. 21)

Bram Stoker's 'Dracula' reminds the viewer that this visual culture culminates with the birth of cinema at the turn of the century. As Dracula parades along the pavement, a barker can be heard promoting this most recent development in optical entertainment: 'See the amazing cinematograph – a wonder of modern civilisation, the latest sensation, the attraction of the century, the new wonder of the world!' Earlier it was suggested that the ensuing street scene provides a snapshot of metropolitan experience: 'snapshot' is the wrong (if appropriately modern) metaphor to use, for the scene, introduced through an 'iris-in', is briefly shot in the style of an early film. In this way, Coppola documents 'the early film's fascination with the hustle of street-level *actualité* footage'.[18] A street scene was screened at the premier of the Lumière Cinématographe in Paris. Méliès recalls how,

> ... a horse pulling a wagon began to walk towards us, followed by other vehicles and then pedestrians, in short all the animation of the street. Before this spectacle we sat with gaping mouths, struck with amazement, astonished beyond all expression.[19]

Interestingly, this brief sequence is partly shot from the Count's point of view, reinforcing the association in the film between the vampire and cinema. To use Baudelaire's description of the kaleidoscopic *flâneur*, Dracula is as it were a Pathé camera 'gifted with consciousness' here (p. 10).

As for the films on view themselves, the titillating short watched by Dracula and Mina ironises his paean to science to some degree. The film shows two semi-naked women sitting on a man's lap. The trick of stop action transforms them into a dour looking woman, presumably his wife,

---

[18] Joe Kember, 'Popular Sensations: Institutional Modernity and the Textual History of *The Long Strike*', in *Visual Delights Two: Exhibition and Reception*, ed. by Vanessa Toulmin and Simon Popple (Eastleigh: John Libbey Publishing, 2005), pp. 46-60 (p. 47).

[19] Shepley, M., 'Méliès and Early Film' (n.d.) <http://www.mshepley.btinternet.co.uk/melies2.htm> [accessed 30 April 2006]. All further references will be given in the body of the text.

'The Amazing Cinematograph'

and he despondently pushes her away. The theme of unlicensed desires is central to Bram Stoker's 'Dracula', of course. The man may remind the viewer of Jonathan, who cuts a repressed figure at home, but succumbs easily to the temptations of the vampire brides at the castle before marrying his outwardly straight-laced fiancée. Mina herself has been conducting her own affair in his absence with Dracula, who is also brought into mind by the man in the film, where the two women would signify Mina and Lucy. 'Infidelity', to use Van Helsing's word to describe Jonathan's relations with the vampire brides, is the norm. There is also a black and white peep show in the booth. In this way, Coppola documents the early film's additional fascination with the erotic image and comments on the appeal of the vampire genre itself, the sexual voyeurism with which *Bram Stoker's 'Dracula'* is unapologetically complicit. As Jacqueline LeBlanc notes, 'Featuring bare breasts and erotic scenes of orgasmic passion, Coppola's film provides the 1990s version of the early cinema's titillation. It offers up a blatant version of the sexuality more prudishly figured in Stoker's novel'.[20]

The erotic films give the cinematograph a sleazy air, 'which must leave the viewer wondering why Dracula would risk taking Mina to such a place', according to Alain Silver and James Ursini.[21] As a public space in which privacy of sorts is possible, it makes a convenient locale for

---

[20] Jacqueline LeBlanc, '"It is not good to note this down": *Dracula* and the Erotic Technologies of Censorship', in *Bram Stoker's* Dracula: *Sucking Through the Century, 1897-1997*, ed. by Carol Margaret Davison (Toronto: Dundurn Press, 1997), pp. 261-281 (pp. 261-262).

[21] Alain Silver and James Ursini, *The Vampire Film: From 'Nosferatu' to 'Interview with the Vampire'*, 3rd Limelight edn (New York: Limelight Editions, 1997), p. 158.

her vampiric seduction. It could also be argued that Dracula is hardly going to worry about offending her middle class sensibilities, when he is intent upon biting her neck and drinking her blood. In symbolic terms, it is highly appropriate that the character who has been 'seducing' women on film for much of the twentieth century, indeed, whose screen popularity attests to the seductive attraction of the vampire for the cinema audience, should lure one of his potential victims to this darkened space and it is deeply ironic that he cannot perform on this occasion. Besides, the fact that this is not somewhere a woman like Mina should be, let alone in the company of a handsome stranger, as she soon realises, is rather the point.

We saw earlier how the modern city is characterised by its 'sensory stimulation'. In 'The Metropolis and Mental Life' (1903), Georg Simmel describes how the city dweller is overwhelmed by 'the rapid crowding of changing images, the sharp discontinuity in the grasp of a single glance, and the unexpectedness of onrushing impressions'.[22] Critics like Vanessa Schwartz have noted that these 'words could serve as a description of the cinema; the experience of the city set the terms for the experience of other elements of modernity'.[23] This makes the cinematograph the logical destination for the vampire eager to experience 'the whirl and rush'. The idea of 'the

---

[22] Georg Simmel, 'The Metropolis and Mental Life: [Extract]', in *The Nineteenth-Century Visual Culture Reader*, ed. by Vanessa R. Schwartz and Jeannene M. Przyblyski (London: Routledge, 2004), pp. 51-55 (p. 51).

[23] Vanessa R. Schwartz, 'Walter Benjamin for Historians', *The American Historical Review*, 106.5 (2001)
<http://www.historycooperative.org/journals/ahr/106.5/ah0501001721.html> [accessed 29 November 2005] [para. 30 of 50]

unexpectedness of onrushing impressions' is especially applicable to *Arrival of a Train at the Station* which also plays in the booth, whether or not we take seriously the reports of audiences ducking behind their seats. Tom Gunning has identified 'a basic aesthetic of early cinema' that he calls '"the cinema of attractions", which envisioned cinema as a series of visual shocks'.[24] Films like *Arrival of a Train at the Station* 'present the shock of cinema in an exaggerated form' (p. 824). Gunning actually debunks the idea of the spectator who is fearful of the oncoming train, and in *Bram Stoker's 'Dracula'* it takes the escaped wolf that roams the booth, rather than an illusory engine, to send the audience into panic. Nevertheless, the inclusion of *Arrival of a Train at the Station* inevitably brings with it the image of the terrified spectator 'hypnotised and transfixed' like the very victim of the vampire (p. 819). This image will recur in accounts of the reception of late twentieth-century horror films like *The Exorcist* (1973), which *Bram Stoker's 'Dracula'* references, most obviously when the vampire Lucy vomits blood over Van Helsing.[25] Sequences like this one are themselves obviously intended to shock or assault

---

[24] Tom Gunning, 'An Aesthetic of Astonishment: Early Film and The (In)Credulous Spectator', *Art and Text*, 34 (1989). Reprinted in *Film Theory and Criticism: Introductory Readings*, ed. by Leo Braudy and Marshall Cohen, 5th edn (New York: Oxford University Press, 1999), pp. 818-32 (p. 824). All further references will be given in the body of the text.

[25] John Nicholson describes how, with *The Exorcist*, 'The stunt of having emergency staff to save the terrified moved up a notch. Cinemas had to cope with patrons being physically overcome. Stories spread of vomiting, possession, even death in the auditorium': see 'Scared Shitless: the Sex of Horror', in *Creepers: British Horror and Fantasy in the Twentieth Century*; ed. by Clive Bloom (London: Pluto Press, 1993), pp. 120-35 (p. 124).

the viewer. In the mirror scene, for example, Dracula relieves Jonathan of his razor, turns towards the camera and wipes its bloody blade across his tongue.

Returning to where we began, the astonished Count reacts to the cinematograph rather like Méliès, one optical illusion in awe of another. Dracula later reveals his illusory status to Mina by placing her hand over his absent heart. 'There is no life in this body,' he tells her. 'I am nothing. Lifeless, soulless, hated and feared. I am dead to all the world. ... I am the monster the breathing men would kill.' Dracula is less like 'the breathing men' than 'the body that has been filmed – de-realized but also made magically present through its capture by the cinema machine', an analogy that is promoted by the way images momentarily flicker over him in the cinematograph scene.[26] Nicholas Daly refers 'to the extensive set of late Victorian tales that dwell on the existence of "dead" things that have a life of their own – vampires, mummies, portraits', and suggests that 'it is tempting to speculate that the appearance of those tales in or around 1895 is not a coincidence' (p. 60). In other words, Gothic entities like the living portrait in Oscar Wilde's *The Picture of Dorian Gray* (1891), or Stoker's 'undead' Count, confound the distinction between life and death, and in so doing prefigure or resemble the uncanny cinematic body. Indeed, the memorial nature of film subsequently theorised by André Bazin in his essay 'The Ontology of the Photographic Image'[27] was quickly recognised: 'When these gadgets are in the hands of the

---

[26] Nicholas Daly, *Literature, Technology, and Modernity, 1860-2000* (Cambridge: Cambridge University Press, 2004), p. 57. All further references will be given in the body of the text.

[27] André Bazin,'The Ontology of the Photographic Image', in *What is Cinema?: Essays*, sel. and trans. by Hugh Gray, 2 vols (Berkeley: University of California Press, 1967-72), I, 9-16.

'The Amazing Cinematograph'

public', ran the report of the Lumière Cinématographe premiere in *La Poste*, 'then death will no longer be final' (Shepley, 1). This drive to overcome mortality informs Mina's plea to 'Take me way from all this death!' in *Bram Stoker's 'Dracula'*.[28]

Fin-de-siècle Gothic and the birth of cinema are contemporaneous because they are partly produced by, or responses to, the same cultural forces, making cinema 'Gothic' and *fin-de-siècle* Gothic 'cinematic'.[29] According to Brian Coe, 'By the middle of the 1880s everything was ready for the appearance of cinematography'.[30] Significantly, this is when the Gothic re-emerges with the publication of *Strange Case of Dr Jekyll and Mr Hyde* (1886). Siegbert Prawer comments in *Caligari's Children* (1980) how, 'A careful reading of Stevenson's story confirms that there was such a thing as the cinematic imagination before there was a cinema'.[31] Something similar can be said of *The Picture of Dorian Gray*. A parallel can be identified between Dorian's picture and early cinematic technology, as the novel taps into those undercurrents that contribute to the ensuing '"Living Picture" craze' (Coe, p. 76). The idea of the living portrait, the fact that it changes or moves, and

---

[28] For a different reading of this line, see: Ken Gelder, *Reading the Vampire* (London: Routledge, 1994), p. 89.

[29] For a discussion of the Gothic nature of cinema, see Gelder, pp. 87-88.

[30] Brian Coe, *The History of Movie Photography* (London: Ash & Grant, 1981), p. 54. All further references will be given in the body of the text.

[31] Siegbert S. Prawer, *Caligari's Children: The Film as Tale of Terror*, rev. edn (New York: DA Capo Press, 1989), p. 105. Prawer continues: '[Stevenson's] externalization of an inner conflict in the shape of Jekyll-and-Hyde, his description of Utterson's mode of dreaming and apprehending, are cases in point' (p. 105).

the descriptions of the spectator Dorian viewing it, a kind of screen onto which his transgressions are projected, are further examples of the 'cinematic imagination' which is also at work in *Dracula* (one may recall the 'strange optical effect' as the spectator Jonathan gazes intently at the flickering light through the dark) and which makes the addition of the cinematograph in *Bram Stoker's 'Dracula'* paradoxically in keeping with the novel, as has been argued. The significant point about *Dracula* is precisely how it facilitates an early cinematic adaptation.

Bibliography

Primary Works

Bram Stoker, *Dracula*, ed. by Maud Ellmann (Oxford: Oxford University Press, 1996)

Bram Stoker's 'Dracula', dir. by Francis Ford Coppola, ad. by James V. Hart (Columbia Pictures, 1992)

Secondary Works

Barnes, John, *The Beginnings of the Cinema in England* (Newton Abbot: David & Charles, 1976)

Baudelaire, Charles, *The Painter of Modern Life and Other Essays*, trans. and ed. by Jonathan Mayne, 2nd edn, (London: Phaidon, 1995)

Bazin, André, 'The Ontology of the Photographic Image', in *What is Cinema?: Essays*, sel. and trans. by Hugh

'The Amazing Cinematograph' Gray, 2 vols (Berkeley: University of California Press, 1967-72), I, 9-16

Coe, Brian, *The History of Movie Photography* (London: Ash & Grant, 1981)

Coppola, Francis Ford, and James V. Hart, *Bram Stoker's 'Dracula': The Film and the Legend* (New York: Newmarket Press, 1992)

Corbin, Carol, and Robert A. Campbell, 'Postmodern Iconography and Perspective in Coppola's *Bram Stoker's 'Dracula'*", *Journal of Popular Film and Television*, 27 (1999), 40-48

Daly, Nicholas, *Literature, Technology, and Modernity, 1860-2000* (Cambridge: Cambridge University Press, 2004)

Davies, Gill, 'London in *Dracula*; Dracula in London', *Literary London: Interdisciplinary Studies in the Representation of London* (2004) <http://www.literarylondon.org/london/journal/march2004/davies.html> [accessed 30 April 2006]

Dryden, Linda, *The Modern Gothic and Literary Doubles: Stevenson, Wilde, and Wells* (Basingstoke: Palgrave Macmillan, 2003)

Fry, Carrol L., and John Robert Craig, '"Unfit for Earth, Undoomed for Heaven": The Genesis of Coppola's

Byronic Dracula', *Literature/Film Quarterly*, 30 (2002), 271-78

Gelder, Ken, *Reading the Vampire* (London: Routledge, 1994)

Gunning, Tom, 'An Aesthetic of Astonishment: Early Film and The (In)Credulous Spectator', *Art and Text*, 34 (1989). Reprinted in *Film Theory and Criticism: Introductory Readings*, ed. by Leo Braudy and Marshall Cohen, 5th edn (New York: Oxford University Press, 1999), pp. 818-32

Hammond, Paul, *Marvellous Méliès* (London: Gordon Fraser Gallery, 1974)

Kember, Joe, 'Popular Sensations: Institutional Modernity and the Textual History of *The Long Strike*', in *Visual Delights Two: Exhibition and Reception*, ed. by Vanessa Toulmin and Simon Popple (Eastleigh: John Libbey, 2005), pp. 46-60

LeBlanc, Jacqueline, '"It is not good to note this down": *Dracula* and the Erotic Technologies of Censorship', in *Bram Stoker's* Dracula: *Sucking Through the Century, 1897-1997*, ed. by Carol Margaret Davison (Toronto: Dundurn Press, 1997), pp. 249-68

'The Amazing Cinematograph'

Nicholson, John, 'Scared Shitless: the Sex of Horror', in *Creepers: British Horror and Fantasy in the Twentieth Century*, ed. by Clive Bloom (London: Pluto Press, 1993), pp. 120-35

Parsons, Deborah L., *Streetwalking the Metropolis: Women, the City, and Modernity* (Oxford: Oxford University Press, 2000)

Pick, Daniel, *Svengali's Web: The Alien Enchanter in Modern Culture* (New Haven, CT: Yale University Press, 2000)

Prawer, Siegbert S., *Caligari's Children: The Film as Tale of Terror*, rev. edn (New York: DA Capo Press, 1989)

Schwartz, Vanessa R., 'Walter Benjamin for Historians', *The American Historical Review*, 106.5 (2001) <http://www.historycooperative.org/journals/ahr/106.5/ah0501001721.html> [accessed 29 November 2005] [para. 30 of 50]

Shepley, M., 'Méliès and Early Film' (n.d.) <http://www.mshepley.btinternet.co.uk/melies2.htm> [accessed 30 April 2006]

Silver, Alain, and James Ursini, *The Vampire Film: From 'Nosferatu' to 'Interview with the Vampire'*, 3rd Limelight edn (New York: Limelight Editions, 1997)

Simmel, Georg, 'The Metropolis and Mental Life: [Extract]', in *The Nineteenth-Century Visual Culture Reader*, ed. by Vanessa R. Schwartz and Jeannene M. Przyblyski (London: Routledge, 2004), pp. 51-55

Sinclair, Iain, 'Invasion of the Blood', in *Film/Literature/Heritage: A 'Sight and Sound' Reader*, ed. by Ginette Vincendeau (London: British Film Institute, 2001), pp. 101-4

Singer, Ben, 'Modernity, Hyperstimulus, and the Rise of Popular Sensationalism, in *Cinema and the Invention of Modern Life*, ed. by Leo Charney and Vanessa R. Schwartz (Berkeley: University of California Press, 1995), pp. 72-99

Spooner, Catherine, *Fashioning Gothic Bodies* (Manchester: Manchester University Press, 2004)

Stoker, Bram, *Bram Stoker's 'Dracula' Unearthed*, ann. and ed. by Clive Leatherdale (Westcliff-on-Sea: Desert Island Books, 1998)

Part 2

Adapting the Twentieth-Century Novel

ADAPTING THE TWENTIETH-CENTURY NOVEL

The process of screen adaptation, and perhaps also the academic study of the literature/film relationship, finds its most intriguing, troubling and difficult cases in the attempts to film the experimental fiction of the twentieth century. There have been film versions of modernist literary works such as Woolf's *Mrs Dalloway* (1997), James Joyce's *Ulysses* (1967) and Proust's *À la recherche du temps perdu* (as *Swann in Love*, 1984, and *Time Regained*, 1999). In a sense, perhaps for some modernist novels, this is not so surprising. The fragmentation, self-consciousness of form, collision of different discourses or images, and emphasis on the dislocation and ennui produced by urban modernity are also crucial to the forms of early cinema. What Walter Benjamin identified as the 'shock' of modernity is reproduced in the collision of images in cinematic montage, and films such as Dziga Vertov's *Man with a Movie Camera* (1929) attempt to present, in cinematic form, the kaleidoscopic subjective experience of the city that is also the focus of much modernist writing and art. While cinema may not find a simple analogue for the representations of interiority achieved by modernist literary forms, in the work of Vertov or Laszlo Moholoy-Nagy film finds an 'expressionism' which can be related to the impetus towards abstraction and away from mimetic representationalism which can be found across art forms in the first half of the twentieth century.

Some modernist writers embraced the cinema: the poet H.D. and novelist Dorothy Richardson were both heavily involved with the film journal *Close-Up* at the end of the 1920s and beginning of the 1930s; and writers such as the American John Dos Passos were clearly influenced by filmic technique in their novels, such as in Dos Passos's compendious *U.S.A.* (1930-6), which includes 'Camera Eye' and 'Newsreel' sections. Others, such as Woolf, were less sympathetic. However, Woolf's experiments with representing psychological interiority – the so-called 'stream of consciousness', a coinage of William James – were strongly influenced by the philosopher Henri Bergson. Bergson's conception of time was of a mobile fluidity which he called *durée* or 'duration', which can only be perceived using intuition, not through the mechanical divisions of 'clock time'. Bergson's ideas are crucial to Woolf's method, and Deniz Baker examines these influences in her essay in this section. For contemporary film theorists, Bergson is also important, because of his influence on the French philosopher (and film theorist) Gilles Deleuze, whose work on cinema is currently highly visible. For Deleuze, *time* and *movement* are crucial in thinking cinema, perhaps vice versa: that cinema is a fundamental tool for thinking temporality and human existence.[1]

The difficulties in finding visual or cinematic analogues of modernist or postmodernist literary techniques are exposed in the film version of *Mrs Dalloway* that Deniz Baker investigates in her essay. How does a film adapt a modernist text without resorting to a laborious (and perhaps too obvious) formal tricksiness, or the reverse, a flattening of the source text into a quasi-realist continuity-style diegesis? William Stephenson, in his essay, explores the decisions made by the film-makers in adapting John Fowles's *The French Lieutenant's Woman*, and their search for *cinematic* means to present the formally experimental novel. The answer, in this case as in others – such as the

---

[1] See Gilles Deleuze, *Cinema 1: The movement-image*, trans. by Hugh Tomlinson and Barbara Habberjam, new edn (London: Continuum, 2005); Gilles Deleuze, *Cinema 2: The time–image*, trans. by Hugh Tomlinson and Robert Galeta, new edn (London: Continuum, 2005).

adaptation of the 'unfilmable' *Tristram Shandy*, titled *A Cock and Bull Story* (2005) – is to turn to the device of a film-within-a-film, and a high level of self-reflexivity and self-consciousness within the adaptation itself.

This self-consciousness leads us to another connection between Deniz Baker's essay and that of William Stephenson, in their approach to their respective texts: both suggest a kind of multiple model of adaptation. Stephen Daldry's film of *The Hours* (2002) is both an adaptation of Michael Cunningham's novel, and a refraction of Woolf's *Mrs Dalloway*; and the novel of *The French Lieutenant's Woman* is dramatised through Harold Pinter's script, the director's decisions, the work of the actors and, most intriguingly, in negotiation with the perception of the audience. For both the essays that follow, adaptation is intertextual in many, surprising ways.

MODERNIST WRITING, THE CINEMATIC IMAGE AND TIME

Deniz Baker

Modernism developed at around the same time as cinema. Experimental writers like H.D. and Dorothy Richardson contributed to discussions of film, in magazines such as *Close-Up* (1927-1933). The literary attributes of modernism have been discussed by critics and scholars in terms of a 'cinematic' language, its prose possessing features that can be identified as analogous to the close-up, long shot, cut and flashback. In this chapter I will explore some of the relationships between film and literary modernism, looking particularly at the way in which Virginia Woolf and her writings have come to occupy such a prominent place in the literary and cultural field and then go on to explore the ways in which Woolf inscribes narrative time and the implications of this for adaptations of her work into narrative film.[1]

Modernism and representations of time

Discussions of literary modernism have suggested that a sense of movement characterises the writing.[2] The

---

[1] For a selection of writings by modernist writers on film from a key cinema journal of the period, see *Close Up, 1927-1933: Cinema and Modernism*, ed. by James Donald, Anne Friedberg and Laura Marcus (London: Cassell, 1998). See also Maggie Humm, *Modernist Women and Visual Cultures: Virginia Woolf, Vanessa Bell, Photography and Cinema*. (Edinburgh: Edinburgh University Press, 2002).

[2] See Michael Hollington, 'Svevo, Joyce and Modernist Time', in *Modernism: A Guide to European Literature 1880-1930*; ed. by Malcolm Bradbury and James McFarlane, new edn (Hassocks: Harvester Press,

Modernist Writing, the Cinematic Image and Time

narrative method of modernist prose can be discussed in terms of a movement of the eye across the surface of life. In her essay 'Street Haunting' (1930), Woolf presents us with the following image:

> The shell-like covering which our souls have excreted to house themselves, to make for themselves a shape distinct from others, is broken, and there is left of all these wrinkles and roughnesses a central oyster of perceptiveness, an enormous eye.[3]

Woolf returns throughout the essay to two ideas contained in this quotation. One is the importance of the *visual*; and the other is the *construction of subjectivity*, here imaged as being fluid (the central oyster of perception), but which requires boundaries between self and other for protection (the shell-like covering). Woolf is attentive to the qualities of visual perception: 'We are only gliding smoothly on the surface. The eye is not a miner, not a diver, not a seeker after buried treasure. It floats us smoothly down a stream; resting, pausing, the brain sleeps perhaps as it looks.'[4] But the eye does not provide total satisfaction for the writer: 'We are in danger of digging deeper than the eye approves; we are impeding our passage down the smooth stream by catching at some branch or root.'[5] The Woolfian subject

---

1978), pp. 430-42. In relation to Dorothy Richardson, see Jean Radford, *Dorothy Richardson* (New York: Harvester Wheatsheaf, 1991).

[3] Virginia Woolf, 'Street Haunting: A London adventure', in *Collected Essays*,.4 (London: Hogarth Press, 1967), pp. 155-166 (p. 156).

[4] Woolf, 'Street Haunting', p. 156.

[5] Woolf, 'Street Haunting', p. 157.

apprehends urban life in the way that a spectator views a film. The *flâneur* or *flâneuse*⁶ exists as a disembodied eye consuming a series of separate impressions. Spectatorship is here associated with 'the surface' and the rendering passive of 'the brain'. Balanced against the passive motion of the eye is an attentive stillness.⁷

Relating Woolf's writing strategies to Henri Bergson's ideas of time and its perception/construction, it can be seen that modernist writing moves across the surface of life, but also resists the motion of urban modernity by means of the 'epiphany'. The epiphanic moment is one of expanded consciousness, not characterised by motion but by *stasis*. It is represented in modernist literature by Proust's 'madeleine moment', in which the protagonist of *À la recherche du temps perdu* is viscerally connected to an earlier moment and an earlier self by the simple act of dipping a cake into a drink.⁸ Modernity's disjointed and

---

⁶ For the *flâneur*, see Walter Benjamin, 'On some motifs of Baudelaire', in *Illuminations*, ed. by Hannah Arendt, trans. by Harry Zohn, new edn (London: Fontana, 1992), pp. 152-196; Walter Benjamin, *The Arcades Project*, trans. by Howard Eiland and Kevin McLaughlin (Cambridge MA: Belknap Press, 1999); and the essays in *The Flâneur*; ed. by Keith Tester (London: Routledge, 1994). For the implications of gender on the *flâneur*, see Deborah L. Parsons, *Streetwalking the Metropolis: Women, the City, and Modernity* (Oxford: Oxford University Press, 2000).

⁷ For the importance of attention as a psychological phenomenon in the nineteenth century and after, see Jonathan Crary, *Suspensions of Perception: Attention, Spectacle, and Modern Culture* (Cambridge MA: MIT Press, 1999), and Jonathan Crary, *Techniques of the Observer: On Vision and Modernity in the Nineteenth Century* (Cambridge MA: MIT Press, 1990).

⁸ Marcel Proust, *Remembrance of Things Past* [*À la recherche du temps perdu*], trans. by C. K. Scott Moncrieff and Stephen Hudson, 7 vols (London: Chatto and Windus, 1922-31). The 'madeleine moment' is from volume 1, *Swann's Way*.

Modernist Writing, the Cinematic Image and Time

fragmented reality resolves into such moments of consciousness. The speed of modern life is stopped and encapsulated in an image.[9]

Woolf called these epiphanies 'moments of being'. In 'A Sketch of the Past' (1939), Woolf described everyday life as being 'embedded in a kind of nondescript cotton'. 'Moments of being' are rare interludes in existence otherwise embedded in cotton wool. She writes: 'behind the cotton wool is hidden a pattern; that we – I mean all human beings – are connected with this; that the whole world is a work of art; that we are parts of the work of art'. The idea that relations between elements rather than their sequence provide meaning is explored by other modernists, notably Dorothy Richardson.[10] The ambivalence of literary modernism to the linear movement in the cinematic image is contained in the desire to condense the subject's experience of modernity to a static

---

[9] Ezra Pound's imagist poem, 'In a station of the metro', is a good example of this: bustling urban life is rendered as fixed image. See *Collected Early Poems of Ezra Pound*, ed. by Michael John King (London: Faber, 1977).

[10] Virginia Woolf, 'A Sketch of the Past', in *Moments of Being*, edited by Jeanne Schulkind, 2nd edn (London: Grafton, 1989), pp. 69-174 (p. 79; p. 81). Dorothy Richardson describes the aesthetic in the following terms in an essay from 1948, 'Novels', from *Life and Letters Today*, 56, 127, (March 1948):

> Today there are novels wherein the interest of any single part is no longer dependent for the reader upon exact knowledge of what has gone before or upon frothy excitement …as to what next will happen. Such novels may be entered at any point, read backwards, or from the centre to either extremity and will reveal, like a mosaic, the inter-dependence of the several parts, each one bearing the stamp of the author's consciousness. (p. 92)

moment. For the philosopher Henri Bergson, the mechanism of film is analogous to the way in which human beings conceptualise time. Indeed, this is the basis of his critique of film.[11] Fragmented, discontinuous moments (images) are run together (through a projector) to give the illusion of continuous motion, in the same way that the intellect segments and fragments time in order to represent it.

The phrase 'the hours', a working title for *Mrs Dalloway*, which Michael Cunningham gives as title to his adaptation of (and homage to) Woolf's work and her life, takes us to the heart of Woolf's concerns with chronological or clock time. The *public* realm is characterised by a linear unravelling of time. It is measured in seconds, minutes, hours and days. The momentum is always forward and contrasts sharply with Woolf's depiction of the psychological perception of time. The narrative of *Mrs Dalloway* holds external time in tension with internal time. Big Ben chimes the hours of the one day in which the story unfolds and the novel progresses through the course of that day from morning to midnight. However, that day contains all of life.

Through the course of the narrative of *Mrs Dalloway* the chimes of Big Ben echo. The clock marks the passage of the hour and the half-hour through the day and is heard by several of the main protagonists. In fact, clock time does

---

[11] Henri Bergson, *Time and Freewill: An Essay on the Immediate Data of Consciousness*, trans. by F. L. Pogson, 2nd edn (1899; London: Allen and Unwin, 1912). For Gilles Deleuze's application of Bergsonian ideas of time and the *durée* to cinema, see his (currently highly influential) volumes *Cinema 1: The Movement-Image,* trans. by Hugh Tomlinson and Barbara Hammerjam, new edn (London: Continuum, 2005), and *Cinema 2: The Time-Image,* trans. by Hugh Tomlinson and Robert Galeta, new edn (London: Continuum, 2005).

the opposite of what Clarissa does. It fragments. She binds: 'Shredding and slicing, dividing and subdividing, the clocks of Harley Street nibbled at the June day, counselled submission, upheld authority.'[12] Big Ben marks our passage through the narrative: 'a suspense ... before Big Ben strikes. There! Out it boomed. First a warning musical; then the hour irrevocable. The leaden circles dissolved into air' (p. 6).

The narrative impedes the apparently inexorable progress of chronology by means of the excursions or digressions that it makes, primarily, though not exclusively, into Clarissa Dalloway's past. Woolf presents the reader with a story which is unfolding in the present, but which is also always looping back or ahead of itself. The tension in the prose, therefore, is between *movement* and *stasis*, or surface and depth. Characters are shown physically existing in the present but psychologically dislocated, inhabiting the past or future. Septimus Smith is a man who is caught in an anterior moment of trauma, the death by exploding bombshell of his friend and fellow soldier, Evans. He is trapped in, and always repeating, the moment before Evans's death. Clarissa too is prone to remembrance, but is also prone to anticipation. The past provides a memory of joy while the future brings anxiety. Though these fictional characters live in clock time, their inner worlds are dislocated from it and their sense of self is derived largely from the acts of re-memorisation or anticipation.

While it is true to say that the events of *Mrs Dalloway* take place on one day, it is also true to say that they encompass the whole of Clarissa's existence, and by

---

[12] Virginia Woolf, *Mrs Dalloway*, new edn (1925; London: Grafton, 1976), p. 91. All further page references will be given in the body of the text.

extension the lives of those people in London whose paths cross hers. Furthermore, the narrative aspires to embody history and prehistory in the anonymous and mythic female vagrant singing her tuneless song. She exists *in* time and is seen by several of the novel's characters. She has a spatial presence which is indicated by her connection with the prehistory of London. Almost archaeologically the figure connects the past with the present:

> A frail quivering sound, a voice bubbling up without direction, vigour, beginning or end, running weakly and shrilly and with absence of all human meaning into:
>
> ee um fah um so
> foo swee too eem oo –
>
> the voice of no age or sex, the voice of an ancient spring sprouting from the earth; which issued, just opposite Regent's Park Tube Station, from a tall quivering shape, like a tunnel, like a rusty pump, like a wind-beaten tree for ever barren of leaves which lets the wind run up and down its branches singing
>
> ee um fah um so
> foo swee too eem oo,
>
> and rocks and creaks and moans in the eternal breeze.
>
> Through all ages – when the pavement was grass, when it was swamp, through the age of tusk and mammoth, through the age of silent sunrise – the battered woman – for she wore a skirt – with her

Modernist Writing, the Cinematic Image and Time

right hand exposed, her left clutching at her side, stood singing of love – love which lasted a million years. (pp. 73-4)

The singer is outside, or underneath society and her meaningless song, a series of obscure sounds, pre-exists language. Her mouth is 'a mere hole in the earth, muddy … matted with root fibres and tangled grasses … through the knotted roots of infinite ages' (p. 73). She herself exists in a state prior to subjectivity. She does not use language. She laughs and sings and her song is millions of years old. She is a sexualised personification of the prehistory of London, embodying its development from swamp to city. Like some pagan deity who is associated with water, she stands for fertility and for life. She is herself a song of love and the song endures. Woolf images a connection between all the inhabitants of London as well as all the stages of London's history, from prehistory to the modern day, as captured and given voice to by the 'song' of the female vagrant. We can see the nameless, timeless figure as a personification of Bergsonian duration.

Woolf's novel can be viewed as being strongly influenced by Bergson's philosophy, especially his doctrine of 'duration' found in *Time and Freewill* (1899). He proposed that the future, like the universe, is not static, but is constituted by a creative process. For Bergson, science and mathematical models of the universe can only give the subject access to time by separating them from their experience. Bergson posits the view that human logic represents time by spatialising it as a set of discrete points joined together. There is sequence in this model of time. Bergson distinguished between this temporal construct and 'real time' or *duration* which is not fragmented. For Bergson, time *as duration* can only be lived through intuition, and not the intellect. For Woolf's fictional characters, time is experienced in one or both of these ways: as interior and simultaneous, or as the linear juxtaposition of one moment followed by another discrete moment. That is why Clarissa Dalloway experiences herself as, simultaneously, the young girl falling in love *and* the middle-aged mother and wife.

So, time passes, but is also ever present. Time is mapped onto space as the characters traverse the city. However, a series of still moments check this linearity. The movements can be thought of in terms of horizontal and vertical axes (surface and depth), which recalls the images from 'Street Haunting' that I cited earlier. The moments of stillness connect the *present* subject with her *past* selves, as well as connecting disparate individuals within the city space. In Mrs *Dalloway*, Clarissa reaches an understanding about her life. Her experience of the day draws on past memories and future anticipation. A sense of collective experience is also represented and unites the inhabitants of London in moments of shared observation. The many examples of these include the car backfiring and speculation as to who is within the dove grey vehicle; the aeroplane looping letters in the sky; and the singing of the homeless woman. Drawing upon another visual analogy, we can say that Woolf connects these dislocated moments to suggest a coherence and a community in the same way that spatial relations unify atomised colour in post-Impressionist painting.[13]

---

[13] See Ann Banfield, 'Time Passes: Virginia Woolf, Post-Impressionism and Cambridge Time', *Poetics Today*, 24 (2003), 471-516, for a fuller discussion of this idea.

Modernist Writing, the Cinematic Image and Time

"The Hours", Hollywood continuity cinema and time

Michael Cunningham's novel, *The Hours*, adapts both Woolf the writer and *Mrs Dalloway*, her novel, in a contemporary (American) consideration of themes that are often cited as recurring concerns of Woolf.[14] I will now focus on two linked themes: the construction of sexual/social identity through the subject's experience of time, and time itself as mediated by city space, especially through the act of walking.

Cunningham shifts the terms of the novel's discussion of these themes in order to encompass shifts in the debates over the past century. Although *Mrs Dalloway* intimates the experience of same-sex desire through the kiss shared by Sally Seton and Clarissa, it turns away from an overt exploration and returns the two women to normative female roles as wives and mothers. Cunningham refocuses what could be seen as a modernist debate about the differences between men and women to consider the spectrum of sexual identities including heterosexuality and homosexuality, while also seeking to move beyond the binaries these terms construct and reflect. In Cunningham's text, gender identity and its exploration are dispersed among four key characters. The first, Virginia Woolf (a fictionalised version of the biographical/historical writer, played by Nicole Kidman), is a woman defined by her creative rather than her sexual identity. Laura Brown's entrapment, as a young mother in 1950s American suburbia (she is played by Julianne Moore), is clearly within the confines of marriage and motherhood. Clarissa Vaughan (Meryl Streep) has achieved both

---

[14] Michael Cunningham, *The Hours*, new edn (1998; London: Fourth Estate, 2003).

motherhood (albeit outside the confines of the heterosexual nuclear family) and professional satisfaction. Richard Brown, a published author (played by Ed Harris), is the fourth character who may be considered in this context. In him we find aspects of Woolf's creativity and sexual complexity. Richard is also connected with Septimus Smith in Woolf's *Mrs Dalloway*, primarily through his mode of death and his status as sacrificial visionary. Richard, like Woolf and like Septimus, commits suicide. The particular definition this act gives to life is also significant. Both Woolf and Cunningham present the suicide as sacrifice which redeems another.

The film of *The Hours* attempts to translate these updated ideas through the cinematic text to a film audience.[15] In *The Hours*, the filmic conventions of contemporary Hollywood cinema countermand the revolutionary politics of literary modernism. Conventions of Hollywood continuity style mitigate against the idea of circularity or stasis in the narrative.[16]

We can link the determinism of Hollywood continuity style to Bergson's theories in *Time and Freewill*. For Bergson, a consequence of what, in his view, was the confusion of space and time, is the idea that everything is determined by a prior cause. According to such a model (challenged by Bergson) human action is conceived of as being *determined by causality*. When two or more events are placed next to one another in sequence the effect is to give

---

[15] *The Hours* [Motion picture], dir. by Stephen Daldry, ad. by David Hare (Miramax , 2003).

[16] For a detailed explanation of Hollywood continuity style, see David Bordwell, Janet Staiger, and Kristin Thompson, *The Classical Hollywood Cinema: Film Style & Mode of Production to 1960* (London: Routledge, 1988).

the appearance of causality. A happened, and then B happened is understood as B happened *because* A happened. In Bergsonian duration there is no juxtaposition of events, no placing them in a spatial relationship and therefore *no causality*. For Bergson, freewill and freedom can only be experienced through duration and the *rejection* of a chain or sequence of events. Freedom for Clarissa Dalloway comes when she pauses from her ceaseless to-ing and fro-ing. Cunningham ultimately confers a similar freedom on his Clarissa.

In Bergson's duration, there is no sequence and no causality. Woolf's modernist text aspires to this freedom from cause and effect by means of a narrative structured around moments of expanded consciousness (Bergsonian duration), moments of memory. Crucially for Bergson, it is only through *memory* that the subject can apprehend the present moment, therefore the distinction between past and present is abolished. The modernist narrative is organised around seemingly disconnected fragments of experience, and is focalised through Clarissa Dalloway; but, it must be noted, through other characters too. These fragmentary and disjointed moments do not add to the forward momentum of plot: they simply appear to reinforce the text's key motifs.

Mrs Dalloway refuses to present the reader with a series of causes and effects which lead to a resolution. The epiphanies serve less to explain 'why?' or 'how?'; instead they reveal states of mind. In a sense, Woolf's text is attempting to *avoid* plot, the satisfaction for the reader being not so much in the resolution of events as in the revelation of a state of being. The text stresses relationships *between* events rather than their sequence.[17] If we

---

[17] Richardson writes:

Textual Revisions

distinguish between story and plot we can see that events that make up a particular narrative can be presented in such a way as to either suggest causality or to problematise the sense of sequence. Our minds always look for meaning, seek structure. As readers and viewers, we infer causality even in purely chronological accounts. We look for plot in even the most abstract and fragmented narrative.

In *The Hours*, Cunningham presents the reader with the familiar figure of the singing woman:

> Ahead under the Arch, an old woman in a dark, neatly tailored dress appears to be singing, stationed precisely between the twin statues of George Washington, as warrior and politician, both faces destroyed by weather. It's the city's crush and heave that move you; its intricacy; its endless life. You know the story about Manhattan as a wilderness purchased for strings of beads but you find it impossible not to believe that it has always been a city; that if you dug beneath it you would find the ruins of another, older city, and then another and another. Under the cement and grass of the park (she has crossed into the park now, where the old woman throws back her head and sings) lay the bones of those buried in the potter's field that was simply paved over, a hundred years ago, to make Washington Square. Clarissa walks over the bodies of the dead as men whisper offers of drugs (not to her) and three black

---

> Now that the stillness had returned, life was going on, dancing, flowing, looping out in all directions, able to bear its periods of torment in the strength of its certainty of recovery, so long as time stayed still. Life ceased when time moved on. Out in the world life was ceasing all the time. All the time people were helplessly doing things that made time move.... (Dorothy Richardson, *Deadlock* [1921]; republished in *Pilgrimage*, III, new edn [London: Virago, 1979], p. 188.)

girls whiz past on roller skates and the old woman sings, tunelessly, iiiiiii.[18]

In this allusion to *Mrs Dalloway*, Cunningham preserves the sense of vertical time in the figure of the anonymous woman. She mitigates against chronological time and links the stages of the city's development. However, Cunningham's text is more 'realist' than Woolf's, his structures more linear. He presents three narrative strands which run in parallel with one another, seemingly close to modernist experimentation; however, the individual narratives are linear and the momentum is towards a resolution which connects and explains the relationships between the lives of the key female protagonists: Virginia Woolf, Laura Brown and Clarissa Vaughan (known as 'Mrs Dalloway' to her former lover, Richard, and identified as such in the section headings). If we exclude the prologue in both book and film, there are three time schemes and also three locations, although the fictional present of the narrative occupies a single day in each case. Although the fictional present occupies one day, the narrative *does* move forward in anticipation and backwards in remembrance, in an echo of Woolf's method. The characters can be said, therefore, to inhabit more than simply the present moment.

Cunningham shows Clarissa reflecting on her epiphany, her moment of happiness as a young student, holidaying with Richard and Louis at Wellfleet. Clarissa remembers a kiss and the feeling that happiness was beginning. However, retrospectively she recognises that it was not the *beginning* of anything, it was *the thing itself*. She can inhabit that moment, relive it and recognise it for

---

[18] Cunningham, p. 14. All further page references will be given in the body of the text.

what it was. It did not lead to anything; it was not part of a causal chain that increased happiness for her.

Cunningham celebrates the solitary and unconnected epiphanies which neither have an origin nor lead onto anything more than the moment itself, and in so doing questions the idea of teleology, the chain of cause and effect. His narrative method relates these ideas rather than embodying them: he *tells* rather than *shows*. There is, as we have seen, a distinction between the novel's presentation of time and that of the film which, it seems, is more bound to Hollywood continuity conventions. This, in turn, leads the viewer to expect coherent psychological motivations and satisfying narrative resolution.

Selfhood, in these texts, is apprehended through time. Clarissa Vaughan spends her day rushing to organise the party. She is mostly anticipating the future, although as we have seen she also evokes events long after they have taken place (the Wellfleet moment). Richard is dislocated from time because of his illness and the medication he takes. In the film, he is depicted crucially as being bound to the trauma of maternal abandonment. He aspires to represent the whole of life in his writing and is the artist/visionary figure, but he believes that he has failed. The film's only flashback proper (if we exclude the prologue and voice-over at the end) is one in which we see again Richie running after his mother as she drives away. The image of him remembering being left by his mother at Mrs Latch's house foreshadows and stands for the eventual absolute abandonment when she leaves her family. In the context of the film, then, we read this as causal. Richie is abandoned by his mother and we infer that this has a causal connection to his suicide.

By emphasising causality rather than contingency, the film renders Richard a victim. In identifying him as the boy in the Laura Brown sequence, the viewer makes sense of the story and understands the connection between Laura Brown and Clarissa Vaughan. The viewer wants to make sense of the events in the three stories and so it is logical to reach this particular narrative resolution. Richard *is* Richie. He links the two stories and Laura Brown (his mother, 'the monster' who abandoned him) finally appears in Clarissa's story after her son's death. The mystery is solved and the quest for meaning satisfied; but, at the cost of demonising the mother.

The film ends with Clarissa, whose narrative trajectory frees her from identification with Woolf's character. With the death of Richard, that name and that identity cease to be. She is freed from her past and from future anticipation and able to live in the present moment. It appears that, at the end of the film, Clarissa has found liberation from remembrance and anticipation and is finally alive. This is affirmed through the kiss she gives Sally, the first demonstration of affection that we have seen between them. In Cunningham's book, in contrast, there is more closeness and communication. Woolf is given a final voice-over and her words appear to convey the message that life is imperfect, fleeting but beautiful and to be celebrated nonetheless.

The voice-over, giving primacy to the novelist whose work lives beyond the bounds of her life, seems to suggest that creativity is a privileged sphere and one which can confer meaning on an absurdly meaningless existence. If we interpret the closing words and images as a celebration of life, despite the recognition of its limitations, they seem to say that life is absurd in that it makes no sense. Humans desire that life *should* make sense and have recourse to the twin poles of hope and nostalgia. Looking life straight in the face involves forgoing the illusion of hope (in the afterlife, for example, or future fulfillment in this life) and resisting living in anticipation, just as it involves forgoing nostalgia (a melancholic looking backwards in the longing for meaning). Clarissa finds a stoic joy in the *imperfection* of the present. In this sense, the film could be seen as attempting to communicate the spirit of the books, despite the differences of the media and audience expectation.

The death of the author

Both the book and the film of *The Hours* begin with the death of the author, literally. But this death does not undercut the authority of Woolf as a poet-visionary; it establishes her presence ever more firmly in the narrative that unfolds. The book opens with a section entitled 'Prologue', in which Cunningham narrates Virginia Woolf's suicide in the present tense. The prologue ends with a paragraph in which Woolf, now drowned, is curiously still a part of the world which continues without her. Significantly, a mother and a son are the other two individuals in this paragraph, and their presence can be seen as foreshadowing the crucial mother/son dynamic, so important to a narrative resolution in *The Hours*:

> Here they are, on a day early in the Second World War: the boy and his mother on the bridge, the stick floating over the water's surface, and Virginia's body at the river's bottom, as if she is dreaming of the surface, the stick, the boy and his mother, the sky and the rooks. An olive-drab truck rolls across the bridge, loaded with soldiers in uniform, who wave to the boy who has just thrown the stick. He waves back. He demands that his mother pick him up so he can see the soldiers better; so he will be more visible to them. All this enters the bridge, resounds through its wood and stone, and enters Virginia's body. Her face, pressed sideways to the piling, absorbs it all: the truck and the soldiers, the mother and the child. (p. 8)

Modernist Writing, the Cinematic Image and Time

One striking feature about this passage is its vertical spatiality: the boy and mother on a bridge, which is above a stick, which floats on the surface of the water, beneath which lies the body of Virginia. Although her role is a passive one, clock time continues despite her death, events 'enter' her body and her face 'absorbs' all. She is still part of that world; indeed, she appears to be 'dreaming' it. Woolf, though dead, is depicted as somehow giving rise to the external world: it is her dream. Because of the way the book's chapters are arranged and the arrangement of scenes in the film, Woolf's book *Mrs Dalloway* appears to *precede* life. In other words, life is shown to be mirroring art. The prologue of the book anticipates Woolf's role in the lives of Laura Brown and Clarissa Vaughan, as even in death her words and her life continue to resonate to the extent that the literary text seems to inscribe, to *write* the lives of the other two female protagonists. This can be read as Cunningham's reinterpretation of Woolf's notion that the act of writing has the power to annihilate clock time and, by extension, mortality. Writing replaces the author, paper replaces flesh; and it, at least, endures.

    The opening sequence of the film also presents Virginia Woolf's suicide, and foregrounds the idea of alienation between people through the way the bodies are filmed (its gestural economy), and through the way that both characters are imaged in the same *space* but not at the same *time*. It is prologue-like in that it sets itself outside the frame of the film proper and contains the opening titles. As was the case with the book, the opening establishes the authority of Virginia Woolf at the same time that it depicts her death. Woolf stands as a literary/historical figure and a fictionalised character and so occupies a twofold space.

    If we consider the opening of the film, we can see how it presents time to suggest that life continues beyond the death of the individual. The cross-cutting of two sequences suggests two things: firstly, that words endure. Presumably, Virginia is dying or dead by the time Leonard reads her letter; however, her words remain with the viewer and assert her presence despite her absence. The second thing is alienation, in the face of attempts to achieve contact. Virginia is not seen in the same shot as Leonard, although the location unites the two of them in spatial terms. They are in the same place, but not at the same time.

The miniature Gothic arch of the corridor (which leads to the outside door) is an image which is repeated. First of all, Virginia leaves the house through it, and its shape is mirrored in the tunnel-like archway of roses in the garden. Leonard enters the house by the same door, and the use of the same distinctive location links the characters in terms of place, but not in terms of time. It is important that Virginia and Leonard are not in the same space at the same time during this sequence, as it is a clue to the preoccupation of both Cunningham and Woolf with time, as we shall see in a moment.

With Leonard's reading of the letter (which comes to the end as the voice-over ends, Kidman speaking the words and signing herself Virginia) it appears that the two time schemes converge. Leonard's presence acquires a sense of belatedness (like Laura Brown's at the end of *The Hours*). This happens as the name Virginia is spoken (as signature to the letter) and Woolf's head is submerged by the fast flowing water. Tension has been built up by cross-cutting and use of the music track (with shots becoming shorter and shorter to speed up the pace) to suggest that, if only the two time frames might converge, if Leonard *could* reach the river soon, he might pull her out and save her. However, the two characters are kept apart visually and Virginia's figure underwater (the wedding ring framed momentarily to reaffirm the identification of the woman in the water with the writer of the letter) is cross-cut with Leonard running, and the sequence ends with a black screen and the title of the film, *The Hours*.

The voice-over affirms love; however, the images suggest the impossibility of contact and timely communication. As the voice-over says 'I don't think two people could have been happier than we have been', the camera presents us with a medium close-up of Leonard, and moves in to indicate his growing awareness of what has happened. This is followed by an extreme close-up of Virginia placing her hand tenderly on the letter, in a gesture of tenderness and love which we may expect to see expressed to another human being. It is an ambiguous moment, open to interpretation: is it a testimony to the love the couple shared, or an indication of the barriers between individuals? Is the paper contact or separation? This motif and this question echo throughout the novel and the film in which the possibility of connecting with others and the means by which this can be achieved are explored.

Presenting the death of Woolf at the outset of the film does a number of things. It sets an elegiac tone for the entire narrative, it consigns her role to 'the past' (she is the only one of the three female protagonists no longer living in the film's present, which is 2001) and, importantly, it gives her story primacy over the other two women's as it establishes her as a structuring principle around which the complicated time-scheme and thematic parallels can be organised. In this way, although the film represents multiple subjectivities, they are not all given equal importance. Woolf's life acts as a master narrative which enables the elaborate construction to cohere. Perhaps, as a historical person and a writer, Woolf is given some primacy over the fictional characters, Laura Brown and Clarissa Vaughan. She appears to 'write' the life of Laura Brown, and her pen moving across the paper appears to anticipate the crisis and the resolution Laura makes. The novel Woolf is writing casts a shadow over Clarissa Vaughan's life, who states that having once been called Mrs Dalloway by Richard, that identity has 'stuck' and has hampered her from moving on beyond their love affair.

As we have seen, in the film Woolf occupies two temporal fields. She is depicted in 1941, and then in 1923. These represent the point at which she finds the first sentence of the novel she is working on, and the point at which she resolves to die. For the bulk of the film, Clarissa and Laura Brown occupy their own present time: Clarissa in 2001 and Laura in 1951. It is only with the death by suicide of Richard that Laura steps into the film's 'present tense' and also occupies 2001, as a much older figure. The tragedy could be seen as being set in motion by Woolf, when she pens her novel and comes to the understanding that Clarissa will not die. Someone else will, however. This recourse to causality is strengthened by the strong closure offered in the death of Richard, which also conforms to the pattern set out in *Mrs Dalloway* that women survive and men are the casualties of the sexual hegemony reinforced by society.

Instead of Clarissa killing herself, in *Mrs Dalloway* Septimus Smith does. In Cunningham's text, Laura almost kills herself, but cannot; however, her decision to leave her family is seen as causal in the chain of events which leads to Richard's suicide. Although the survivor who is changed and the sacrificial visionary are different characters in Woolf's novel, the Laura Brown and Clarissa Dalloway narratives are both reflected in the Woolf narrative. She survives the crisis of 1923 but ultimately kills herself 18 years later.

Modernist Writing, the Cinematic Image and Time

Conclusion: Out of time

The book of *The Hours* is an adaptation of *Mrs Dalloway* and, to a certain extent, an adaptation of the life of Woolf herself. It is infused with her life, the events of which and glimpses of which, seen through diaries, letters and essays, form yet another textual reservoir to be drawn on. There is no distinction between the life and the work now that the life has become reified through time and the documents which represent it. Like Woolf's texts, Cunningham's *The Hours* rejects a linear structure and the formal delineations of an ordered progression through a narrative signalled by chapter numbers or titles. The material is presented in chapters, but these are not numbered in a chronological way; they are organised around recurring patterns of names and identities. The novel is, however, chronological within each narrative strand. Patterns are established to suggest that the world of *The Hours* moves on in clock time, but the text also contains links across from one life to another. Music is one means whereby circularity of form is intimated.

Woolf's narrative is 'stream of consciousness', whereas Cunningham's is not. He uses the third person omniscient narrator and *describes* what is happening; his text does not enter the minds of characters and animate them from within, and there is extensive use of dialogue. The effect is to render Cunningham's novel more immediately readable than Woolf's. There are long quotations from *Mrs Dalloway* in the sections where Laura is reading the book, and these allow the reader unfamiliar with that novel to link passages from Cunningham's text with its predecessor. There are also long passages in *The Hours* which are inflected with the rhythms and the imagery of Woolf's writing, both from novels and letters. Cunningham's *The Hours*, then, in its intertextuality, is, like *Mrs Dalloway*, a story which is unfolding in the present, but which is also always looping back or ahead of itself.

The Hare/Daldry film, by way of contrast, makes much more accommodation with the linear structures of Hollywood continuity style narrative, even though it is divided into three narrative strands and three locations, intercut. It makes use of visual cues like flowers, food, books and water to provide a symbolic structure which links these three narratives, and embodies themes such as: the power relations between people explored through the presentation of food and feeding (in parental/spousal and class relations); the interconnectedness of life and death (food as nourishment or source of disgust or water imagery signalling birth and death); the acceptance that life and beauty are fleeting (flowers); and books (the possibility that something will endure and continue beyond the life of the individual). The three narratives run contiguously, but are also linked by means of fluid camera work and cuts on action, such as the cuts connecting flowers, women waking to alarm clocks, and washing their faces and dressing their hair in the sequence at the opening of the film.

In Cunningham's *The Hours*, the poet Richard Brown confusedly mixes up the future with the past and asks to see his prize which he has not yet received. 'I seem to have fallen out of time' he says. 'The party can go on just with the idea of me. The party has already happened, really, with or without me' (p. 65). His temporal disjunction (caused by his medication, and the disease that is killing him) makes manifest the feeling that the three central female characters have, to some extent, 'fallen out of time'. A sacrificial death, in the form of Richard's suicide, resolves the crisis afflicting those characters. The narrative resolution, though, is one which brings us *all* into the present. For viewers of the film and readers of the book, there is understanding of how Laura's and Clarissa's lives

Modernist Writing, the Cinematic Image and Time connect, and this replicates the understanding achieved by the characters themselves.

Bibliography

Primary Works

Cunningham, Michael, *The Hours*, new edn (1998; London: Fourth Estate, 2003)

The Hours [Motion picture], dir. by Stephen Daldry, ad. by David Hare (Miramax, 2003)

Woolf, Virginia, *Mrs Dalloway*, new edn (1925; London: Grafton, 1976)

Secondary Works

Banfield, Ann, 'Time Passes: Virginia Woolf, Post-Impressionism and Cambridge Time', *Poetics Today*, 24 (2003), 471-516

Benjamin, Walter, *The Arcades Project*, trans. by Howard Eiland and Kevin McLaughlin (Cambridge MA: Belknap Press, 1999)

Benjamin, Walter, 'On some motifs of Baudelaire', in *Illuminations*, ed. by Hannah Arendt, trans. by Harry Zohn, new edn (London: Fontana, 1992), pp. 152-196

Bergson, Henri, *Time and Freewill: an Essay on the Immediate Data of Consciousness*, trans. by F. L. Pogson, 2nd edn (1899; London: Allen and Unwin, 1912)

Bordwell, David, Janet Staiger, and Kristin Thompson, *The Classical Hollywood Cinema: Film Style & Mode of Production to 1960* (London: Routledge, 1988)

Cardwell, Sarah, 'Present(ing) Tense: Temporality and Tense in Contemporary Theories of Literature-Film Adaptation', *Scope: An Online Journal of Film and TV Studies* (2000) <http://www.scope.nottingham.ac.uk/article.php?issue=jul2000&id=288&section=article>. [accessed 13 August 2008]

Crary, Jonathan, *Suspensions of Perception: Attention, Spectacle, and Modern Culture* (Cambridge. MA: MIT Press, 1999)

Crary, Jonathan, *Techniques of the Observer: On Vision and Modernity in the Nineteenth Century* (Cambridge, MA: MIT Press, 1990)

Deleuze, Gilles, *Cinema 1: The Movement-Image*, trans. by Hugh Tomlinson and Barbara Hammerjam, new edn (London: Continuum, 2005)

Modernist Writing, the Cinematic Image and Time

Deleuze, Gilles, *Cinema 2: The Time-Image*, trans. by Hugh Tomlinson and Robert Galeta, new edn (London: Continuum, 2005)

Donald, James, Anne Friedberg, and Laura Marcus, eds, *Close Up, 1927-1933: Cinema and Modernism* (London: Cassell, 1998)

Hollington, Michael, 'Svevo, Joyce and Modernist Time', in *Modernism: A Guide to European Literature 1880-1930*, ed. by Malcolm Bradbury and James McFarlane, new edn (Hassock: Harvester Press, 1978), pp. 430-42

Hughes, Mary Joe, 'Michael Cunningham's *The Hours* and Postmodern Artistic Representation', *Critique: Studies in Contemporary Fiction*, 45 (2004), 349-361

Humm, Maggie, *Modernist Women and Visual Cultures: Virginia Woolf, Vanessa Bell, Photography and Cinema.* (Edinburgh: Edinburgh University Press, 2002)

King, Michael John, ed., *Collected Early Poems of Ezra Pound* (London: Faber, 1977)

Parsons, Deborah L., *Streetwalking the Metropolis: Women, the City, and Modernity* (Oxford: Oxford University Press, 2000)

Proust, Marcel, *Remembrance of Things Past* [*À la recherche du temps perdu*], trans. by C. K. Scott Moncrieff and Stephen Hudson, 7 vols (London: Chatto and Windus, 1922-31)

Radford, Jean, *Dorothy Richardson* (New York: Harvester Wheatsheaf, 1991)

Richardson, Dorothy, *Deadlock* (1921), republished in *Pilgrimage*, III, new edn (London: Virago, 1979)

Richardson, Dorothy, 'Novels', *Life and Letters Today*, 56 (1948), 188-92

Schiff, James, 'Re-writing Woolf's *Mrs Dalloway*: homage, sexual identity, and the single-day novel by Cunningham, Lippincott and Lanchester', *Critique: Studies in Contemporary Fiction*, 45 (2004), 362-382

Spiegel, Alan, *Fiction and the Camera Eye: Visual Consciousness in Film and the Modern Novel* (Charlottesville: University Press of Virginia, 1976)

Tester, Keith, ed., *The Flâneur* (London: Routledge, 1994)

Woolf, Leonard, *The Journey Not the Arrival Matters: An Autobiography of the Years 1939-1969* (London: Hogarth Press, 1969)

Woolf, Virginia, 'A Sketch of the Past', in *Moments of Being*, ed. by Jeanne Schulkind, 2nd edn (London: Grafton, 1989), pp. 69-174

Woolf, Virginia, 'Street Haunting: a London adventure', in *Collected Essays*, 4 (London: Hogarth Press, 1967), pp. 155-66

Young, Tory, *Michael Cunningham's 'The Hours': A Reader's Guide* (New York: Continuum, 2003)

FROM IMAGE TO FRAME: THE FILMING OF *THE FRENCH LIEUTENANT'S WOMAN*

William Stephenson

Not only has cinema greatly influenced the modern novel, it has shaped modern consciousness. The novelist John Fowles believed that, in the second half of the twentieth century, the mind's eye had become like a camera. He found that when he analysed his dreams, 'I recalled purely cinematic effects: panning shots, close shots, tracking, jump cuts, and the rest. In short, this mode of imagining is far too deep in me to eradicate - and not only in me, but all my generation.'[1]

Fowles's novels often evolved from a static image in his mind, like a frozen frame. He claimed that he saw such mental pictures very often: significantly, he called them 'mythopoeic "stills"' (*W*, p. 14). The image that began *The French Lieutenant's Woman*, his third novel, fitted this pattern: it was of an anonymous woman standing on a quay, looking out to sea. Fowles was thinking like a cinemagoer, in that he saw the 'still' of the woman and projected his fantasy onto her, turning her into Sarah Woodruff, a lonely Victorian governess who defies the social and sexual restrictions her century places upon her by falling in love with a nobleman, Charles Smithson.

---

[1] John Fowles, *Wormholes: Essays and Occasional Writings*, ed. by Jan Relf (1998; London: Vintage, 1999), p. 24. All further references will appear in the main body of the text with the abbreviation *W*. The most important essays in *Wormholes* for students of *The French Lieutenant's Woman* and the Pinter/Reisz adaptation are 'Notes on an Unfinished Novel' (1969) and 'The Filming of *The French Lieutenant's Woman*' (1981).

From Image to Frame

Laura Mulvey has famously pointed out that the male gaze in cinema is part of a patriarchal system in which men live out their 'phantasies and obsessions ... by imposing them on the silent image of woman still tied to her place as a bearer of meaning, not maker of meaning'.[2] Sarah Woodruff does a great deal to challenge Mulvey's claim, as she returns and refutes the male gaze both in Fowles's novel and the subsequent film adaptation: nevertheless, Fowles's initial vision of her was cinematic insofar as it involved camera-like objectification of a silent female image.

Fowles's visualisation of his heroine showed his awareness of the effect of filmic structure on the modern imagination. However, he did not believe that the cinema necessarily offered more than the older form. To Fowles, the chief difference between the two media lay in the freedom given by print. A cinema image 'is virtually the same for all who see it; it stamps out personal imagination, the response from an individual *visual* memory', whereas a prose sentence 'will evoke a different image in each reader': this 'is a privilege of *verbal* form; and the cinema can never usurp it' (*W*, p. 24: emphasis in original).

Fowles here overestimates the capacity of cinema to dominate the reader's or viewer's imagination and of print to liberate it.[3] In both media, reception has a crucial role in determining meaning. Although the reader of a literary

---

[2] Laura Mulvey, 'Visual Pleasure in Narrative Cinema', *Screen*, 16 (1975), 6-18 (p. 7).

[3] Fowles's comment was made in 1969. In later years, his views changed. In 1981, he pointed out the mutual dependency of film and literature: 'A good director is always partly a novelist, and vice versa' (*W*, p. 45). Later still, in 1988, he claimed that the two media share 'a curious feedback': see John Fowles, *Conversations with John Fowles*, ed. by Dianne L. Vipond (Jackson: University Press of Mississippi, 1999), p. 151.

text is engaged in concretising (or imaginatively filling in the gaps) in the narrative, the same can be said of the film viewer. In either case, 'filling in indeterminate places requires creativity'.[4] Writing in 1964, five years before the publication of *The French Lieutenant's Woman*,[5] Marshall McLuhan (whose work was known to Fowles: indeed, his name is used jokingly in the novel as an example of outrageous modernity) argued that film and print are closely bonded, as they both require the reader/viewer to concretise: 'The reader in projecting words, as it were, has to follow the black and white sequences of stills that is typography, providing his own sound track.'[6]

This essay will study the novel, screenplay and film of *The French Lieutenant's Woman* in order to examine the roles of the reader, viewer, actors, director and screenwriter, all of whom have some sort of imaginative investment in creating the multimedia text that *The French Lieutenant's Woman* now is. The essay will argue that Harold Pinter's screenplay and Karel Reisz's film adaptation neither dilute nor strengthen the novel: indeed, such value judgements are irrelevant when confronted by the complex relationship of the postmodern multimedia text with the world. Even in its original printed form, *The French Lieutenant's Woman* is a fluid, adaptable, visually conceived and highly concretisable text: or, put another way, the

---

[4] Robert C. Holub, *Reception Theory: A Critical Introduction* (1984; London: Routledge, 1989) p. 26.

[5] John Fowles, *The French Lieutenant's Woman* (1969; London: Vintage, 1996), p. 41. Further references will appear in the main body of the text with the abbreviation *FLW*.

[6] Marshall McLuhan, *Understanding Media* (1964; London: Routledge, 2001), p. 311.

novel is organised so that the reader (or potential scriptwriter, director or viewer) can, in a sense, screen it.

The blueprint of a metaphor: From novel to script to film

The novel's transition to celluloid was far from easy.[7] Even though Fowles and his agent Tom Maschler began looking for a suitable director and screenwriter before the book was published in 1969 (*W*, p. 39), it took until 1981 for a film adaptation to appear on screen.[8] From early on, Fowles and Maschler knew they wanted Karel Reisz to direct and Harold Pinter to script the film.[9] Fowles greatly

---

[7] Even after 1978, when Pinter and Reisz agreed to work on the film, there were difficulties involved. Warner Brothers initially agreed to fund the project, but withdrew late on: see Eileen Warburton, *John Fowles: A Life in Two Worlds* (London: Jonathan Cape, 2004), p. 401. In the end, Meryl Streep's agent secured the transfer of the film to United Artists. For more views on Fowles and cinema, see: William Stephenson, *John Fowles* (Plymouth: Northcote, 2003), pp. 40-2; William Stephenson, *Fowles's 'The French Lieutenant's Woman': A Reader's Guide* (London: Continuum, 2007), pp. 93-107.

[8] For an account of positive and negative critical reactions to the film, see: Michael Billington, *The Life and Work of Harold Pinter* (London: Faber, 1996), p. 274; Stephanie Tucker, 'Despair Not, Neither to Presume: *The French Lieutenant's Woman: A Screenplay*', *Literature and Film Quarterly*, 24 (1996), 63-9, (p. 64). Despite mixed reactions, the film grossed over £20 million in the USA and £3 million in the UK in the 1980s, making it commercially comparable to such English period dramas as *Tess*, *The Elephant Man* and *A Passage to India*. See Andrew Higson, *English Heritage, English Cinema: Costume Drama Since 1980* (Oxford: Oxford University Press, 2003), p. 93.

[9] Fowles himself was out of the running. He composed the screenplay for the 1968 adaptation of *The Magus*, which was one of the worst films of the 1960s: 'disastrously awful' (Fowles, *Conversations*, p. 66). He was also far from satisfied with the adaptation of his first novel, *The Collector* (1963), that was 'Technicoloured and glossied and blunted out of all

admired Pinter for his economy with words, especially his gift for 'reducing the long and complex without distortion' (*W*, p. 43). Fowles understood that Pinter's task would not be to reproduce the novel, or remain faithful to it, but to produce a script 'faithful to the very different production capability (and relation with audience) of the cinema': the final script, in Fowles's view, was not a mere version of the novel, but 'the blueprint ... of a brilliant metaphor for it' (*W*, p. 43).[10]

Despite Pinter's eventual achievement, *The French Lieutenant's Woman* looked unfilmable, according to at least one screenwriter who was offered the script (*W*, p. 39): even Pinter found it 'bloody, bloody hard'.[11] The reasons for the novel's resistance to adaptation are: its use of a contemporary narrative voice to describe Victorian material; the presence of a pseudo-authorial narrator who frequently interrupts the action with ironic asides, and even on some occasions steps directly into the story (he gets into a train carriage with Charles Smithson); and not least the famous dual ending, where in chapter 60 Charles's and Sarah's affair ends with the couple reconciled, but in chapter 61 they part, seemingly forever. *The French Lieutenant's Woman* is a historical fiction set in 1867-9, but also an account of a writer composing a novel a century later. The novel deliberately (and for a

---

contact with the book': see John Fowles, *The Journals, I*, ed. by Charles Drazin (London: Jonathan Cape, 2003), p. 624.

[10] Fowles had no involvement with the script except to edit the proposal scene between Charles and Ernestina, and the final Victorian reunion of Charles and Sarah, in order to add a happiness and emotional content missing, in his view, from Pinter's version (Warburton, p. 399).

[11] Mel Gussow, *Conversations with Pinter* (London: Nick Hern Books, 1994), p. 53.

screenwriter, infuriatingly) confuses periods and genres: 'Thackeray meets the world of the *nouveau roman*: high-class romance (a kind of corn on the Cobb) mates with Robbe-Grillet and Sarraute'.[12]

In any proposed film version, the century-wide gap between modern narrative voice and Victorian setting would violate any attempt at realist illusion. The novel's narrator could seemingly only have been imitated through voice-over or similarly clumsy devices, or dispensed with altogether. The dual ending, if filmed as in the book, would have alienated a mainstream audience by disrupting the linear narrative demanded by Hollywood convention.

Pinter's solution to this problem (that evolved in conversation with Reisz and was based on the director's original idea) was not to dispense with any possible challenge to the audience, but to deepen it.[13] He introduced a dual chronology, whereby a modern love affair framed the Victorian one and the two narratives commented on and ironised each other. Such complex competition between narratives is at the core of Pinter's methodology: 'Pinter's plays have always been about competing stories and the struggle to make one or another prevail'.[14] Pinter invented two new protagonists, Mike and Anna, actors playing Charles and Sarah in a film based

---

[12] Billington, p. 272. Further references will appear in the main body of the text.

[13] Guido Almansi and Simon Henderson, *Harold Pinter* (London: Methuen, 1983), p. 107.

[14] Francis Gillen, 'From Novel to Film: Harold Pinter's Adaptation of *The Trial*', in *Pinter At Sixty*, ed. by Katherine H. Burkman & John L. Kundert-Gibbs (Bloomington: Indiana U. P. 1993), pp. 137-48 (p. 145).

on Fowles's novel, also called *The French Lieutenant's Woman*. Like that of Charles and Sarah, their affair is illicit, as Mike is already married to Sonia, and Anna has a partner, David.

By juxtaposing the repressed sexuality of the Victorian characters with the repressed love of the modern ones, Pinter's script encourages a critical attitude to both. Sarah and Charles fall in love long before they allow themselves a passionate but clumsy sexual encounter: Mike and Anna have had a sexual relationship for some time before he declares 'I love you'[15] and she in turn realises she loves herself and/or David more than Mike.

At the same time, the script shows how the modern lovers confuse themselves with their roles. Mike's love increasingly focuses on the character Anna plays, rather than Anna herself. In the film's final scene, part of the modern framing narrative, Anna drives away, ending the affair. Mike, bereft and confused, shouts 'Sarah!' from an upstairs window (S, p. 104). Ironically, he is standing in the room where, in the Victorian narrative, Charles and Sarah have just rediscovered their love after a long separation, in the film's equivalent to chapter 60, the novel's first, 'happy' ending. Anna's behaviour replicates that of Sarah, a character who makes her own sexual destiny by loving Charles, then leaving him. Michael Billington sees this as part of Pinter's 'strong feminist line' (p. 273): he argues that Anna's final rejection of Mike at the end of the film suggests that 'Women progress and profit

---

[15] Harold Pinter, *The French Lieutenant's Woman: A Screenplay*, with foreword by John Fowles (Boston: Little, Brown, 1981), p. 83. All further page references will appear in the main body of the text with the abbreviation S.

from the past; men remain insecure and exploitative' (p. 274).[16]

The film has no narrator, but Pinter's script does much of the same work, by creating clearly signposted ironic asides. Charles's chaste kiss with his fiancée Ernestina Freeman, upon her acceptance of his proposal of marriage, is followed by a sudden cut to Mike and Anna in bed in her hotel room (*S*, p. 9). On the soundtrack, the proposal scene's generic pastoral music, overdubbed with Ernestina's chaste gasps of joy, is followed bathetically by Anna's telephone ringing as the cut occurs. This 'sound-bridge'[17] encourages an ironic reading by suggesting that rather more carnal gasps have occurred shortly before in the hotel bed.

By forcing the connections and dissonances between the frame and the enclosed narrative into the viewer's consciousness, Pinter and Reisz avoid the 'decorative aesthetics aimed at uncritical consumption' promoted by

---

[16] Sarah is a model in the novel, but becomes an artist in the film and Pinter's script. Critics are divided over whether this makes a feminist statement. Michael Billington argues that Sarah's new status in the film becomes 'a symbol of her personal growth' (Billington, p. 274). Steven H. Gale reads her drawings as representations 'of the [positive] psychological change that Sarah has undergone': see Steven H. Gale, 'Art Objects as Metaphors in the Film Scripts of Harold Pinter', in *Pinter At Sixty*, ed. by Katherine H. Burkman and John L. Kundert-Gibbs (Bloomington: Indiana U. P., 1993), pp. 163-72 (p. 167). However, Guido Almansi and Simon Henderson believe that the drawings are unconvincing, as there is "no suggestion that the protagonist is endowed with an artistic nature' (Almansi and Henderson, p. 97).

[17] Marie-Claire Simonetti, 'The Blurring of Time in *The French Lieutenant's Woman*, the Novel and the Film', *Literature and Film Quarterly*, 24 (1996), 301-8 (p. 303).

the Merchant-Ivory cycle.[18] If it is true that Reisz's movie 'defined a lush, sexualised, colour-oriented style for the 19th-century period film' and that 'the Merchant-Ivory school was the principal benefactor' of the trend it began,[19] then its imitators clearly ignored the jarring estrangements created by such rapid cuts between the Victorian narrative and the modern frame.[20]

Some of the film's ironies of juxtaposition reveal important differences between film and screenplay. In the film, as Anna falls into Mike's arms in rehearsal, there is a sudden cut to Sarah's similar fall into Charles's arms in the Victorian narrative, creating a shift between time frames that is smooth yet unexpected, and punctures the surface verisimilitude of both the frame and the enclosed narrative: 'The continuous, falling motion of the two characters is contrasted with the break in scenery and costume'.[21] This represents a considerable departure from the version in scenes 78 and 79 of the screenplay (S, pp. 29-31), where the fall occurs entirely in rehearsal, in modern costume.

---

[18] Belén Vidal Villasur, 'Classic adaptations, modern reinventions: reading the image in the contemporary literary film', *Screen*, 43 (2002), 5-18 (p. 6).

[19] Andrew Pulver, 'Adaptation of the Week No 9: Karel Reisz's *The French Lieutenant's Woman* (1981)', *The Guardian*, 22 May 2004, section G2, p. 17.

[20] That said, there is a case for placing *The French Lieutenant's Woman* as an early member of a heritage school of British costume cinema from the 1980s on, which relied on the female audience, foregrounded women protagonists, and was based on romance narratives. See Higson, pp. 22-3.

[21] Simonetti, p. 304.

From Image to Frame

Reisz's choice to edit Anna's and Sarah's falls together not only adds pace, but changes the gender politics of Pinter's scene. By blurring Sarah with Anna, the scene suggests that Sarah is, like her modern counterpart, a vulnerable but sexually assertive woman, whose fall into the man's arms is no accident: Anna is trying to work out what the fall means 'strategically, psychologically, emotionally',[22] both in terms of her role as Sarah and in her own life. In fact, both women adopt combative psychological strategies in their sexual relationships: they refuse to be mere spaces onto which 'the determining male gaze projects its phantasy'.[23]

Moreover, the editing makes the gaze problematic by disturbing the ontology of its object(s): on how many women is the viewer gazing? Which of them is real? On first glance, Anna is real and Sarah merely a role: a second's reflection, though, forces the conclusion that both are roles played simultaneously by Meryl Streep, the actress. Streep aimed to blur Anna and Sarah, and deepen the ambiguity of the character, through creating disparities between her dialogue, gaze and body language. As Reisz commented,

> Meryl is able to say one thing with her lips and another with her eyes. She eludes you all the time …. Meryl is able to create a sense of interior life. The enigma of the character is of the essence'.[24]

---

[22] Almansi and Henderson, p. 97.

[23] Mulvey, p. 11.

[24] Ivor Davis, 'Meryl Streep has been seizing the headlines for her performance in *The French Lieutenant's Woman*', *The Times*, 17 September 1981, p. 9.

The rehearsal scene between Anna and Mike before Anna/Sarah's fall highlights the artificiality of both the modern *and* Victorian narratives by showing how both love affairs are organised through preparation and role playing. This paradoxically makes it all the more easy for Anna to conflate the two, as does Mike (played by Jeremy Irons), whose affectedness as 'an actor in love with the image of himself in love', ironically mimics Charles's attempt to sustain 'the postures of a Victorian gentleman'.[25] The rehearsal scene was originally set by Pinter in an empty billiard room in a hotel (S, p. 29). The decision, presumably by Reisz, to reset the scene in a conservatory, with a few scattered deck chairs and potted plants, and rain pattering on the roof and smearing the windows, creates an ironic contrast to the verdant wilderness of the Undercliff outside the glass. In effect, the *mise-en-scène* of the conservatory forms a metaphor for Anna and Mike's enclosed, somewhat jaded imitation of Sarah and Charles's increasingly less repressed encounters in the pastoral exterior.

The actors play the scene badly, then Anna suggests, 'Let's just do it again, okay?' – a line not in Pinter's screenplay. Their second attempt is completely different, reflecting an ambiguous sexual tension between Anna, Mike and their characters. The shift in tone is not stated by Pinter: instead, it is implied by such directions as 'He looks down at her face, her mouth' (S, p. 31). The anonymous 'he' and 'her' do not make clear whether Mike or Charles is looking, or whether Anna or Sarah is the object of his gaze. Both the Victorian and modern females have become specular objects. So have the males. When Anna stands

---

[25] David Robinson, 'A bold and enthralling experiment in time': [review of *The French Lieutenant's Woman* film], *The Times*, 16 October 1981, p. 12.

with her skirt caught in imaginary brambles, the conservatory glass and the distant sea in the background, her look is a frank, direct return of Mike's: the camera zooms in on her face before she walks towards him, about to rehearse the fall. Her last line preceding this is 'I see you' (not in the screenplay), an implied challenge to the male right to own the gaze. The shot of Anna is preceded by a shot of Mike that records *his* look at her, making the male gaze an object of scrutiny rather than a seemingly natural effect of camera positioning.

Writing the gaze: The novel's cinematic self-consciousness

Even before Pinter's and Reisz's direct references to the gaze, the novel was full of allusions to cinematic viewing. The opening chapter is an account of the scenery around the Cobb (the Lyme Regis harbour breakwater on which Sarah stands), and the progress of Charles and Ernestina, seen from the viewpoint of a local 'spy' with a telescope (*FLW*, p. 10), who turns out later to be the town doctor, Grogan. This is paralleled in the screenplay by Charles's use of a telescope to spy on his valet Sam's flirtation with a servant girl, Mary (*S*, p. 2) as well as by Grogan's voyeuristic claim that he has a telescope to look at 'mermaids', meaning women, who are bathing on the beach below (*S*, pp. 39-40).

In both novel and screenplay, the telescope is a nineteenth-century version of the film camera. It turns inland and out as if panning, and its changes of focus show how it enables surveillance: 'he might, focusing his telescope more closely, have suspected that a mutual solitude interested them' (*FLW*, p. 10). In the novel, the telescopist can judge Charles and Ernestina by their clothes, but Sarah, standing on the quay, remains enigmatic, dressed in light-absorbing black, her gaze focused steadily out to sea, refusing any rapport with the telescope-camera (*FLW*, p. 11).

Fowles here points towards the inability of the visual media to penetrate consciousness. The gaze of the telescopist, it appears, has clear limits, but the vision of the heroine can reach further: when first seeing Charles, Sarah gives him a look that seems to penetrate and wound him: he thinks of her look as 'a lance', and feels 'pierced and deservedly diminished' (*FLW*, p. 16). Sarah appropriates the male gaze in a way that turns Charles into a specular object: the diction even implies a form of ocular rape. Her look, even in print, is already a visual, proto-cinematic device. Not surprisingly, the look was retained in both screenplay and film. Even in Fowles's book, Sarah's stare turns her into one of those 'objects that *return the gaze* .... As a result, the fantasy of the all-powerful desiring gaze is debunked'.[26] Charles looks at Sarah, but she looks right back, drawing attention to his and the reader's role in concretising her as an imaginative object and questioning the politics of that concretisation.

Sarah's look fits her personality, which is anachronistically contemporary: she is 'born with a computer in her heart' (*FLW*, p. 57). As the heroine's modern qualities suggest, the novel is historically alert and subtle. It undermines any sense of complacent hindsight through modern references, such as that to the computer, that establish that the Victorian narrative is a mere fiction, based on how the twentieth century *imagines* nineteenth-century England.

In keeping with this, the narrator makes references to the cinema that suggest, with a degree of ironic distance, how the Victorian novel might be filmed. Mary, a comely

---

[26] Villasur, p. 11: emphasis in original.

Dorset servant-girl, has a famous descendant. Her great-granddaughter's face 'is known over the entire world, for she is one of the more celebrated younger English film actresses' (*FLW*, p. 78). This passage is an example of the novel's foregrounding of its distance from the Victorian era – a defamiliarising strategy or alienation effect. It also playfully anticipates a future film in which the actress could play her own ancestor. Most importantly, the narrator's reference to Mary's descendant casts the novel in cinematic terms, inviting the reader to superimpose the imagined face of a film star over the visual image of Mary's face already conceived. Fowles manipulates the reader's concretisation of Mary by substituting a cinematic, contemporary image of her for the pseudo-Victorian one the reader had begun to form: thus the reader's gaze, in the sense of the capacity to project fantasy onto the framed object, becomes subject to ironic play.

Although the screenplay had no narrative voice to reproduce such tricks, Pinter and Reisz found two ways of conveying the artificiality of Fowles's narrative and its cinematic self-consciousness. These were the introduction of the modern framing narrative of Anna and Mike, and the repeated return of the viewer's gaze by Sarah/Anna/Streep. In doing this, the screenwriter and director were not entirely reworking the novel: rather, they were developing what was already in it. In the notorious chapter 13, Fowles's narrator addresses the reader directly in order to claim, 'I live in the age of Alain Robbe-Grillet and Roland Barthes; if this is a novel, it cannot be a novel in the modern sense of the word' (*FLW*, p. 97). The first half of the sentence refers to Barthes's post-structuralist literary theory and the avant-garde *nouveau roman* of Robbe-Grillet. The second half of the sentence, though, is ambiguous. Does it mean that the novel is too old to be modern, as it is a close imitation of Victorian fiction, or does it mean that it is too avant-garde to be a modern novel as ordinarily understood, and is closer to a *nouveau roman*? The answer is both: Fowles's text looks backward to the Victorian novels it copies and yet reworks them in an experimental way.

This creates the sort of paradox beloved of theorists of postmodern literature such as Linda Hutcheon, who uses *The French Lieutenant's Woman* as a prime example of historiographic metafiction, or those fictions that claim to be able to reference the past historically and yet show themselves, through a number of reflexive devices, to *be* fiction.[27] Thus, when Reisz's film and Pinter's script aim to imitate the past and yet simultaneously to declare their contemporary artificiality, they are not changing Fowles's novel, but building on it.

From still to rhizome: The extending network

In an essay nearly contemporary with Fowles's novel, 'From Work to Text' (1971), Roland Barthes challenges the received idea of what a novel or film is. He argues that the *work*, a property of the author, has been replaced by a more complex, fluid entity, the *text*, which '*is experienced only in an activity of production*'.[28] Barthes's essay is a strong statement of the need to rethink the work in terms that acknowledge the intertextual basis of any cultural production and the reader's active role in concretising the

---

[27] Linda Hutcheon, *A Poetics of Postmodernism: History, Theory, Fiction* (London: Routledge, 1988), p. 5.

[28] Roland Barthes, 'From Work to Text' [1971], in *Image Music Text: Essays*, trans. by Stephen Heath (London: Fontana, 1977), pp. 155-64 (p. 157): emphasis in original. Further references will appear in the main body of the text.

text through his/her understanding of its intertextual links and, often, its multimedia basis. It is thus possible to think of Fowles's novel, Pinter's screenplay and Reisz's film as extensions of one text. If the Barthesian text is experienced only by means of active production, then the viewer or reader interpreting film, screenplay or novel is *producing* the text out of the encounter of all three media.

Barthes argues that the text requires new ways of reading, which ultimately require one 'to abolish (or at the very least to diminish) the distance between writing and reading' in order to join them 'in a single signifying practice' (p. 162). If the work is an organism that grows through development, the text is a network that extends itself through systems of combination, including amalgamation with those things conventionally thought of as outside it, e.g. the reader (p. 161).

In a development of Barthes's idea, Gilles Deleuze and Félix Guattari suggest that the text can be seen as a rhizome, or centreless network, that comes to extend between and through the book/film in its printed/celluloid form and the world of the reader or viewer. A rhizome is 'without an organizing memory or central automaton, defined solely by a circulation of states'.[29] The rhizome is clearly a far cry from the received idea of the book as mimetic mirror of reality. In fact, they argue, the book *never was* a mirror: 'contrary to a deeply rooted belief, the book is not an image of the world. It forms a rhizome with the world.' (p. 11)

The metaphors of the network and rhizome encapsulate the complex interrelationship between the

---

[29] Gilles Deleuze and Félix Guattari, *A Thousand Plateaus: Capitalism and Schizophrenia* [1980], trans. by Brian Massumi (London: Athlone Press, 1988), p. 21. Further references will appear in the main body of the text.

novel, screenplay and film of *The French Lieutenant's Woman* and their various worlds of reception, in which the multimedia text has been concretised in very varying ways by different readers in diverse circumstances. The network or rhizome is not a teleological form: just as it lacks a definitive centre, it refuses closure.

The text's awareness of this is evident in Pinter's solution of the novel's most difficult technical problem, the dual ending in chapters 60 and 61. In the novel, the narrator cannot decide how to end the story, as to put one ending last would give it 'the tyranny of the last chapter' (*FLW*, p. 390), so he declares that he will flip a coin to let chance solve the problem for him. In the screenplay, there are two references to indecision over the ending. David, Anna's partner, asks Mike which of the novel's endings the film will use, and he replies: 'We're going for the first ending - I mean the second ending' (*S*, p. 95). This scene was retained in the film, but an earlier, similar one, was cut, where David asks Anna what has been decided about the ending, and she replies, 'I want to play it exactly as it's written' (*S*, p. 84). Playing *The French Lieutenant's Woman* precisely as written in 1969 would have been pointless, even if technically possible, and Fowles, Pinter and Reisz were well aware of this: instead, Anna seems to mean that Fowles's structural game involving two endings will be retained.

The shared refusal of the film, screenplay and novel to end definitively is not only evidence of the rhizomatic structure of the multimedia text, but also a comment on the extradiegetic world of the reader/viewer: in effect, an extension of the textual network into the world of reception. Stephanie Tucker has drawn attention to a passage from the screenplay, cut out of the movie, in which a Victorian scene is being filmed, but Anna/Sarah, sensing a private joke, bursts out laughing, forcing the director to retake. The realities of the Victorian world and the actors' world 'merge, to remind us again of the fragile and ambiguous boundaries distinguishing our own realities, which, if we heed the screenplay, seem increasingly illusionary.'[30] This analysis can be applied to many scenes that remain within the final film, such as Sarah/Anna/Streep's fall into the arms of Charles/Mike/Irons, which begins in a twentieth-century conservatory and ends in a Victorian wood.

Such scenes serve to textualise the viewer's world. They do this by exposing the viewer's role in creating meaning: they situate the experience of viewing *within* the multimedia text's extended rhizomatic structure. The text is implying that, like the identities of Sarah and Charles (and Anna and Mike, and even Streep and Irons, who are known to us only as screen images), *our* identities are semiotic. Fowles points to this in the novel, when the narrator disputes the reader's intuitive belief that a character is either real or imaginary (and thus the textual world and the reader's lived world are distinct): 'You do not even think of your own past as quite real; you ... fictionalize it, in a word, and put it away on a shelf – your book, your romanced autobiography' (*FLW*, p. 99). The reader's memory is a text: this is typical of the postmodern cultural climate in which 'simulacra prevail over history'.[31]

The film of *The French Lieutenant's Woman* is not a historical adaptation in the sense of a mimetically consistent, faithful reproduction of a bygone reality. Instead it signposts itself as a fake of two earlier fakes, the novel and the historical Victorian world: in both novel and

---

[30] Tucker, p. 67.

[31] Jean Baudrillard, *Symbolic Exchange and Death* [1976], trans. by Iain Hamilton Grant (London: Sage, 1993), p. 56.

film, the modern frame (of the narrator in the novel, and of Anna and Mike in the film) exposes the Victorian world as written/acted, but is itself conspicuously literary/cinematic. The film's first shot is of Anna, in costume, checking her image in a mirror. The second shot boldly announces the film within a film, as it begins with a clapperboard that fills the frame: the off-screen spoken commands 'action' and 'drag' further signify the medium of cinema. The camera then tracks Anna/Sarah's walk along the Cobb to her position at its end. Once there, she copies Fowles's mental 'mythopoeic still' of the woman looking out to sea.

The genesis of the novel is thus reprised, in a retrospective nod to Fowles's creativity that nevertheless transfers to the viewer the role of the observer who must concretise the black figure on the end of the quay. Over Anna/Sarah's walking figure appear the credits to the author, screenwriter and director, in a white font that gives the letters edges with no centre. The names each vanish after a few frames, signifying the insubstantiality of Fowles, Pinter and Reisz, who remain as ghostly presences overlooking the viewer's concretisation of the scene. Thus even as it begins, the multimedia text, the product of an overlapping series of entities (novel, screenplay, film), refuses to be a crude vehicle for one-way communication, and instead invites the viewer to give it meaning: 'If the text is worth its salt, it will survive being "visualized". If it meets its match, then word and image will marry ... and enhance each other.' (*W*, p. 46)

Bibliography

Primary Works

Fowles, John, *The French Lieutenant's Woman* (1969; London: Vintage, 1996)

The French Lieutenant's Woman, dir. by Karel Reisz, ad. by Harold Pinter (United Artists, 1981)

Pinter, Harold, *The French Lieutenant's Woman: A Screenplay*, with foreword by John Fowles (Boston: Little, Brown, 1981)

Secondary Works

Almansi, Guido, and Simon Henderson, *Harold Pinter* (London: Methuen, 1983)

Baudrillard, Jean, *Symbolic Exchange and Death* [1976], trans. by Iain Hamilton Grant (London: Sage, 1993)

Barthes, Roland, 'From Work to Text' [1971], in *Image Music Text: Essays*, trans. by Stephen Heath (London: Fontana, 1977), pp. 155-64

Billington, Michael, *The Life and Work of Harold Pinter* (London: Faber, 1996)

The Collector, dir. by William Wyler (Columbia, 1965)

Deleuze, Gilles, and Félix Guattari, *A Thousand Plateaus: Capitalism and Schizophrenia* [1980], trans. by Brian Massumi (London: Athlone Press, 1988)

Davis, Ivor, 'Meryl Streep has been seizing the headlines for her performance in *The French Lieutenant's Woman*', *The Times*, 17 September 1981, p. 9

Fowles, John, *Conversations with John Fowles,* ed. Dianne L. Vipond (Jackson: University Press of Mississippi, 1999).

Fowles, John, *The Journals, I,* ed. by Charles Drazin (London: Jonathan Cape, 2003)

Fowles, John, *Wormholes: Essays and Occasional Writings,* ed. Jan Relf (1998; London: Vintage, 1999)

Gale, Steven H., 'Art Objects as Metaphors in the Film Scripts of Harold Pinter', in *Pinter At Sixty*, ed. by Katherine H. Burkman and John L. Kundert-Gibbs (Bloomington: Indiana University Press, 1993), pp. 163-72

Gillen, Francis. 'From Novel to Film: Harold Pinter's Adaptation of *The Trial*', in *Pinter At Sixty*, ed. by Katherine H. Burkman and John L. Kundert-Gibbs (Bloomington: Indiana University Press, 1993), pp. 137-48

Gussow, Mel, *Conversations with Pinter* (London: Nick Hern Books, 1994)

Higson, Andrew, *English Heritage, English Cinema: Costume Drama Since 1980* (Oxford: Oxford University Press, 2003)

Holub, Robert C., *Reception Theory: A Critical Introduction* (1984; London: Routledge, 1989)

Hutcheon, Linda, *A Poetics of Postmodernism: History, Theory, Fiction* (London: Routledge, 1988)

The Magus, dir. by Guy Green (Twentieth Century Fox, 1968)

McLuhan, Marshall, *Understanding Media* (1964; London: Routledge, 2001)

Mulvey, Laura, 'Visual Pleasure in Narrative Cinema', *Screen*, 16 (1975), 6-18

Pulver, Andrew, 'Adaptation of the Week, No 9: Karel Reisz's *The French Lieutenant's Woman* (1981)', *The Guardian*, 22 May 2004, section G2 p. 1

Robinson, David, 'A bold and enthralling experiment in time': [review of *The French Lieutenant's Woman* film], *The Times*, 16 October 1981, p. 12

Simonetti, Marie-Claire, 'The Blurring of Time in *The French Lieutenant's Woman*, the Novel and the Film', *Literature and Film Quarterly*, 24 (1996), 301-8

Stephenson, William, *John Fowles* (Plymouth: Northcote, 2003)

Stephenson, William, *Fowles's 'The French Lieutenant's Woman': A Reader's Guide* (London: Continuum, 2007)

Tucker, Stephanie, 'Despair Not, Neither to Presume: *The French Lieutenant's Woman: A Screenplay*', *Literature and Film Quarterly*, 24 (1996), 63-9

Villasur, Belén Vidal, 'Classic adaptations, modern reinventions: reading the image in the contemporary literary film', *Screen*, 43 (2002), 5-18

Warburton, Eileen, *John Fowles: A Life in Two Worlds* (London: Jonathan Cape, 2004)

Part 3

Adapting Drama

ADAPTING DRAMA

As was noted in the Introduction, Kamilla Elliott has argued that the closest literary form to the cinema is *not* the nineteenth-century proto-cinematic realist novel, but the theatre. One can easily understand the force of this argument. Both theatre and narrative film require the performance of actors, in an imaginative space constructed by a director and crew, presented to an audience in a darkened auditorium. Elliott also suggests that the negotiations of time and space are more similar in theatre and film; and in terms such as *mise-en-scène*, film reveals its debt to theatrical production. If we think of the exhibition of films – in an auditorium, in the dark, with curtains that part before the performance, and with a screen (especially prior to widescreen technologies) that mimics the dimensions of the proscenium arch – then other similarities suggest themselves.

However, there *are* crucial differences. Actors are used in both forms to present the action but, in theatre, the audience's experience of the performance is directly produced by the *presence* of the actors and, in many cases, the dynamic established between acting company and audience on any given night. By contrast, the cinematic performance is fixed and reproducible in the cinema, on DVD, or downloaded onto the computer. The circumstances of reception might change, but the performance does not. Film performance is *iterable*; theatrical performance is not. No two performances of the same play, with the same cast, in the same space, and even with the same audience, would be alike. Of course, the gestural range of theatrical acting differs from the cinematic; the 'stagy' acting that estranges the modern viewer when watching early cinema was often produced by theatrical actors who had not comprehended the need to limit their expressiveness, especially in relation to the filmic resources of medium shot and the close-up. A gesture made to be comprehensible to an audience member in the back of the Circle would seem wildly and inappropriately over-emphasised in film close-up. The very nature of film form in continuity cinema – the editing of shots together to form scenes and sequences, often filmed out of narrative chronology – differs markedly from both theatrical form and theatrical performance, and the construction of (and manipulation of) time and space in film surely has greater expressive possibilities than the theatre. The instantaneous cut from shot to shot, scene to scene, place to place, gives the cinema a mobility that theatre cannot have.

The adaptation of the stage play to the screen, in contrast to the compression and selection required in adapting the large nineteenth-century realist novel, often requires 'opening out' the play: increasing the number of locations, introducing new scenes, altering speeches to move away from the set-piece theatrical monologue. Not to do so, or not to do so *enough*, means the film-maker runs the risk of making 'filmed theatre' rather than a film text in its own right. Both Graham Atkin and Ashley Chantler make this point, and Chantler in particular emphasises the difference between Pinter's play of *The Caretaker* and the film he analyses: the film is, and should be considered as, a separate artwork.

For screen versions of Shakespeare, other issues are crucial. There have been several collections of essays produced on Shakespeare on screen and, of course, film versions of *Twelfth Night* or *Macbeth* are often used in the teaching situation to 'illustrate' how a text (studied on the

Adapting Drama

page) might appear in performance.[1] They are thereby reduced to a form of 'filmed theatre' despite themselves, rendered entirely secondary to (and illustrative of) the Shakespeare text. All the debates about the 'classic' text, and the cultural capital that also accrues to the 'classic' (and which must be negotiated by the film adaptation) are magnified in the case of Shakespeare on screen. There may be impulses towards Elizabethan dress or 'heritage' productions of the play, partly to correspond to received ideas about the play or about Shakespeare's works in the popular imagination; but for adaptations of Shakespeare plays, the fidelity issue is actually more complicated. What must be taken into account is the long history of Shakespeare *in theatrical production*, some of which are clear 'adaptations' of the play in that they offer clear readings of the play text (set in modern dress, or relocated period, or refracted transculturally) that attempt to bring forth certain aspects or elements of the play that have been previously unregarded. This history of performance means that the film-maker who adapts Shakespeare to the screen has a greater degree of flexibility than in some other genres or modes. Baz Luhrmann's *William Shakespeare's Romeo + Juliet*, for example, relocates the play to a modern-day 'Verona Beach', where Montagues and Capulets are rival crime families in armed conflict; while Richard Loncraine's

---

[1] See, for example, *Shakespeare the Movie: Popularizing the Plays on Film, TV, and Video*, ed. by Lynda E. Boose and Richard Burt (London: Routledge, 1997) and *Shakespeare the Movie II: Popularizing the Plays on Film, TV, Video, and DVD*, ed. by Richard Burt and Lynda E. Boose (London: Routledge, 2003); *Screening Shakespeare in the Twenty-First Century*, ed. by Mark Thornton Burnett and Ramona Wray (Edinburgh: Edinburgh University Press, 2006); or *Shakespeare and the Moving Image: The Plays on Film and Television*, ed. by Anthony Davies and Stanley Wells (Cambridge: Cambridge University Press, 1994).

Richard III, starring Ian McKellen, reads the king as a dictator in a version of 1930s Britain. While the latter film was based on a particular theatrical staging of the play, in execution it becomes entirely cinematic. Most strikingly, Richard's 'winter of discontent' speech cuts from a triumphal public oration to an intimate to-camera speech in the toilet.

The interconnection of film and drama is significantly attested to by the path between stage and screen for actors and directors alike. McKellen, now an actorly institution almost as well known as the Royal Shakespeare Company itself, played Gandalf in Peter Jackson's films of *The Lord of the Rings* and Magneto in the *X-Men* franchise; Kevin Spacey, an excellent Hollywood character actor, has spent some years as artistic director of the Old Vic Theatre in London. This intercourse has not weakened either form, made theatre more filmic or cinema more theatrical. It is evidence of the ongoing cross-fertilisation between these two dramatic forms, a dialogue still vital despite their differences.

'THE RAIN IT RAINETH IN EVERY FRAME': A DEFENCE OF TREVOR NUNN'S *TWELFTH NIGHT* (1996)

Graham Atkin

Kevin Jackson's rejection of Trevor Nunn's film version of Shakespeare's *Twelfth Night* in *The Independent on Sunday* was typical of the negative critical response to the film. His claim that 'murk is drowning every frame' is, however, wrong-headed, for Nunn's vision genuinely reflects the cruelty in the play's humour, the play's strong sense of loss in love and its recurring anxiety about ageing and death. This chapter will endeavour to redress unnecessarily dismissive views of Nunn's enterprise by demonstrating the film's essential integrity in dramatising the play's concerns. Indeed Nunn's film version of the play, it will be argued, is perhaps not dark enough.

Jackson criticised the opening of Nunn's film in no uncertain terms:

> ... Nunn has come up with a tacky little back-story sequence about our heroine's shipwreck off the coast of Illyria – a misconceived aid to comprehension for the darkly ignorant that almost scuppers the film before we've heard so much as a syllable of Shakespeare's verse or prose. We do hear other text, though – an embarrassing cod-Jacobean voice-over which spells out the life histories of Viola and Sebastian ... , who are performing a drag act (cute, eh?) for their fellow passengers just as the ship hits rock.[1]

---

[1] Kevin Jackson, 'Film: The rain it raineth in every frame': [review of Nunn's *Twelfth Night*], *The Independent on Sunday*, 27 October 1996

To be sure, the voice-over does seem to be an error of judgment on Nunn's part, but there have been mistaken voice-overs before that have not prevented a film achieving overall excellence (consider the 1982 theatrical release of Ridley Scott's *Blade Runner*,[2] for example). The opening sequence, however, far from almost scuppering the film, sets up the dramatic situation effectively, seizes our attention through the excitement of shipwreck, and allows us a first view of an emotive Viola, feelingly played by Imogen Stubbs, washing up on a strange shore.

The opening

The genius of Nunn's opening scene is that he suggests that it is the very playfulness of the twins that creates a disruption in the cosmos, the tempest that sees the ship wrecked. As Viola, having been stripped of her moustache and thereby, to the amusement of those gathered for the entertainment, identified as female, raises her hand to her brother's upper lip and prepares with thumb and forefinger to strip off his moustache, the boat lurches, the storm increases in its intensity, and the great tragic event from which the whole story springs crashes and splashes before our eyes. As Rothwell has it, Nunn is working through 'a *Titanic* trope' here, with Viola and Sebastian cast into the perilous seas from the 'passenger vessel on the edge of doom'.[3]

<http://www.independent.co.uk/life-style/film-the-rain-it-raineth-in-every-frame-1360414.html> [accessed 14 April 2009]

[2] *Blade Runner*, dir. by Ridley Scott (Warner Bros, 1982).

[3] Kenneth S. Rothwell, *A History of Shakespeare on Screen* (Cambridge: Cambridge University Press, 1999), p. 227.

'The Rain It Raineth in Every Frame'

When Viola, the sea captain and other survivors gather on Illyria's shore, they soon have to evade detection by Illyrian soldiers. On the effect of stressing the state of war in Illyria, Rothwell rightly points out that, by turning 'Illyria into a police state', Nunn 'robs Viola of some of the mystery that Shakespeare surrounded her with'.[4] Take, for example, the fact that Viola, in Nunn's film, no longer speaks perhaps the most encouraging and reassuring lines in the play:

> O time, thou must untangle this, not I,
>
> It is too hard a knot for me t'untie. (II, 2, 39-40)

They are encouraging and reassuring in the sense that the lines clearly tell us we are in the world of *comedy*, where insoluble problems will be solved and wounds salved. Here time will untie knotty problems, time will solve, time will bring in a better world. In Shakespeare's *tragic* cosmos, time will always confound and quell, but here, Viola's surrender to time's agency will be vindicated by her resurrected twin and the ecstasy of requited love. Here, what is currently monstrous (love-sick Cesario) will metamorphose into the perfect form, the form fit for purpose (the in-love Viola). In tragedy, it is the serpent that writhes from the innocent flower, as it dawns on us that happiness is lost forever.

Viola's final words are clearly not her finest lines, and it is not overly disappointing that Nunn has cut them (though they have important implications for the extent to which we sympathise with the imprisoned Malvolio, for we learn in these lines that Malvolio has himself had the

---

[4] Rothwell, p. 227.

Textual Revisions

helpful sea captain imprisoned):

> The captain that did bring me first on shore
> Hath my maid's garments. He upon some action
> Is now in durance at Malvolio's suit,
> A gentleman and follower of my lady's. (V. 1.272-5)

A more serious omission is surely Viola's penultimate speech, which is charged with a passion unmatched by any other character in the play, except perhaps Antonio and Malvolio:

> And all those sayings will I overswear,
> And all those swearings keep as true in soul
> As doth that orbed continent the fire
> That severs day from night. (V.1.267-70)

This is fine swearing and over-swearing, reaching Player King-like levels of emotional intensity (with the word 'orbed' putting us in mind of the Player King's:

> Full thirty times hath Phoebus' cart gone round
> Neptune's salt wash and Tellus' orbed ground).[5]

Nunn robs Viola of some of her majesty by not having her speak these towering words of commitment. Nunn gives Viola only the first of these lines, 'And all those sayings will I over-swear', which, while delivered by Stubbs with some feeling, nevertheless falls somewhat short of the

---

[5] William Shakespeare, *Hamlet*, III.2.151-2.

'The Rain It Raineth in Every Frame'

rhetorical majesty of Shakespeare's full speech. Given that these are the last words that Viola speaks in Nunn's film, it does seem a lost opportunity for further wonder at the imperious force of love manifested in the film's heroine, especially given the widely-praised excellence of Stubbs's performance throughout the film. But the omission of lines in renditions of Shakespeare seems almost inevitable and the refusal to pare down the text seems likely to lead to box-office failure (such as in Kenneth Branagh's full-text film version of *Hamlet*). The significance is not so much in the lines Nunn has cut, but in what he does with what remains.

Shakespeare begins his play with Orsino's famous line, 'If music be the food of love, play on', but Nunn chooses to begin with a storm, the song 'O mistress mine' sung by the cross-dressing twins, and Feste's own words, spoken by Ben Kingsley, as we watch the oceanic catastrophe. This leads into Shakespeare's second scene, and the first spoken words (after Kingsley's voice-over) are Viola's mournful, 'What country, friends, is this?' Before we see Orsino, we have Viola stumbling across the funeral of Olivia's brother. The sense of loss and grief is thus firmly established, and we are permitted a privileged view of the process by which Viola then transforms herself, taking off her female clothes and binding herself with a red sash. As Hatchuel has it: 'Through this chronological series of shots, Nunn stresses Viola's heart-breaking decision to change physically. Deciding to appear as a boy is not a mere game, but a resolution which has drastic, tormenting consequences on her body.'[6] This ignores the fact that Nunn's sequence presents Viola's transformation as comically liberating and

---

[6] Sarah Hatchuel, *Shakespeare, From Stage to Screen* (Cambridge: Cambridge University Press, 2004), p. 47.

playfully erotic, skilfully setting the tone while the credits are still rolling.

Viola masculinises herself with the assistance of the sea captain, and then heads off to St Michael's Mount, to Orsino's court, across the sun-streaked natural cobbling. The brooding Duke is clearly a figure of fun: our first view of him leads us into smiles, at the melodrama of his rhetoric and the moodiness of his changeability. The slow panning shot, which ends by revealing Viola/Cesario at the piano, reveals an array of attendants, some of whom look distinctly unimpressed with their Count's self-indulgence. Nunn's re-jigging of Shakespeare's opening means that Orsino's lines gain in dramatic intensity, as the excellent Stubbs pulls a pained face while Toby Stephens's Count bemoans the fact that Olivia pays 'this debt of love but to a brother'. The sadness in Viola is driven home by Nunn's inter-cutting of the seemingly drowned Sebastian (played by Stephen Mackintosh). Nunn has more than justified the decision to add the opening shipwreck. By employing a flashback which allows the audience access to the pangs of Viola's suffering, we are able to see that Viola is 'playing' (or acting/performing) the persona of her own brother, as it were, as a debt of love *to* that lost brother. When Nunn cuts back, he uses the sea to connect us to Viola's new male life and, in a scene which sets the film's tone of suppressed eroticism, Stubbs is shown fending off the innocently placed hand of the fencing instructor, but through the mesh of her mask we see an unmistakeable smile that also suggests pleasure. Kevin Jackson may complain about an 'impossibly sexy Cesario', but the situation Nunn has contrived here, while mildly comic, is powerfully suggestive of the complex levels of erotic interplay allowable in a 'what you will' world.

The wild sea setting of the following scene, in which Orsino confesses that he has 'unclasped' to Viola/Cesario

'The Rain It Raineth in Every Frame'

'the book even of my secret soul', visually concretises the sense of torrents of feeling and passion sweeping over individual characters. We cannot but concur with Orsino's judgment that Viola has a 'constellation' which is 'right apt for the affair' as we see Stubbs, in her soldier's uniform, pace along the Cornish cliff-tops with her three attendants, on her way to enchant Olivia.

First meetings

The change of scene to Olivia's household begins with a close-up. The music changes to the playful bombastic tune accompanying Malvolio (Nigel Hawthorne) as he tours the kitchen, preparatory to the funeral reception. His mood is contradicted by the music, gently mocking his gravity. We are then immediately introduced to Malvolio's true counterpoint, the drunken Sir Toby Belch, brilliantly played by Mel Smith. Nigel Hawthorne's fingernail-inspecting, bespectacled disapproval of the sterling efforts of the sizable kitchen staff (numerically speaking), and especially his supercilious double-clap (suggesting hup-two) and mimed whisking direction, expertly form an immediate and strong impression of Malvolio's priggish self-love and self-aggrandisement. Conversely, Sir Toby is hardly aware of himself at all – asleep, with bottle in hand, he is quickly revealed to be, not only a drunk, but also a sponge. The casting here is faultless. Hawthorne's Sir Humphrey Appleby, the fussy but Machiavellian mandarin civil servant of the BBC comedy series *Yes, Minister*, provides a crucial intertext for the British audience in decoding the character of Malvolio.[7] Mel

---

[7] The satirical sitcom *Yes, Minister*, written by Antony Jay and Jonathan Lynn, was shown by the BBC from 1980 to 1984. It was followed, with the same cast, after the promotion of the minister in question, Jim Hacker MP (Paul Eddington), by *Yes, Prime Minister*, from 1984 to 1988.

Smith's ebullient Sir Toby, especially as he throws back the curtains to allow the sunshine to flood in, clearly heartens us, as we sense the coming confrontation of two opposing attitudes towards life.[8] Toby has the assistance – the love – of the busy and serious Imelda Staunton as Maria, her aiding role suggested here with great economy by her providing Sir Toby with a hangover remedy which he takes gratefully. As Toby speaks, Sir Andrew, played by Richard E. Grant, cavorts (Grant's capering galliard is a magnificent display of absurd comic dancing, complete with 'buck-kick'), but in the distant door frame the figure of Malvolio appears, then in close-up, framed between the doors, a figure of utmost rigidity and order. Sir Andrew performs an ungainly dance to reveal laughably his 'virtues', and the precise figure of Malvolio in the doorway nips the levity of Belch's belly laugh in the bud. Belch had enthusiastically asked, 'Is this a world to hide virtues in?' and Nunn's decision to confront the hedonistic duo with the haughty figure of Hawthorne's Malvolio seems to answer the question with a disapproving, 'Yes, if the virtues you have to display are so frivolous, yes, hide them.' The audience must disagree. We know that the virtue of Grant's dancing is in the pleasure it brings, not only to the accompanying Sir Toby, but also to us, the amused viewers of such excellent slapstick. Smith and Grant are also employed by Nunn to present the viewer with a fine scene of drunkenness when they return late at night to Olivia's quiet house. This scene is a comic highlight of Nunn's film, emphasising the role of strong physical comedy in the portrayal of Sir Andrew and Sir

---

[8] Mel Smith has also been a very well-known British television comedic actor, particularly in the BBC comedy series *Not the Nine O'Clock News* (1979 to 1982) and *Alas Smith and Jones* (1982 to 1988).

'The Rain It Raineth in Every Frame'

Toby. Smith and Grant's crashing and clattering about, followed by their ridiculous dancing, injects the kind of chaotic tomfoolery and hubbub that Shakespeare's characterisation demands.

The *mise-en-scène* and editing here add to the sense of the scene in the play text, as does the opening of the next scene, a shot of Maria (Imelda Staunton) at her accounts – interrupting herself to attend to Feste, who she sees from the window. Feste surrenders to Maria's authority, as Maria reminds Feste how a fool can mend – with her wit, her corruption of words. He smiles – 'Well, go thy way'. It is a small indication of the capacity of words to heal, and Kingsley's Feste responds to Maria's demonstration of care for him by giving a wry smile, suggesting his intention to resume his complex but crucial role in this house of mourning. This complex mending role is first witnessed in the scene with Olivia outside the church. His refusal to indulge Olivia in her mourning, pointing out that she is a fool to grieve while believing her brother to be in heaven, achieves a crucial victory and a sweet smile, as Olivia asks 'doth he not mend?' Hawthorne's Malvolio here responds with evil eyes, showing us the bitterness that will be avenged – 'Yes, and shall do, till the pangs of death shake him'. It is a vital moment, for it starts the whirligig spinning, as Nunn's direction implies with a tracking shot, the camera-eye circling the figures.

This then is our second sight of Feste (first seen as an omniscient overseer on the cliff-tops), the 'clinical depressive' as Jackson has it. Feste is humoured into laughter by Staunton's intelligent Maria. This works well – Kingsley and Staunton and Smith, Grant and Hawthorne provide a depth of acting talent equal to their evocative surroundings. Nunn likes to employ parallels, and Feste's plaintive shrugging walk around the kitchen table contrasts effectively with Malvolio's inspection parade.

Maria goes before Feste, providing a chair for the weary clown to be seated.

Jackson's judgement of Nunn's film, that 'murk is drowning every frame', is particularly supported by his account of the first meeting between Olivia and Viola, much of which, he claims, 'is so tenebrous that a sceptic might suspect industrial action on the part of the lighting crew.' This is a cheap journalistic shot from Jackson, for the 'murkiness' of this scene serves as a pointed and thoroughly effective contrast to the bright light of the following garden scene, in which the film reaches an emotional climax with Cesario/Viola's passionate and song-like exclamation of 'Olivia'. Cesario achieves entry to the inner sanctum – the screen filled with shadows, candlelight, dark clothing and drapes, with occasional glimpses of light beaming from his/her hair and face – and as Olivia (the pale Helena Bonham Carter) moves, she sounds interested and dismisses the surprised Maria. Cesario's direct speech, 'let me see your face', moving out of Orsino's text, achieves another victory. Olivia removes her veil with,

> '... we will draw the curtain and show you the picture.... Is't not well done?' (I.5.236-8);

but Cesario is not as impressed as Olivia expects him to be, disdainfully suggesting that the beauty may not all be natural: 'Excellently done, if God did all.' Stubbs's pulling back of the curtain here is a fitting action for the moment. She has moved Olivia to the lectern, but now moves from student to tutor. Olivia's unveiling is an act of pride and vanity, though Bonham Carter's attractive features justify Cesario's judgment, ''Tis beauty truly blent'. The wincing Bonham Carter turns away from the rays of light which

'The Rain It Raineth in Every Frame'

expose her like a search-beam to the gaze of her candid tormentor – but when she turns back again it seems she looks with new eyes. Stubbs rapidly approaches with her most direct line thus far:

> Lady, you are the cruel'st she alive
> If you will lead these graces to the grave
> And leave the world no copy. (I, 5, 244-6)

We now hear a different Olivia – capable of self-mockery and flirtation. But Cesario is relentless – judging Olivia in a quick and telling phrase: 'you are too proud'.

There follows the near kiss, with the rising music suggesting that love or desire is in the air. This is one of the two most highly-charged erotic moments in Nunn's film (the other is the even-nearer kiss between Viola and Orsino as they listen to Feste's 'Come away, death'). Jackson claims, 'There's hardly a sexual spark anywhere in the romance, even at the oddly inconsistent moment when Viola and Orsino sit together in inevitable darkness, listen to a glum song sung by Feste ..., close their eyes and nearly snog'; but perhaps Jackson is looking in too obvious a place for the sexual sparks, which fly more unpredictably from the wheels of confusion set in play. It is another near kiss that is truly charged with erotic energy, when the feisty disguised Viola comes to within a hair's breadth of the dazzled and dazzling Olivia.

This scene is played with consummate skill. The air crackles with the electrical charge of desire and their hair seems to touch even though their lips do not. Olivia is then drawn out into the garden, followed by Cesario, imagining himself in his master's place, and Olivia plays along, falling in love, catching the plague: 'Why, what would you?' Cesario's passion, the threat of that passion to the status quo, is summed up in a quick cut to the surprised Malvolio as he hears the exuberant (and loud) 'Olivia' hallooed by Stubbs. Cesario's outburst shocks Olivia into an open-mouthed, open-eyed awe, while Malvolio is stopped in his official tracks and made to do an about-face for the film audience. We clearly see Viola's spirit of love shaking up the Illyrian scene, like a cross between Venus and Cupid – somewhat blindly firing her incendiary love darts willy-nilly into the gloom of Olivia's household. Olivia's 'Shhh' here is too late – love will not be shushed in Illyria now that Viola is present. Nunn is right here: it is Viola who drives the play; it is she who commands an end to grief, an end to mourning. Viola plays no part in the gulling of Malvolio – indeed, in Nunn's film she remains wonderfully neutral to Malvolio, who, in his condescending tossing of 'her' ring, does more than enough to provoke her.

Malvolio immediately turns to come to Olivia's assistance and is made to pursue the young man of unknown parentage in an undignified bicycle ride. Malvolio is told to 'run after' Cesario, and is even encouraged by the besotted Olivia: 'Hie thee'. The mockery of Malvolio has begun in his inability to ride a bicycle properly and to stand it up effectively, more physical comedy that adds to his out-of-breath discourtesy towards the confused Cesario. The ring, however, is a clear sign of love – a sign Viola does not fail to interpret correctly. Nunn's handling of this scene, with the truth dawning on Viola managed through intercut flashbacks that illustrate her realisation that 'she loves me', is capped by Stubbs's amused punctuating laugh following 'I am the man'; a most unmanly, pubescent laugh that mocks the notion that she *is* the man: 'I am the man. Uh – uh'. The laugh is a little blip – almost an electronic noise – an error – a non-human sound fitting for the disguised 'monster' who is neither

'The Rain It Raineth in Every Frame'

male nor female. Stubbs does not move her mouth as she makes this noise, so suggestive of puzzled amusement, from the pharynx. Nunn, however, cuts Viola's following lines on time and how time must undo the knot of this error, 'not I'. This is a pity, for these lines go further than any in the play to make Viola the voice of comic surrender, the voice of sweet submission to fate and fortune, the voice of patient optimism. This is a key aspect of Viola which should not really be neglected. To drive home the uncertainties here as to who is the man, we immediately encounter the pained Sebastian, and the even-more-pained Antonio, on whose shoulder Sebastian can manfully weep. 'Let me be your servant' implores Antonio – and there is more than a hint of desire in his plea. The love-sick Antonio, played with an entirely fitting emotional intensity by Nicholas Farrell, seems on the verge of grieved tears throughout the film.

From carnival to torture

The conflated scenes between Orsino and Viola and between Sir Andrew, Sir Toby, Maria, Feste and Malvolio create a powerful central movement in the film. The noise of Sir Andrew, Sir Toby and Feste is hugely disruptive, anarchic mayhem. This is the height of the carnivalesque eruption, and Malvolio is interrupted during his private enjoyment of a bedtime restorative drink while reading *Amour* magazine (an image of hypocritical self-indulgence). Feste sings his mournful love song with squeeze-box accompaniment while sitting atop the kitchen table cross-legged, and Nunn's editing effectively introduces Feste's song through Viola and Orsino's exchange. 'How dost thou like this tune?' asks the Count, to which Viola replies, feelingly,

Textual Revisions

> It gives a very echo to the seat
> Where love is throned. (II, 4, 21-2)

The same tune that Feste sings for Toby and Andrew is played on the piano in the Count's games room, unifying the scenes through the genius of music.

These are scenes which show lovers knowing their love for others – or feeling them as a mournful pain. Orsino's posturing is juxtaposed with Viola's, Toby's, even Andrew's truly felt suffering. Maria's singing and her knowing glance at the smouldering, rumbling Sir Toby add another dimension of love and loss to the scene. Kingsley's aggressive delivery of the song's 'Youth's a stuff will not endure' communicates a sense of the unfairness of ageing, of loss, of death. It is Sir Toby who has to rescue us from the gloom and drive the party to more revels with his clattering of pans. This carnivalesque scene sets up the great confrontation of revelry with respect, of fun versus duty. The revellers show no respect, though Maria seems to fear repercussions as Belch attacks Malvolio:

> Art any more than a steward? Dost thou think because thou art virtuous, there shall be no more cakes and ale. (II, 3, 113-5)

> Go sir, rub your chain with crumbs. A stoup of wine Maria! (II, 3, 118-9)

This is a key moment, as the forces of carnival and excess collide with the force of Malvolio's disapproval and sense of propriety. Battle is joined, and the whirligig of time spins faster.

Malvolio's madness is so capably handled by Hawthorne as to be ridiculous and disturbing at the same time. It is, as Fabian comments, an 'improbable fiction' that we see played out, and it is at this juncture that the play shifts into another tone, with the joke pushed too far by the increasingly malevolent and less and less likeable Sir Toby. Malvolio's madness is foreshadowed by the scene in which he discovers and interprets the letter, where the final birth of Hawthorne's smile is truly monstrous. In a play of monstrosity, this is the most comic monster yet – a grimace of pain and strangulation, something forced against nature – or a nature so misled and malformed by repression, so ill-nurtured, that is speaks more of pain than pleasure. As Toby, Maria and Fabian giggle infectiously on the sofa, the ominous line from Mel Smith,

> Come, we'll have him in a dark room and bound ... for our pleasure (III, 4, 136-8),

jars with both on-screen and off-screen audiences. Staunton's Maria looks truly disturbed, and the shift in our perception of Malvolio from deserving butt of the joke to victim of cruelty commences.

Aguecheek's idiocy, presented memorably by a posturing Grant, replete in yellow stockings and practising his fencing, signifies that he now becomes the principal object of humour. His letter challenging Cesario is truly absurd and his pomposity outdoes Malvolio's. The pack play with Aguecheek as they had gulled Malvolio previously, but even Aguecheek later solicits our sympathy when Grant shuffles away, crestfallen, after the wounded Sir Toby turns on him. It puts us in mind of the earlier claim that 'I was adored once too' from Sir Andrew, a comment that hints at a sadness beneath the ridiculous façade.

Textual Revisions

By this stage, the film has managed to make Sebastian's key question seem wholly apposite: 'Are all the people mad?' Olivia augments this sense of lunacy:

> How runs the stream
>
> Or I am mad, or else this is a dream. (IV, 1, 59-60)

Sebastian is the true player, the true dreamer, the missing piece who has to be fitted in, and Steven Mackintosh's fresh-faced innocence serves well. We are approaching the end, and it is necessary for there to be a number of rejections. Sir Toby is rejected by Olivia: 'Rudesby, be gone!' Aguecheek is hurtfully rejected by Sir Toby (Mel Smith, with wounded head, is particularly loathsome in this moment; indeed, from this point on all the levity has seeped out of this characterisation, and as he leaves with Maria under the amused eye of Feste there seems to be no joy at all in the prospect of their marriage).

The darkest part of this comedy is surely the imprisonment and torment of Malvolio, and Nunn's treatment of this scene, while disturbing, is not disturbing enough. The scene of Malvolio's imprisonment is, I would argue, *insufficiently* dark in Nunn's film. Not only is Malvolio shown in some light in his captivity but, more importantly, the scene is intercut with other scenes. The effect is a diminishment of the torment Malvolio suffers. The grief and torture of the scene are thus glossed over and some of the real impact of the play is lost. Kingsley and Hawthorne do their best to draw out the darker aspects here, and Smith's Belch and Maria also draw the play away from laughter and hilarity into something more sombre and dispiriting, an entertainment we would all be well rid of. However, Nunn's editorial decisions undoubtedly detract from any potential for presenting Malvolio as a figure we might pity, just as they dilute the sense that Feste is somewhat demonic. We cannot really feel much for Malvolio the way Nunn presents it, and this takes away from the real pain of this moment and the real cruelty. As the film cuts back to Malvolio's tears, they seem a sideshow. Feste is a vicious man here, similar to the old Vice of the morality plays. Kingsley here captures the sense of the old Vice capably, while adding an almost *Clockwork Orange*-like menace to the performance (and for any who have seen Kingsley's terrifying Don Logan in *Sexy Beast* (2000) there are other sinister connotations);[9] but Nunn's editing prevents his audience from experiencing a sufficiently sustained exposure to such an uncomfortable (though, perhaps for the early modern audience, somewhat familiar) presence. Feste's performance here, far from driving Malvolio mad, is a malevolent form of madness in itself; Feste turns into a deranged mannequin. As he spies from the corner of the church on Sebastian and Olivia, cynically watching their marriage, his parting song grates. The mad capers have taken a sinister turn, and even Belch begins to tire of the sport.

The notion of sport which has become mixed with something far from entertaining is captured in the oxymoron of Fabian's description of proceedings as 'sportful malice', a line sadly not kept by Nunn. It is perhaps surprising that bear-baiting is specifically mentioned in only two of Shakespeare's plays. In *The Winter's Tale* we hear that Autolycus 'haunts wakes, fairs and bear-baitings'; but in *Twelfth Night* there are two mentions of the 'sport' of bear-baiting, one from Sir Andrew:

---

[9] *Sexy Beast*, dir. by Jonathan Glazer (FilmFour, 2000).

Textual Revisions

> I would I had bestowed that time in the tongues that I have in fencing, dancing and bear-baiting. (I.iii.90-92)

and one from Fabian

> ... he brought me out of favour with my lady about a bear-baiting here. (II.v.6-8).

It is pleasing to note that Nunn, while omitting the first reference, has retained the latter, for the idea of bear-baiting as sport is crucial to our understanding of the treatment of Malvolio. Accounts of bear-baiting from the period make evident the ferocity of the cruelty involved and the popularity of the spectacle. Shakespeare's theatre was in direct competition with such entertainment. In place of a bear, a kind of Puritan is placed at the stake for the wild pack of hedonistic practical jokers to savage.

Toby and Maria are spectators to Feste's tormenting of Malvolio in the guise of Sir Topaz. Toby eats an oatcake and drinks his wine, watching from a distance, the very archetype of the idle spectator. Master Topaz opens the slatted window of Malvolio's cell, and Hawthorne's mouth and fingers appear at the hatch in a powerful image of tormented, imprisoned humanity. Staunton's Maria, slightly bad-tempered, concerned and serious, augments the sombre mood. The humour is palling as Feste continues, and then we cut from this scene to Olivia and Sebastian kissing. Mackintosh's Sebastian cannot quite believe his luck. The frivolity and indignity of love is made real. By cutting in this way, Nunn does allow a juxtaposition of Sebastian's 'I am mad', with Malvolio's 'I am not mad', a neat effect; but the editorial decision, I would reiterate, still diminishes the impact of the cruelty of the treatment of Malvolio. Nunn's choice places before us

'The Rain It Raineth in Every Frame'

more obviously the fascinating exploration of love and madness that is *Twelfth Night*. Malvolio rattles his cage like a trapped animal. Sir Toby roughly kisses Maria, but there is little joy in it. Kingsley's Feste provides a nod of acceptance or permission, but Maria does not look content or happy, and neither does Toby.

Feste's revenges

Feste is 'unaccountably anguished', according to Jackson, yet Feste's anguish *is* accounted for. He is, like Olivia, in mourning. When Orsino enquires into the identity of the man who has previously sung him a song that pleased him ('Who was it?'), Curio replies:

> Feste the jester, my lord, a fool that the Lady Olivia's father took much delight in. (II.i4.11-2)

So we can assume that Feste grieves for his dead master – and this explains his morbidity of mind (for example, in the centrally placed song of death, the Clown's song). In the film Feste performs this song as if it were the song closest to his heart. He has been discovered by Orsino and Cesario hiding in an out-building – drinking alone – the drinker who drinks to drown his sorrows or be drowned in his sorrows. Seeing Feste here suggests that his earlier words to Olivia when she asks, 'What's a drunken man like, fool?', are to be seen as more personally felt than objectively observed:

> Like a drowned man, a fool, and a madman: one draught above heat makes him a fool, the second mads him, and a third drowns him. (I.5.132-4)

Textual Revisions

In his hovel, Feste resembles an outcast – a beggar – who chances to be able to meet the mood of those he performs for. Orsino strikes a melancholy pose, but Feste is the truly melancholy man of *Twelfth Night* – grieving, bitter, more intelligent that the others. He changes his mask for his audience – or does he? His criticism of Orsino turns the tables:

> Now the melancholy god protect thee, and the tailor make thy doublet of changeable taffeta, for thy mind is a very opal. (II.4.73-5)

Kingsley's slurred, almost bad-tempered 'Farewell' from the doorway, to an Orsino who it seems does not hear him, is indicative of an essential loneliness and sorrow.

The subsequent scene is brilliantly managed by Nunn and his two actors, Toby Stephens and Imogen Stubbs. The tempestuous sea provides a fitting backdrop for Orsino's passionate outburst – but it is the gentle counterpoint of Viola's heartfelt words which move the audience to share her tears. Making full use of the intimacy film affords, Nunn closes in on the grieved Stubbs as she feelingly appeals to the foolish Count. Stubbs's tears and near tears in her eyes through the film are indeed moving. They, assisted by close-up camera work, produce the deepest sense of pity that the film evokes. Orsino's tetchy sentence, 'And what's her history?,' cues the revelation – the telling of the love never told. Nunn's rendition captures all the ironies of Shakespeare's scene. Viola speaks from the heart to the deluded, narcissistic Orsino – she tells her love while saying she says nothing: 'A blank'. This is the true melancholy of the play – the melancholy of pining in thought – of wasting away while the world passes us by. Love here is no pleasure – it is a pain, a torment. This torment is felt throughout the play and properly communicated in Nunn's interpretation.

The brilliance of the casting is here particularly evident: Grant's Aguecheek, Smith's Belch, Staunton's Maria, Hawthorne's Malvolio, Stubbs's Viola, Kingsley's Feste, and, most hopelessly, Farrell's Antonio, all convey a deep sense of the melancholic grief of love. Olivia and Orsino, though more demonstrative, are less believable. Indeed, it seems that the more a character in Illyria professes love, the less believable that character becomes. Hence, we cannot believe Orsino, Olivia becomes more ridiculous as the play unfolds, and Malvolio is an over-performing fool – until, that is, his final heartfelt anguish. One thing that Nunn's version leads us to feel concerning Malvolio is that his most real moment is his closing ominous threat: 'I'll be reveng'd on the whole pack of you!' Hawthorne here achieves tragic presence, and the play's content and contrived resolution wobbles and veers off kilter. 'Anything that's mended', we remember Feste saying, 'is but patched'.

The reunion of Sebastian and Viola is also skilfully handled, with the pleasing echo of the film's opening in the removal of Cesario's false moustache. Nunn overcomes one of the difficulties encountered in rendering this moment by shrewd management of the lead-up to the twins' intense meeting. Grant's Aguecheek here, as throughout, brings necessary energy for Stubbs to play off and invokes sympathy in his crestfallen response to the cruelty of his rejection by the Smith's venomous Belch:

> 'Will you help? An ass-head, and a coxcomb, and a knave, a thin-faced knave, a gull?' (V, 1, 204-5)

Our concern for Aguecheek is led by Viola, who follows him as he staggers disconsolately away, allowing Sebastian to take centre frame. Brother and sister are finally brought face to face, or rather framed profile to profile, in front of the Lanhydrock Gate House. The setting reinforces the sense of symmetrical stability which the play's end suggests. Lanhydrock works because it is a place out of time, Edwardian in a way, but not quite Edwardian; somehow timeless, like Nunn's film.

The final image of Kingsley's Feste spinning away down the hillside echoes again the whirligig of time which, as we have seen, will bring in his revenges. This complicates Feste's parting laughter and lines. In what way will Feste strive to please us every day (repeated three times)? Perhaps the enigmatic clown strives to please as an agent of time's vengeful whirligig, by visiting us and taunting us in our dark tormented cells of unrequited love.

In the end, perhaps it is most fitting to judge Nunn's film by his own yardstick. In an article in *The Guardian* published in 2005, Nunn writes that the legend of certain productions survives 'because of their daring, their unexpectedness and their determination to provide fresh insight, new stimuli and increased relevance.' He also writes that Shakespeare works 'much more through storytelling than symbolic gesture and that every play of his is unique, different and particular, and won't be solved by the application of a formula.'[10] When we watch Nunn's film of *Twelfth Night*, we have to admit that he subordinates any desire to gesture symbolically to the primary importance of storytelling and that, in the clarity

---

[10] Trevor Nunn, 'Play for Today', *The Guardian*, 24 September 2005 <http://www.guardian.co.uk/stage/2005/sep/24/theatre.classics> [accessed 13 August 2008]

'The Rain It Raineth in Every Frame'

of that storytelling, the selection of settings, and the excellence of his actors, his film provides fresh insight, new stimuli and increased relevance at least a decade after its first screening.

Bibliography

Primary Works

Shakespeare, William, *Twelfth Night*, ed. by J. M. Lothian and T. W. Craik, 2nd edn (London: Methuen, 1975)

Twelfth Night, dir./ad. by Trevor Nunn (Entertainment, 1996

Secondary Works

Blade Runner, dir. by Ridley Scott (Warner Bros, 1982)

Hatchuel, Sarah, *Shakespeare: From Stage to Screen* (Cambridge: Cambridge University Press, 2004)

Jackson, Kevin, 'Film: The rain it raineth in every frame': [review of Nunn's *Twelfth Night*], *The Independent on Sunday*, 27 October 1996 <http://www.independent.co.uk/life-style/film-the-rain-it-raineth-in-every-frame-1360414.html> [accessed 14 April 2009]

Nunn, Trevor, 'Play for Today', *The Guardian*, 24 September 2005 <http://www.guardian.co.uk/stage/2005/sep/24/theatre.classics> [accessed 13 August 2008]

Rothwell, Kenneth S., *A History of Shakespeare on Screen: A Century of Film and Television*. (Cambridge: Cambridge University Press, 1999)

Sexy Beast, dir. by Jonathan Glazer (FilmFour, 2000)

Shakespeare, William, *Hamlet*, ed. by Ann Thompson and Neil Taylor, 3rd edn (London: Arden Shakespeare, 2006)

THE FILM OF HAROLD PINTER'S *THE CARETAKER*

Ashley Chantler

> Donner: [Donald Pleasance and I] met Harold for luncheon one day...
> Pinter: I paid for the lunch.
> Donner: He paid for the lunch. We said, 'We think a film could be made of [*The Caretaker*].'
> Pinter: I was very suspicious.
> Donner: He was very suspicious.[1]

Harold Pinter's suspicions about a film of *The Caretaker* were unnecessary and he later acknowledged its success:

> You can say the play has been 'opened out' in the sense that things I'd yearned to do, without knowing it, in writing for the stage, crystallised when I came to think about it as a film. Until then I didn't know that I wanted to do them because I'd accepted the limitations of the stage.[2]

---

[1] Harold Pinter and Clive Donner, 'Filming *The Caretaker*', interview by Kenneth Cavander, in *Harold Pinter: 'The Birthday Party', 'The Caretaker', 'The Homecoming': A Casebook,* ed. by Michael Scott (London: Macmillan, 1986), pp. 124-33 (p. 125) (first publ. in *Transatlantic Review*, 13 (Summer 1963), 17-26).

[2] Pinter and Donner, p. 127. The film, directed by Clive Donner and starring Alan Bates (Mick), Donald Pleasance (Davies) and Robert Shaw (Aston), was shot in Hackney, London, in January 1962; was first screened in June 1963 at the Berlin Film Festival; and was released in Britain in February 1964. It won the Berlin Film Festival Silver Bear (1963) and the Edinburgh Film Festival Certificate of Merit (1963); for

Textual Revisions

In an early review of the film, the influential *New Republic* film and theatre critic Stanley Kauffmann reinforces Pinter's view and suggests that the film is superior to previous stage versions:

> It is a fascinating, funny, eerie film, a work of murky evocations boiling out of grubby naturalistic minutiae. That is, of course, the Pinter method, but in the film we are seeing that method used at its best so far.... One feels that, at last, the work has been fully revealed.[3]

It must be emphasised, though, that the film is not the play on celluloid. It is a separate work, and it could be argued that to call it *'The Caretaker'* is misleading.[4] Between the play and the film, there are numerous substantive variants. When writing the screenplay, Pinter created new scenes to take the action outside the room and the house, and he deleted, moved and added dialogue. Furthermore, the film has close-ups, zooms, pans to left and right, shifts in point of view, cuts that do not follow the play's breaks, electronically-created sound effects, and was filmed in black and white on grainy Kodak 4X. The film is a new text; thus viewers interpret a different text.

---

further details, see Steven H. Gale, *Sharp Cut: Harold Pinter's Screenplays and the Artistic Process* (Lexington: University Press of Kentucky, 2003), pp. 97-98.

[3] Stanley Kauffmann, *'The Guest'*, *New Republic*, 25 January 1964; as quoted in Gale, *Sharp Cut*, p. 98.

[4] The film was released in the United States as *The Guest*, 'perhaps to avoid confusion with Hal Bartlett's *The Caretakers*, which had been released in 1963' (Gale, *Sharp Cut*, p. 97); ideally, the British version should also be titled thus.

The Film of Harold Pinter's *The Caretaker*

Students studying the play should not, therefore, use the film as if it is a verbatim recreation of the text or a stage version on screen; viewing the film is not the same as reading or watching the play. The film is perhaps best used by literature students as a catalyst for further reflection on the text. Students studying the film should be careful when using secondary sources about the play: the texts are, of course, of academic interest, but their statements about the characters or meaning might not necessarily apply to the film. Students studying the film should also approach with caution the secondary material that favours general statements rather than detailed filmic analysis and that which has a tendency to blur the boundaries between the two works;[5] as illustrated later in this essay, a detailed comparison of the film and the play generates a deeper and more nuanced understanding of both works.

The Caretaker as a play was first presented at the Arts Theatre, London, on 27 April 1960, and it transferred to the Duchess Theatre a month later.[6] It was Pinter's first major success as a playwright: 'I've had two full-length plays produced in London. The first [*The Birthday Party*] ran a week and the second ran a year.'[7] It had a total run of four

---

[5] Steven H. Gale, for example, who has written informatively and astutely on Pinter's screenplays, asserts that 'the meaning of the film version of *The Caretaker* is the same as the meaning of the stage version of the play. As a matter of fact, the film ... confirms, emphasizes, and further elucidates the meaning gleaned from the drama'; see Steven H. Gale, 'Film and Drama: The Opening Sequence of the Filmed Version of Harold Pinter's *The Caretaker* (*The Guest*)', in *Pinter at 70: A Casebook*, ed. by Lois Gordon (New York: Routledge, 2001), p. 125.

[6] Two of the cast (Alan Bates and Donald Pleasance) repeated their roles in the film; Peter Woodthorpe played Aston.

[7] Harold Pinter, 'Writing for the Theatre': speech made at the National Student Drama Festival in Bristol in 1962, in Harold Pinter, *Various*

hundred and forty-four performances[8] and has gone on to generate numerous interpretations. Steven H. Gale captures neatly the two poles of interpretation, ranging from the metaphysical and abstract to the prosaic and reductive:

> Terence Rattigan claims that, 'When I saw *The Caretaker* I told Pinter that I knew what it meant. "It's about the God of the Old Testament, the God of the New, and Humanity, isn't it?" Pinter said blankly, "No, Terry, it's about a caretaker and two brothers."'[9]

Pinter has also said that the play is 'about love',[10] but statements by authors about their work should perhaps not be granted special authority:

> ... it can never be too much insisted upon: *there is no true meaning to a text* – no author's authority. Whatever he may have *wanted to say*, he has written what he has written. Once published, a text is like an apparatus that anyone may use as he will and according to his ability: it is not certain that the one who constructed it can use it better than another. Besides, if he knows well what he meant to do,

---

Voices: Prose, Poetry, Politics, 1948-2005 (London: Faber & Faber, 2005), pp. 20-26 (p. 20) (first publ. in Harold Pinter, *Plays One* (London: Methuen, 1962)).

[8] Michael Billington, *Harold Pinter* (London: Faber & Faber, 2007), p. 114; this is a revised and updated edition of *The Life and Work of Harold Pinter* (1996).

[9] Gale, *Sharp Cut*, pp. 107-08.

[10] Gale, *Sharp Cut*, p. 108.

The Film of Harold Pinter's *The Caretaker*

this knowledge always disturbs his perception of what he has done.[11]

And categorical statements must certainly never be taken as 'the truth', as Pinter reminds us: 'A categorical statement ... will never stay where it is and be finite. It will immediately be subject to modification by the other twenty-three possibilities of it.'[12] It might be found that the play is about 'love', the film not. It might be found that Pinter has thrown us a red herring; when once asked what his plays are 'about', he famously replied: 'The weasel under the cocktail cabinet.'[13]

Given that the film of *The Caretaker* is such a fertile work, it is impossible, in the space available, to engage with everything that can be said about it. This essay has, therefore, been divided into four sections, centring on various definitions of 'alienate' and 'alien',[14] that will hopefully illuminate several key scenes and prompt reflection on and further analysis of both the film and the play.

'Alienate': 'To estrange'

Mark Batty has written that the first minutes of the stage version of *The Caretaker* 'set an enigma into operation'

---

[11] Paul Valéry, 'Concerning *Le Cimetière Marin*', in *The Art of Poetry*, trans. by Denise Folliot (New York: Vintage, 1961), p. 152 (first publ. as 'Au Sujet du *Cimetière Marin*' in *La Nouvelle Revue Française*, 234 (March 1933)).

[12] Pinter, 'Writing for the Theatre', p. 20.

[13] Billington, *Harold Pinter*, p. 204.

[14] The definitions are from the *Shorter Oxford English Dictionary* [SOED].

through which 'Pinter is perpetrating an act of menace upon his audience': 'we find ourselves contracted into a theatrical experience which is relatively less comfortable than might normally be expected.'[15]

The play, first published in 1960, opens thus:

> MICK *is alone in the room, sitting on the bed. He wears a leather jacket.*
>
> *Silence.*
>
> *He slowly looks about the room looking at each object in turn. He looks up at the ceiling, and stares at the bucket. Ceasing, he sits quite still, expressionless, looking out front.*
>
> *Silence for thirty seconds.*
>
> *A door bangs. Muffled voices are heard.*
>
> MICK *turns his head. He stands, moves silently to the door, goes out, and closes the door quietly.*[16]

The first impression of Mick, '*a man in his late twenties*' (p. v), is confusing. He is perhaps a figure of isolation and solitariness, and his anonymity on the stage at this point would reinforce this impression. His looking '*slowly ... about the room*' at the mass of incongruous junk surrounding him suggests that he is burdened and helpless; the bucket on the ceiling seems to be a rather pathetic attempt at controlling his environment, a tenuous gesture in an imposing world. When he looks '*expressionless*' at the audience, it is likely that sympathy is invoked, but the emotional connection is limited as he

---

[15] Mark Batty, *Harold Pinter* (Plymouth: Northcote House, 2001), pp. 8-9.

[16] Harold Pinter, *The Caretaker,* new edn (London: Faber & Faber, 2000), p. 1. All further references will be given in the body of the text.

gives nothing away, remaining aloof and isolated. His exit at the sound of voices might suggest a fear of others.

But Mick is wearing a leather jacket, the significance of which is emphasised by it being the only article of clothing specified by Pinter, which is in contrast to the detail given to Aston, who *'wears an old tweed overcoat, and under it a thin shabby dark-blue pinstripe suit, single-breasted, with a pullover and faded shirt and tie'*, and Davies, who *'wears a worn brown overcoat, shapeless trousers, a waistcoat, vest, no shirt, and sandals'* (p. 1). In the early 1960s, a leather jacket suggested youthful rebellion (to rebel is to do, to try to make decisions for oneself in the face of familial and social expectations) and being part of a subculture.[17] The jacket contradicts the audience's other impressions; it is a fissure running through the opening that destabilises conclusions about Mick and affects how he is responded to later. The opening thus establishes that the world of the play is not black and white, where people are easily defined and the audience's relationship with them simple, where assumptions can be relied on and interpretation unproblematic; it a world of uncertainty and questioning.

The film opens at night with the view of a van, the driver's window down, the inside black, parked in an unlit

---

[17] *Rebel Without a Cause* (dir. by Nicholas Ray), in which James Dean wears a now iconic leather jacket, was released in 1955; Rockers (and Mods) were at their peak in the late 1950s and early 1960s. *The Wild One* (dir. by Laslo Benedek), in which Marlon Brando wears a leather biker jacket, was released in America in 1953, but public screenings of the film were banned in Britain until 1968; the film was deemed by the British Board of Film Censors to be subversive. For more on 1950s/1960s British subcultures and the fears of the Establishment, see Dominic Sandbrook, *Never Had It So Good: A History of Britain from Suez to the Beatles* (London: Little, Brown, 2005).

street opposite dark Victorian terraced houses.[18] A spectral sound breaks the silence, then in the distance a steam train is heard moving. As the opening titles appear, the train whistles; as soon as the titles have finished, the back of a hand flashes into view from inside the van, then darkness, then the embers of a cigarette glow for a moment, then darkness. The cigarette is tossed from the van and a man in a leather jacket gets out abruptly, with energetic purposefulness; the spectral, eerie music begins again and continues. He slams the van door, walks to the right and out of shot, then back into shot across the street, away from the static camera, towards one of the houses; his black clothes merge with the dark bushes and walls.

As with the play's opening, there is a confusion that complicates interpretation. According to Steven H. Gale:

> Collectively, Mick's movements are sending mixed signals, thereby intensifying the audience's subconscious discomfort. A left-to-right movement across the screen is considered natural and therefore comforting; movement to offscreen is disturbing and suggests that the character does not abide by socially imposed restrictions – he determines his own course and limitations. The movement away from the camera is confusing, because the threatening figure is retreating, but this movement likewise reduces the audience's ability to verify the nature of the character.[19]

Furthermore, the van implies labour, enterprise and assistance, but the man's waiting (and presumed watching

---

[18] *The Caretaker*, dir. by Clive Donner (Caretaker Films, 1963; on bfi DVD video, 2002).

[19] Gale, *Sharp Cut*, p. 105.

of a house), his throwing of the cigarette – perhaps an echo of the 'gangster- or cowboy-film convention of a character purposefully discarding a cigarette just before initiating a violent action'[20] – his dark clothes and leather jacket, and the *mise-en-scène* suggest that he is a criminal with sinister intentions.[21]

The conflict of signals is repeated when he gets to the door of the house:

> When Mick arrives at the top of the stairs there is another cut and Mick is shown in a medium close-up – but the closed form and the tight framing, together with Mick's three-quarter-turn positioning, is confining and retains an atmosphere of mystery because he is still partially concealed.... Mick's threatening anonymity is undercut, however, when he produces a set of keys and unlocks the door. The discordant musical tones that accompany him on his walk across the street indicate that he is up to no good, yet it is suddenly apparent that he belongs there.[22]

If he 'belongs there', his criminality and threat are displaced, but they are immediately reinstated when he ascends the stairs inside: the camera is positioned on the landing so that we look down on the dark figure, his face

---

[20] Gale, *Sharp Cut*, p. 105.

[21] Gale says that Mick is 'somewhat menacing' and that his 'leather Teddy-Boy-style jacket along with the cascading, atonal music that accompanies him as he crosses the street support this impression' (*Sharp Cut*, p. 104). Teddy Boys were not known for their leather jackets, rather their 'Edwardian style' (Sandbrook, *Never Had It So Good*, p. 415).

[22] Gale, 'Film and Drama', pp. 123-4.

obscured, as he climbs the first flight, then watch him from behind as he climbs the second. The camera angles, sinister shadows on the walls and alienating sound effects are *film noir*. Indeed, there is perhaps a double echo here of the opening of *The Third Man* (directed by Carol Reed, 1949), when the innocent Holly Martins (Joseph Cotton) ascends the hotel steps to visit Harry Lime (Orson Welles), and the ending of that film, when the criminal Lime is pursued through the labyrinthine sewers of a diseased post-war Vienna. The double echo, with its combination of innocence and guilt, good and bad, certainly fits with the initial presentation of the Janus-form figure at the start of *The Caretaker*.[23]

As Mick climbs the stairs, there seems to be the sound of dripping water, but it is irregular and unnatural. Regarding the sound effects, Michael Birkett, the film's producer, has said that he and Clive Donner:

> … persuaded [Ron Grainer] that what we wanted him to do was not to have him write music but to score the effects we had in the film, which is to say the door handles turning, the sound of footsteps, the windows shutting, noise of traffic outside – all of those things – the drip of a bucket; and we wanted to have them somehow 'treated' …; we had a friend at the BBC who worked in the radiophonic workshops. Unfortunately, the BBC weren't allowed to hire the electronic workshops out, and that was where all the equipment was, all the good technical devices where all those extraordinary cross-faders [were], and all those amplifiers that break sound up into their components …, so [our friend] left a

---

[23] The issue of doubling and the characters as Janus-form is returned to later in this essay.

The Film of Harold Pinter's *The Caretaker*

window open for us at night, and at the end of the day Ronnie Grainer and I would go and get through the window of the BBC radiophonic workshop and with this friend we would do the score.[24]

The sounds are distorted and given an echo so that they are 'slightly stranger than the real sound';[25] this gives them, as Donner has said, a 'mysteriousness' that heightens 'the mysteriousness of everything else that's going on'.[26] The 'treated' dripping sound in the opening furthers the audience's alienation from Mick, increasing the sense that he is a problematic character.

The audience's first view of Mick out of the shadows is when he enters the cluttered room after several strange actions on the landing: if it is his house, why did he not know the door was locked, and why does he turn off the landing light? The shot of Mick as he pauses in the doorway is through the junk at a low angle, and this continues as he walks in and around. The framing, angle, his body language and facial expression clarify that he 'belongs', in the sense that he has been there before, but that he is also alien to the surroundings. It is here, of course, that the opening of the film 'catches up with' the opening of the play, and there are similarities between the two. Both Micks look *'slowly ... about the room'* (p. 1) at the

---

[24] Michael Birkett, in 'Commentary': extra feature, by Alan Bates, Clive Donner and Michael Birkett, in *The Caretaker*, dir. by Clive Donner (Caretaker Films, 1963; on bfi DVD video, 2002).

[25] Birkett, in Bates, Donner and Birkett.

[26] Donner, in Bates, Donner and Birkett.

junk, but Mick in the film does not seem burdened by it; he surveys it dispassionately. There is also no sympathy for him. He is far more sinister than in the play, more subversive, threatening and potentially dangerous. And the audience's alienation is increased even more when Aston and Davies arrive at the house.

'Alien': 'Inconsistent with'

In the play, Mick hears people arrive at the house, *'stands, moves silently to the door, goes out, and closes the door quietly'*; Aston then enters with Davies *'following, shambling and breathing heavily'*; Aston *'puts the key in his pocket and closes the door'*, Davies *'looks about the room'*; Aston says to Davies, 'Sit down', and Davies replies politely: 'Thanks' (pp. 1-2). In the film, we first see Aston and Davies while Mick is looking at the junk: there is a cut to a high-angled shot of a shop-lined, noisy street; a tall, broad, straight-backed man is walking with purpose, seemingly trying to ignore who is following him, a tramp *'shambling'*, gesticulating and speaking fairly inaudibly but obviously angrily.[27] Our first

---

[27] Regarding the scenes outside the house, Pinter has said: 'What I'm very pleased about myself is that in the film, as opposed to the play, we see a real house and real snow outside, dirty snow, and the streets. We don't see them very often but they're there, the backs of houses and windows, attics in the distance. There is actually a sky as well, a dirty one, and these characters move in the context of a real world – as I believe they do. In the play, when people were confronted with just a set, a room and a door, they often assumed it was all taking place in limbo, in a vacuum, and the world outside hardly existed, or had existed at some point but was only half remembered' (Pinter and Donner, p. 130). Arnold P. Hinchliffe incorrectly states that the scenes outside 'do not alter the play', but is right to affirm that 'they remind us of what we should never have forgotten in the first place' (*Harold Pinter* (Boston: Twayne, 1981), p. 89). For more on the outside scenes, see Gale, *Sharp Cut*, pp. 100-07.

impression of Davies in the film, then, is that he is bothersome and, like Mick, someone to be avoided. The opening of the film thus foregrounds an important question that might not be asked at the start of the play: Why does Aston invite Davies in?

Before the shot of Aston and Davies approaching the front of the house, there are two key shots from inside the room: the first is of Mick looking at the statue of Buddha; the second of him looking at the bucket on the ceiling. The Buddha's significance is emphasised by the close-up and the lighting, its incongruity with its surroundings underlined by its whiteness.[28] The bucket is given significance by the film cutting quickly from it to Davies talking repeatedly about buckets (to increase the repetition, Pinter has fused Davies's 'Comes up to me, parks a bucket of rubbish' speech (p. 5) with his 'I told him what to do with his bucket' speech (p. 6)). The two objects are strange, perhaps alienating, and seem unconnected (the beautiful and the ugly; the pure and the dirty; the spiritual and the physical; the foreign and the everyday), but it is their disparateness that suggests that their owner is strange, incongruous, Janus-form, someone who is inconsistent with society's assumptions about being 'normal', perhaps schizophrenic.

This impression of Aston is, of course, supported later in the play and film, notably during his long monologue. He speaks of being in a local café and factory, talking to the people and eventually telling them about him seeing

---

[28] Steven H. Gale has written that 'the Buddha, like Davies, does not belong in the dark, compressed, junky world that Aston inhabits' ('Art Objects as Metaphors in the Filmscripts of Harold Pinter', in *Pinter at Sixty*, ed. Katherine H. Burkman and John L. Kundert-Gibbs (Bloomington: Indiana University Press, 1993), p. 166).

Textual Revisions

'everything' 'very clearly', of 'clear sight', and of how 'everything used to get very quiet':

> Anyway, someone must have said something. I didn't know anything about it. And ... some kind of lie must have got around. And this lie went round. I thought people started being funny. In that café. The factory. I couldn't understand it. Then one day they took me to hospital, right outside London. They ... got me there. I didn't want to go.... Then one day ... this man ... doctor I suppose ... the head one ... he was quite a man of ... distinction ... although I wasn't sure about that. He called me in.... He said ... but I can't ... exactly remember ... how he put it ... he said, we're going to do something to your brain. He said ... if we don't, you'll be in here for the rest of your life, but if we do, you stand a chance. You can go out, he said, and live like the others. (pp. 89-90) [29]

In the café and factory, Aston starts being abnormal (deviating from what is deemed 'normal'), so is judged as mentally unstable;[30] his removal to a hospital is so that he can be made 'normal', be 'like the others'.

To 'cure' him, he is administered electroconvulsive therapy (also know as electroshock therapy): 'They used to come round with these ... I don't know what they were ... they looked like big pincers, with wires on, the wires were

---

[29] For the film, Pinter made numerous elisions from the original monologue, most notably the part when Aston talks about his escape attempt; his passivity emphasises his defeat and the abandonment of his mother, and gives more significance to his later fight with doctors.

[30] Interestingly, 'alienation' can mean 'Loss or derangement of mental faculties; insanity' (SOED).

attached to a little machine. It was electric' (p. 90).[31] Electroconvulsive therapy was introduced in the 1930s as a treatment for schizophrenia,[32] which is defined in the *New Oxford Dictionary of English* as: 'a long-term mental disorder of a type involving a breakdown in the relation between thought, emotion, and behaviour, leading to faulty perception, inappropriate actions and feelings, withdrawal from reality and personal relationships into fantasy and delusion, and a sense of mental fragmentation.' Several terms used in the definition – 'disorder', 'breakdown', 'faulty', 'inappropriate', 'withdrawal', 'delusion',

---

[31] Pinter has said that 'the one thing that people have missed is that it isn't necessary to conclude that everything Aston says about his experiences in the mental hospital is true' ('Harold Pinter', interview by Lawrence M. Bensky, in *The Paris Review Interviews: Playwrights at Work*, ed. George Plimpton (London: Harvill Press, 2000), p. 260). Pinter does not deny that Aston was in hospital, but correctly suggests that his story might not be reliable; see also Bernard F. Dukore, *Harold Pinter* (London: Macmillan, 1985), p. 49, and John Russell Brown, 'Gesture and Movement', p. 138, and Ronald Knowles, 'The "Point" of Laughter', p. 155; both as repr. in Scott.

[32] By the late 1950s, ECT had become increasingly controversial, especially when administered 'unmodified' (without the prior administering of muscle relaxants); in 1957, a man sustained fractures to his hips during unmodified ECT and took legal action against the London hospital; see J. C. Barker, 'Electroplexy (ECT) Techniques in Current Use', *Journal of Mental Science*, 104 (1958), 1069-78, and Richard Abrams, *Electroconvulsive Therapy*, 4th edn (Oxford: Oxford University Press, 2002). Aston's references to the doctors potentially breaking his spine and him not being able to 'walk very well' when he 'got out of the place' (p. 91) suggest that Pinter knew about modified and unmodified treatments, and was perhaps aware of the aforementioned court case. Contemporary to *The Caretaker* is Ken Kesey's *One Flew Over the Cuckoo's Nest* (New York: Viking Press, 1962), which draws on the author's experience of ECT. Many plays labelled 'Theatre of the Absurd' (such as Pinter's, Beckett's and Adamov's) are interested in madness; see Martin Esslin, *The Theatre of the Absurd*, 3rd edn (London: Methuen, 2001).

'fragmentation' – reinforce the view that schizophrenia indicates abnormality, that the schizophrenic is anti-social, 'other' and needs to be re-conformed.[33] Difference is subversive, it challenges the status quo.

Pinter tackles a similar subject in his previous play, *The Birthday Party* (first performed 1958; first published 1960). Goldberg and McCann, 'the hierarchy, the Establishment, the arbiters, the socio-religious monsters',[34] verbally batter Stanley, saying, among many other things, 'You can't see straight', 'You'll be re-orientated', 'You'll be adjusted', 'You'll be integrated', and push him to mental breakdown. Goldberg notes this and says: 'He needs special treatment.'[35] In *The Caretaker*, Aston does not have 'faulty perception', rather 'clear sight'. But he is not able to set the definition of 'faulty', hence the judgement of him being mentally unstable.

To return, then, to why Aston invites Davies in. When Aston in the film asks Davies, 'Do you want to sit down for a couple of minutes?', the film has suggested why, which is confirmed later: Aston and Davies are similar. They have a connection through the judgement of others that they are

---

[33] For an interesting challenge to assumptions about schizophrenia and the schizophrenic, see Gilles Deleuze and Félix Guattari, *Anti-Oedipus: Capitalism and Schizophrenia*, trans. by Robert Hurley, Mark Seem and Helen R. Lane (New York: Viking Press, 1977); for a short but clear summary of *Anti-Oedipus*, see Madan Sarup, *An Introductory Guide to Post-Structuralism and Postmodernism*, 2nd edn (New York: Harvester Wheatsheaf, 1993), pp. 93-97.

[34] Harold Pinter, 'A Letter to Peter Wood', in *Harold Pinter*, repr. in Scott, p. 82.

[35] Harold Pinter, *The Birthday Party*, 2nd rev. edn (London: Faber & Faber, 1991), pp. 82, 83, 84, 85.

The Film of Harold Pinter's *The Caretaker*

outsiders, 'aliens' (p. 2); that they are abnormal.[36] But why is Mick, who does not judge Aston, so bothered by Davies that he resorts to verbal and physical assault?

'Alien': 'Belonging to another person, place, or family'

As Aston and Davies ascend the stairs, Mick creeps out of the room, re-locks the door and hides on the opposite side of the landing, behind a half-opened door. There are then two important shots of Mick. The first is from the room Mick has just entered: the camera is behind and to the right of him, looking over his shoulder to the landing and the other door, which Aston unlocks, opens and enters, followed by Davies. The second is from the position of the landing, the camera, medium-low-angled, looking at Mick peering out from behind the door at the now shut other door, his face obscured partially by shadows. The camera lingers on his face; there is a sinister harp-like sound effect. The two shots, with their shifting perspectives and angles, the lighting and the sound effect, reaffirm Mick as sinister and potentially dangerous, but they also introduce the themes of spying and possession (being possessed/controlled; controlling/lacking control; being possessive), which are reinforced by the shots' echoes of two influential horror films: Tod Browning's *Dracula* (1931) – especially of its shots of Dracula's malevolent face in half-

---

[36] When Mick says to Davies that Aston 'doesn't like work' (p. 77), he is having a joke at Davies's expense, but he also unintentionally points up another parallel between the two men; whether or not Mick dislikes work or ever works, the play and film leave open: Aston tells Davies that Mick is 'in the building trade' (p. 62), and Mick's knowledge of interior design (pp. 96-97, 116) suggests that this is (or was) true, but he seems to have a lot of spare time. Perhaps the three men are connected through their lack of employment.

shadow – and Alfred Hitchcock's *Psycho* (1960) – of its medium-low-angled shots and shadowed faces – two films that are interested in various forms of voyeurism and possession.

In the play, Mick is an eavesdropper: at the start of Act 2, when he repeatedly asks Davies what his name is, the implication is that he has heard Davies tell Aston what his 'real' name is (pp. 25, 33). In the film, Pinter has cut the first revelation that Davies is called Davies, not 'Bernard Jenkins' (p. 25), and reduced the number of times Mick asks Davies what his name is (pp. 43-48 passim). The reduction is because Mick is outside in the van watching the house, rather than on the landing listening in, when Davies tells Aston again what his name is. But in the film there are still enough questions by Mick about 'Jenkins' for it to suggest that he heard them talking earlier about Davies's 'assumed name' (p. 24); he also asks wittily, 'Are you a foreigner?' (p. 49), which reminds us that when he was skulking behind the door he heard Davies talking about 'the Blacks, Greeks, Poles' (p. 2). In the film, then, Mick is a double spy: an eavesdropper (in the house) and voyeur (outside the house). Why, though, the film resists from clarifying for a while, and the answer is linked to possession.

Mark Batty has observed: 'When Mick returns in the final moments of the first act silently to watch Davies and then attack him, we still do not know who he might be and what danger he might represent to either established character.'[37] In the play and the film, it is soon revealed, in Mick's long 'You're stinking the place out' speech (pp. 53-55), that he is Aston's brother, but in the play it really only becomes apparent that Mick cares for (feels affection for;

---

[37] Batty, p. 8.

The Film of Harold Pinter's *The Caretaker*

looks after; is protective of) Aston when Davies says that Aston is 'a bit of a funny bloke':

> MICK: What's funny about him?
>
> *Pause.*
>
> DAVIES: Not liking work.
>
> MICK: What's funny about that?
>
> DAVIES: Nothing.
>
> *Pause.*
>
> MICK: I don't call it funny.
>
> DAVIES: Nor me. (pp. 79-80)

The film, however, clarifies Mick's feelings much earlier. After the 'You're stinking the place out' speech, Aston enters and sits on his bed, and Mick is, for the first time, unsure what to say. '*A drip sounds in the bucket*', Mick and Davies look at the bucket (unlike all three characters in the play), and Mick says to Aston: 'You still got that leak' (p. 55). As Ronald Knowles has said astutely of Alan Bates's performance of the line:

> In that simple observation Bates packed the mixed emotions of a fraught, long-term relationship. Caught partly offguard [sic], his Mick could not say what he felt and perhaps doesn't himself know the meaning of his own feelings. His tone hesitantly attempted sarcasm but the weight of feeling broke through into a compounded appeal and protest – resentment, hope, frustration, love, anxiety and bewilderment.[38]

---

[38] Ronald Knowles, *'The Birthday Party' and 'The Caretaker'* (Basingstoke: Macmillan Education, 1988), p. 75.

In response to Mick, Aston says that he will tar over 'the cracks' to stop the leak 'for the time being' (p. 56). In the play, these statements might not resonate profoundly; in the film, however, due to Bates's and Robert Shaw's acting and the set-up of the shot, the audience suddenly see: what is preventing Aston fragmenting mentally, from cracking up, is not just the tinkering with and buying of electrical goods and the dream of a shed, it is Mick. But also that Mick needs Aston. Why? In the light of what the audience has seen of him previously, it is surely because Mick has the potential to be schizophrenic to the point of being hospitalised. (Mick must have wondered how different he is from his brother.) Aston gives him a centre and prevents him from possible fragmentation. Mick is, therefore, possessive of Aston for common familial reasons: he loves Aston and his love is linked to (self-centred) need. Between the brothers, there is, therefore, a reciprocal and beneficial, if problematic, possession, a possession that Davies could fissure.

'Alienate': 'To turn away'

Why does Mick not just throw Davies out?

> It is clear that Mick recognizes Davies as an opponent from the very beginning, and it is also clear that he would have little trouble driving the intruder out with physical force.... Instead, he initiates a plan whereby Aston will himself eventually reject the old man voluntarily and therefore will not turn against his brother for having banished his friend....[39]

---

[39] Gale, *Sharp Cut*, p. 109.

Towards the ends of the play and film, Aston suggests to Davies that he 'better go' (p. 110), then at the end Mick and Aston smile *'faintly'* (p. 120). It is a subtle reminder of their fraternal bond, but also of their 'need' for each other.[40]

It seems, then, that the play and the film are 'about love', but that the film, through its presentation of Mick, problematises further what 'love' is.

Bibliography

Primary Works

The Caretaker, dir. by Clive Donner (Caretaker Films, 1963; on bfi DVD video, 2002)

Pinter, Harold, *The Birthday Party*, 2nd rev. edn (London: Faber & Faber, 1991)

Pinter, Harold, *The Caretaker*, new edn (London: Faber & Faber, 2000)

Secondary Works

Abrams, Richard, *Electroconvulsive Therapy*, 4th edn (Oxford: Oxford University Press, 2002)

Barker, J. C., 'Electroplexy (ECT) Techniques in Current Use', *Journal of Mental Science*, 104 (1958), 1069-78

---

[40] Gale, *Sharp Cut*, p. 110. Gale does not clarify why the brothers 'need' each other.

Bates, Alan, Clive Donner and Michael Birkett, 'Commentary': extra feature, in *The Caretaker*, dir. by Clive Donner (Caretaker Films, 1963; on bfi DVD video, 2002)

Batty, Mark, *Harold Pinter* (Plymouth: Northcote House, 2001)

Billington, Michael, *Harold Pinter* (London: Faber & Faber, 2007)

Brown, John Russell, 'Gesture and Movement', in *Harold Pinter: 'The Birthday Party', 'The Caretaker', 'The Homecoming': A Casebook,* ed. by Michael Scott (London: Macmillan, 1986), pp. 133-40 (first publ. in John Russell Brown, *Theatre Language: A Study of Arden, Osborne, Pinter and Wesker* (London: Allen Lane, 1972)

Burkman, Katherine H., and John L. Kundert-Gibbs, eds, *Pinter at Sixty* (Bloomington: Indiana University Press, 1993)

Deleuze, Gilles, and Félix Guattari, *Anti-Oedipus: Capitalism and Schizophrenia*, trans. by Robert Hurley, Mark Seem and Helen R. Lane (New York: Viking Press, 1977)

Dracula, dir. by Tod Browning (Universal Pictures, 1931)

Dukore, Bernard F., *Harold Pinter* (London: Macmillan, 1985)

The Film of Harold Pinter's *The Caretaker*

Esslin, Martin, *The Theatre of the Absurd*, 3rd edn (London: Methuen, 2001)

Gale, Steven H., 'Art Objects as Metaphors in the Filmscripts of Harold Pinter', in *Pinter at Sixty*, ed. Katherine H. Burkman and John L. Kundert-Gibbs (Bloomington: Indiana University Press, 1993), pp. 163-72

Gale, Steven H., 'Film and Drama: The Opening Sequence of the Filmed Version of Harold Pinter's *The Caretaker* (*The Guest*)', in *Pinter at 70: A Casebook*, ed. by Lois Gordon (New York: Routledge, 2001), pp. 119-28

Gale, Steven H., *Sharp Cut: Harold Pinter's Screenplays and the Artistic Process* (Lexington: University Press of Kentucky, 2003)

Gordon, Lois, ed., *Pinter at 70: A Casebook* (New York: Routledge, 2001)

'Harold Pinter', interview by Lawrence M. Bensky, in *The Paris Review Interviews: Playwrights at Work*, ed. by George Plimpton (London: Harvill Press, 2000), pp. 257-78

Hinchliffe, Arnold P., *Harold Pinter* (Boston: Twayne, 1981)

Kesey, Ken, *One Flew Over the Cuckoo's Nest* (New York: Viking Press, 1962)

Textual Revisions

Knowles, Ronald, *'The Birthday Party' and 'The Caretaker'*. (Basingstoke: Macmillan Education, 1988)

Knowles, Ronald, 'The "Point" of Laughter', in *Harold Pinter: 'The Birthday Party', 'The Caretaker', 'The Homecoming': A Casebook,* ed. by Michael Scott (London: Macmillan, 1986), pp. 146-61 (first publ. as *'The Caretaker* and the "Point" of Laughter' in *Journal of Beckett Studies,* 5 (Autumn 1979), 83-97)

Pinter, Harold, 'A Letter to Peter Wood', in *Harold Pinter: 'The Birthday Party', 'The Caretaker', 'The Homecoming': A Casebook,* ed. by Michael Scott (London: Macmillan, 1986), pp. 79-82 (first publ. in *Drama* (Winter, 1981), pp. 4-5)

Pinter, Harold, 'Writing for the Theatre': speech made at the National Student Drama Festival in Bristol in 1962, in Harold Pinter, *Various Voices: Prose, Poetry, Politics, 1948-2005* (London: Faber & Faber, 2005), pp. 20-26 (first publ. in Harold Pinter, *Plays One* (London: Methuen, 1962))

Pinter, Harold, and Clive Donner, 'Filming *The Caretaker*', interview by Kenneth Cavander, in *Harold Pinter: 'The Birthday Party', 'The Caretaker', 'The Homecoming': A Casebook,* ed. by Michael Scott (London: Macmillan,

The Film of Harold Pinter's *The Caretaker* 1986), pp. 124-33 (first publ. in *Transatlantic Review*, 13 (Summer 1963), 17-26)

Plimpton, George, ed., *The Paris Review Interviews: Playwrights at Work* (London: Harvill Press, 2000)

Psycho, dir. by Alfred Hitchcock (Paramount Pictures, 1960)

Rebel Without a Cause, dir. by Nicholas Ray (Warner Bros, 1955)

Sandbrook, Dominic, *Never Had It So Good: A History of Britain from Suez to the Beatles* (London: Little, Brown, 2005)

Sarup, Madan, *An Introductory Guide to Post-Structuralism and Postmodernism*, 2nd edn (New York: Harvester Wheatsheaf, 1993)

Scott, Michael, ed., *Harold Pinter: 'The Birthday Party', 'The Caretaker', 'The Homecoming': A Casebook* (Basingstoke: Macmillan, 1986)

The Third Man, dir. by Carol Reed (London Film Production, for British Lion Film Corporation, 1949)

Valéry, Paul, 'Concerning *Le Cimetière Marin*', in *The Art of Poetry*, trans. by Denise Folliot (New York: Vintage, 1961), p. 152 (first publ. as 'Au Sujet du *Cimetière Marin*' in *La Nouvelle Revue Française*, 234 (Mar. 1933))

Textual Revisions

The Wild One, dir. by Laslo Benedek (ColumbiaPictures, 1953)

Part 4

Adaptation and Genre

ADAPTATION AND GENRE

In many ways, science fiction as a genre is very close to literary realism. I am not the first to notice this, of course: Joseph Conrad called H. G. Wells a 'realist of the fantastic', and Christine Brooke-Rose's monograph on the literary fantastic is punningly entitled *A Rhetoric of the Unreal*.[1] Realist techniques of transparency of storytelling, avoidance of ambiguity, the assumption of a knowable world (described with full recourse to Barthes's 'reality effect'), no matter that the world described might consist of alien planets, societies and cultures, are crucial to mainstream or popular science fiction (SF).[2] The SF 'New Wave' of the 1960s compromised these tenets, introducing modernist or postmodernist techniques, and in fact Philip K. Dick, the writer that Brian Baker focuses on in his essay in the following chapter, consistently destabilises the narrative 'real' in his SF novels and short stories. However, this is relatively unusual – and is certainly so in SF cinema, where principles of spectacle tend to prevail, as they often do in fantasy. Despite the *literary* differences between the genres of SF and fantasy, the imperatives of spectacle and micro-detailed world creation – to present a believable, concrete world – are shared by SF and fantasy film. As Chris Walsh notes, Tolkien's universe is perhaps the most finely and deeply wrought imaginative realm ever set down; the responsibility of the Jackson *Lord of the Rings* trilogy of films to impart this concrete materiality, as part

---

[1] Christine Brooke-Rose, *A Rhetoric of the Unreal: Studies in Narrative and Structure, Especially of the Fantastic* (Cambridge: Cambridge University Press, 1981).

[2] See the introduction to the section on adapting the nineteenth-century novel for a lengthier discussion of these issues.

of the *mise-en-scène*, narrative, dialogue and so on, should not be underestimated.

While SF and fantasy cinema share certain emphases, each differs from their literary counterpart. Written SF texts do not have the same emphasis on spectacle and 'epic' sweep (though may have strong adventure elements), because of their linguistic rather than visual rhetoric. Literary SF is therefore able to develop a greater sense of interiority, or even paint upon a domestic canvas, where such a focus in an SF film would leave it on the borders of mainstream SF.[3] Fantasy film often has to temper the heroic with a sense of the everyday or domestic, to 'layer' a sense of material reality. (In contrast to the *Lord of the Rings* trilogy of films, see John Milius's film of *Conan the Barbarian* (1982),[4] which does *not* work to present the richness and depth of materiality that Jackson's films do.)

The generic difference between SF and fantasy is also a long standing focus of critical debate: the charge of 'escapism'. Chris Walsh refers to these accusations in relation to Tolkien and fantasy, but, to be fair, these charges have also been laid at SF's door. In fact, the accusation can be made against all texts that do not directly represent the world that we know, or that attempt to figure 'the Other of what is', in Fredric Jameson's phrase.[5]

---

[3] For instance, Steven Soderbergh's *Solaris* (2002), an SF film which largely pushes effects and spectacle to the margins of the frame in order to concentrate on psychological and romance elements, gained only a very limited release in the UK, despite starring George Clooney.

[4] *Conan the Barbarian*, dir.by John Milius (Universal Pictures, 1982).

[5] Fredric Jameson, 'Of Islands and Trenches: Neutralization and the Production of Utopian Discourse', in *The Ideologies of Theory: Essays 1971-86, Vol. 2: The Syntax of History* (London: Routledge, 1988), pp. 75-101 (p. 77).

Jameson was writing of the political import of Utopian writings when using this phrase, but his understanding of SF (as a Marxist critic of SF and many other literary and filmic forms) is informed by the necessity of imagining otherness to try to think outside, through imaginative frameworks, the ideological frameworks of our own sociocultural circumstances. Another Marxist critic of SF, Darko Suvin, suggested that 'estrangement' was a defining formal feature of SF, in that, in imagining other worlds, SF always casts the reader back finally onto our *own world* – we read through the lineaments of alienness and see ourselves, *differently*.[6] This is, of course, the ultimate rebuttal to the 'escapism' argument: imagining other worlds is in fact a *political necessity* rather than escapism. Brian Baker's essay, for example, considers how the film of *Minority Report*[7] encodes a debate about (and critique of) the so-called Bush Doctrine of Pre-emption that followed the 9/11 attacks in New York.

By way of contrast, I am not convinced that estrangement is central to the workings of fantasy. It seems to me that the world of Tolkien, produced from his immersion in the literatures of the medieval period and before, are too distant from modernity to feel that *Lord of the Rings* casts us back upon our own world, except in the most general terms (power, or kingship, or brotherhood, for instance). In any case, Tolkien explicitly repudiated the idea that his texts were allegorical in any way. I see no reason to denigrate *Lord of the Rings*, however, in suggesting that its imaginative power is in its ability to

---

[6] Darko Suvin, *Metamorphoses of Science Fiction: On the Poetics and History of a Literary Genre* (New Haven: Yale University Press, 1979).

[7] *Minority Report,* dir. by Steven Spielberg (Twentieth Century Fox, 2002).

allow us to 'escape', to be transported into what feels like a fully imagined world. This is no small feat on its own, and the millions of readers who enter into, and are fascinated by, Middle Earth attest to that very imaginative power.

Finally, I will return to Philip K. Dick, author of 'The Minority Report'. Towards the end of his life, Dick was involved in the pre-production, and then production process, that would eventually adapt his novel *Do Androids Dream of Electric Sheep?* (1968)[8] into the film *Blade Runner*.[9] The film was originally released in 1982, the year of Dick's death, and though he saw some material from the production (of which he very much approved) he never saw the complete theatrical cut. *Do Androids Dream...?* and *Blade Runner* share some elements, but in others differ markedly. I do not have the space to detail them here (there have been many essays on the subject, including an entire critical collection), but I would like to cite what Dick thought of the differences between his book and the film. He was unconcerned about the issue of 'fidelity', about the divergences between *Do Androids Dream...?* and *Blade Runner*; instead, he wrote that his text, and Ridley Scott's film (from a script from Hampton Fancher and David Peoples) were two halves of one 'meta-text'; two separate, but equal, elements that comprise one whole. Dick, after reading the shooting script, wrote: 'After I finished reading the screen play, I got the novel out and looked through it. The two reinforce each other .... You read the screenplay and then you go to the novel, and it's like they're two

---

[8] Dick, Philip K., *Do Androids Dream of Electric Sheep?* (Garden City, NY: Doubleday, 1968).

[9] *Blade Runner*, dir. by Ridley Scott (Warner Bros, 1982).

Adaptation and Genre

halves of one meta-artwork, one meta-artifact'.[10] Brooks Landon suggests that

> Dick's own conception of novel and screenplay as "two halves of one meta-artwork" posits [another approach to adaptation]: that we attempt to see both written text and film as part of the same hermeneutic system, one whose interpretation emerges from dialectical comparison – a search for equivalences rather than a gleeful cataloguing of apparent infidelities. Instead of looking for the written text within a film adaptation, in effect thinking of the film as a frame around its antecedent, we should at least consider the possibility that the film might provide an experience equivalent to that of the written text.[11]

Curiously, this idea has found its way into screen adaptations discourse, through the work of Sarah Cardwell. Developing J. Dudley Andrew's suggestion that, because of the frames of ideology and culture and intertextuality, all adaptations refer to what Andrew calls a 'prior whole', Cardwell proposes that the literary 'source' text, and the screen adaptation form one 'meta-text'. As Cardwell writes, 'this view recognises that a later adaptation may draw upon any earlier adaptations, as well

---

[10] Brooks Landon, '"There's Some of Me in You": *Blade Runner* and the Adaptation of Science Fiction Literature into Film', in *Retrofitting* Blade Runner*: Issues in Ridley Scott's* Blade Runner *and Philip K. Dick's* Do Androids Dream of Electric Sheep?, ed. by Judith B. Kerman (Bowling Green, OH: Bowling Green State University Popular Press, 1991), pp. 90-102 (p. 92).

[11] Landon, p. 99.

as upon the primary source model.'[12] Both 'source' and 'adaptation' are versions of a kind of prior *ur*-text; the process of adaptation is multiple. This emphasis on intertextuality, as well as the meta-text's anteriority, of course defuses charges of parasitism with regard to the adapted text: *there are no originals, only copies*. It seems adaptation discourse has itself finally strayed into science fiction: the screen adaptation, like the literary text it is adapted from, is a replicant text.

---

[12] Sarah Cardwell, *Adaptation Revisited: Television and the Classic Novel* (Manchester: Manchester University Press, 2002), p. 25.

'CAN YOU SEE?': SPIELBERG'S SCREEN ADAPTATION OF PHILIP K. DICK'S 'THE MINORITY REPORT'[1]

Brian Baker

The fiction of Philip K. Dick has been a rather mixed source for science fiction cinema and the screen adaptation. While Ridley Scott's *Blade Runner*[2] is now seen as a classic of science fiction (SF) film, and has appeared on cinema and video/DVD in at least three different versions over a period of 25 years, others, such as *Screamers* (1991)[3], adapted from the Dick short story 'Second Variety', have been less successful. The deformative effects of screen adaptation can be seen most clearly in Paul Verhoeven's 1990 film *Total Recall*[4] (which adapted the short story 'We Can Remember It for You Wholesale'), in which the casting of Arnold Schwarzenegger in the central role transformed the project into a 'blockbuster' action movie; while the most adventurous screen version of a Dick narrative is probably Richard Linklater's *A Scanner Darkly* (2006)[5], where the technique of rotoscoping (producing an animated 'layer' from live action photography) imparts the

---

[1] Philip K. Dick, 'The Minority Report', in *The Collected Short Stories of Philip K. Dick, 4: The Days of Perky Pat*, new edn (London: HarperCollins, 1994), pp. 99-140.

[2] *Blade Runner*, dir. by Ridley Scott (Warner Bros, 1982).

[3] *Screamers*, dir. by Christian Duguay (Columbia, 1995).

[4] *Total Recall*, dir. by Paul Verhoeven (TriStar, 1990).

[5] *A Scanner Darkly*, dir. by Richard Linklater (Warner Independent, 2006).

dislocation of that text's psychologically damaged narrator/central character, Bob Arctor (Keanu Reeves).

The adaptation of *A Scanner Darkly* is of considerable interest, though I do not have space for a detailed analysis of the film here. In part, *A Scanner Darkly* compromises Scott Bukatman's statement that: 'unlike the western or, say, film noir, science fiction is not really a director's genre'[6], because Linklater's use of rotoscoping connects the film to his other, earlier film, *Waking Life* (2001)[7]. Linklater is not a director, it must be said, who is identified with science fiction; but the visual texture of the film marks it as an *auteur* film (as does the hip, drop-out milieu, which can also be found in such Linklater films as *Slacker* (1991)[8]). Is Bukatman correct? Are there no *auteur* directors in SF cinema? Perhaps, if we consider SF film alongside the cinematic history of the Western, for instance, where directors such as John Ford or Howard Hawks have been understood by critics to shape the material they direct, to inscribe a 'signature' on the film, even though the film medium is a collaborative (and indeed, industrial) process that involves hundreds of people. The elevation of the director to author, the so-called *auteur* theory, began in the 1950s. It was the theoretical cornerstone of a group of young French critics (and later film-makers), including Jean-Luc Godard and François Truffaut, both of whom wrote for the film journal *Cahiers du Cinéma*. The 'politique des auteurs' is or was the finding of recurrent motifs, themes and subjects in the films of certain directors, which

---

[6] Scott Bukatman, 'Zooming Out: the End of Offscreen Space', in *The New American Cinema*, ed. by Jon Lewis (Durham, NC: Duke University Press, 1998), pp. 248-72 (p. 249).

[7] *Waking Life*, dir. by Richard Linklater (Twentieth-Century-Fox, 2001).

[8] *Slacker*, dir. by Richard Linklater (Orion, 2001).

'Can You See?'

privileged the director as the source of coherent filmic meaning. Unusually, the *Cahiers* group found these signs of individual expression within what was formerly seen in the impersonal and production-line operations of the Hollywood studio system. Directors such as Howard Hawks, Nicholas Ray and Alfred Hitchcock were seen to express a coherent world-view, which could be revealed by film criticism.[9]

Subsequent film history, and indeed popular discourse about the cinema, is indebted to the idea of the director as *auteur*.[10] One of the most powerful and well-known Hollywood directors, who has directed many science-fiction (or SF-informed) films – *Close Encounters of the Third Kind* (1977)[11], *E.T.* (1982)[12], *Jurassic Park* (1993)[13], *A.I.* (2001)[14], *War of the Worlds* (2005)[15] – is also the director of the film I will look at in this chapter, the adaptation of Philip K. Dick's 'The Minority Report', shortened to

---

[9] For more detail, see *The Cinema Book*, ed. Pam Cook and Mieke Bernink, 2nd edn (London: BFI, 1999), part 6: Authorship and Cinema.

[10] Not only in terms of how the history of film is written, which has foregrounded the director and downgraded the screenwriter (to the detriment of the many women screenwriters in Hollywood in the 1930s and 40s), but also in how Hollywood itself has understood authorship.

[11] *Close Encounters of the Third Kind*, dir. by Steven Spielberg (Columbia, 1977).

[12] *E.T.: The Extra-Terrestrial*, dir. by Steven Spielberg (Universal, 1982).

[13] *Jurassic Park*, dir. by Steven Spielberg (Universal, 1993).

[14] *Artificial Intelligence: AI*, dir. by Steven Spielberg (Warner Bros, 2001).

[15] *War of the Worlds*, dir. by Steven Spielberg (Paramount, 2005).

Minority Report (2002)[16]: Steven Spielberg. While Scott Bukatman displaces the SF film *auteur* onto the 'visual designers and special effects supervisors', focusing particularly on Douglas Trumbull (who designed the effects for *Blade Runner* among many other films, including *2001: A Space Odyssey* (1968)[17], and who has also directed two films in his own right), it is clear that Spielberg is the most highly visible Hollywood director to have a long-term investment in science fiction as a cinematic genre. What is not clear, perhaps, is whether Spielberg is an *auteur*, or is simply the most gifted creator of filmed entertainment in post-classical Hollywood.

The case for the prosecution, that Spielberg is *not* an *auteur*, is not an 'artist' whose signature is written upon the films he directs, can call up a wealth of evidence from Spielberg's own filmography. What connects, for instance, the Indiana Jones films, *Always* (1989)[18], *Saving Private Ryan* (1998)[19] and *Catch Me If You Can* (2002)[20]? Not much, perhaps. However, it is clear from Spielberg's later career that, in films such as *Amistad* (1997)[21], *Schindler's List* (1993)[22] and *Munich* (2005)[23], he is attempting to leaven his

---

[16] *Minority Report*, dir. by Steven Spielberg (Twentieth Century Fox, 2002).

[17] *2001: A Space Odyssey*, dir. by Stanley Kubrick (Metro-Goldwyn-Mayer, 1968).

[18] *Always*, dir. by Steven Spielberg (United Artists, 1989).

[19] *Saving Private Ryan*, dir. by Steven Spielberg (DreamWorks, 1998).

[20] *Catch Me If You Can*, dir. by Steven Spielberg (DreamWorks, 2002).

[21] *Amistad*, dir. by Steven Spielberg (DreamWorks, 1997).

[22] *Schindler's List*, dir. by Steven Spielberg (Universal, 1993).

'Can You See?'

'entertainments' with 'serious' treatments of difficult subjects; or, that he has constructed, in a sense, a 'twin track' directorial career for himself. He is clearly aware of his own status as *auteur* (or not). While often critically taken to task for his sentimentality, especially in his recurrent focus upon children, it seems clear that sentimentality is in fact a Spielbergian signature motif, rather than an index of his failure as an artist. Furthermore, in *E.T.* and in *A.I.*, the experience and point of view of the child itself is central to the film (though in both of these, in *Jurassic Park*, and in the Spielberg 'produced' *Poltergeist*[24] (1982), the child is put in danger); in *Close Encounters*, in the figure of Roy Neary (Richard Dreyfus), the child-man is the focus of the sense of wonder; and in *Hook* (1991)[25], anxieties surround the man (Peter Banning, played by Robin Williams) who has forgotten what it is to be a child. Complementing this focus on the child is the recurrent motif of fatherhood, particularly anxious fatherhood: from Chief Brody's fears of water and fears for his children in *Jaws* (1975)[26], to Banning's troubled relationship with his son in *Hook*, to Indy's desire to impress his father in *Indiana Jones and the Last Crusade* (1989)[27]. At the end of this line is John Anderton (Tom Cruise) in *Minority Report*, whose own son has been abducted and his wife 'lost', and whose relationship with Lamar Burgess (Max von Sydow) is that of father and son, but which is not all that it might seem.

---

[23] *Munich*, dir. by Steven Spielberg (Universal, 2005).

[24] *Poltergeist*, dir. by Tobe Hooper (MGM/UA Entertainment, 1982).

[25] *Hook*, dir. by Steven Spielberg (TriStar, 1991).

[26] *Jaws*, dir. by Steven Spielberg (Universal, 1975).

[27] *Indiana Jones and the Last Crusade*, dir. by Steven Spielberg (Paramount, 1989).

Textual Revisions

If we understand fatherhood to be a recurrent Spielbergian motif, this begins to make sense of the changes between Dick's 'The Minority Report' and Spielberg's *Minority Report*. In Dick's short story, Anderton is approaching retirement. He thinks to himself, when meeting his young antagonist Witwer, 'I'm getting bald. Bald and fat and old.'[28] Anderton is the head of Pre-Crime, a division of the Police who use three 'Pre-Cog' talents (human beings who can see the future, or possible futures) to intercede and prevent murders before they can be committed. The narrative of 'The Minority Report' is organised around a power struggle between the Police and the Army, in which a plot to frame Anderton for murder (and therefore produce the ultimate irony for Pre-Crime) would bring the whole operation into question. The narrative proceeds to a crucial point in which Anderton must make a moral decision: to *not* commit murder and bring the system of Pre-Crime crashing down; or to fulfill the predicted future murder and uphold the system. After first considering the former, Anderton decides upon the latter. I will return to the changes made in this scenario in Spielberg's *Minority Report* later in this chapter.

The crucial relationships in the Dick short story are between Anderton and his wife (who Anderton sees as a threat, rather than as a source of support), and Anderton and Witwer (who Anderton distrusts as a younger man who appears to be planning to supplant him). There is no 'Lamar Burgess' character, just as there is no 'lost son'. Spielberg introduces both to make *his* John Anderton, played with boyish energy by Tom Cruise, both father *and*

---

[28] Dick, p. 99.

son.[29] As in *Hook* and *Jaws*, fatherhood in *Minority Report* is suffused with irony and anxiety. Through little fault of his own, though he blames himself to such an extent that we see him reliant upon the illegal drug Clarity, Anderton is traumatised, and fatherhood is synonymous with loss and intolerable grief. The film suggests, as motivation, that Anderton's involvement with Pre-Crime is a direct consequence of, and thereby symptom of, this originary trauma, and his intercessions to prevent murders are a fantasy replaying of his own scenario of loss. He attempts to undo the past through 'undoing' or forestalling a traumatic future. Anderton's interactions with holographic video images of his son at play, treating photographic images as real, torture him while seeming to sustain. Spielberg's Anderton is a broken man, 'split' even, between Pre-Crime cop and tortured father/drug user, between intolerable past and unacceptable future. In fact, Spielberg splits Dick's Anderton into *two* separate fathers: a younger head of Pre-Crime, and an older father-figure (Burgess) who constructed and oversees the system. The reason for this, I would argue, is to make Anderton a much more physically mobile figure, utilising Cruise's 'action star' persona to the full. The translation from short story to film is also a generic transformation here: from science fiction to science fiction 'spectacle film'.

Special effects, spectacle and science fiction cinema

A critical narrative has emerged in the last fifteen years or

---

[29] While a similarly deforming effect on the adaptation of 'The Minority Report' as in the translation from 'We Can Remember It For You Wholesale' to *Total Recall* is certainly a possible reading of the casting of Cruise, the employment of a younger man as the central actor allows Spielberg to investigate a fuller range of father-son dynamics.

so which has redefined the role of special effects in science fiction film (often previously derided, or seen as detrimental to, or in competition with, 'serious' narrative or thematic elements). Brooks Landon, in his 1992 text *The Aesthetics of Ambivalence*, was among the first to rethink special effects as formal elements which define SF film as inherently spectacular, in that the 'technological wonder' of the effects sequences become an 'attraction' in itself. Therefore, rather than lamenting the way in which 'special effects have overshadowed or usurped narrative elements', as previous critics might have done, Landon suggests that science fiction film returns cinema to its oldest representational and formal strategies, the 'cinema of attractions' identified by the film historian and theorist Tom Gunning.[30] Gunning, in a series of seminal articles, complicated what has been regarded as the history of cinema.[31] In the 'classical' conception of film history, early

---

[30] Brooks Landon, *The Aesthetics of Ambivalence: Rethinking Science Fiction Film in the Age of Electronic (Re)production* (Westport, CT: Greenwood Press, 1992), pp. 72-4.

[31] See Tom Gunning, '"Animated Pictures": Tales of Cinema's Forgotten Future, After 100 years of Film', in *Reinventing Film Studies*, ed. by Christine Gledhill and Linda Williams (London: Arnold, 2000), pp. 316-31; Gunning, 'An Aesthetic of Astonishment: Early Film and The (In)Credulous Spectator', in *Film Theory and Criticism: Introductory Readings*, ed. by Leo Braudy and Marshall Cohen, 5th edn (New York: Oxford University Press, 1999), pp. 818-32 (first publ. in *Art and Text*, 34 (1989), 31-45); Gunning, 'The Cinema of Attractions: Early Film, its Spectator and the Avant Garde', in *Early Cinema: Space, Frame, Narrative*, ed. by Thomas Elsaesser with Adam Barker (London: BFI, 1990), pp. 56-62; Gunning, '"Primitive Cinema": A Frame Up? or, The Trick's on Us', in *Early Cinema: Space, Frame, Narrative*, pp. 86-94; Gunning, '"Now You See It, Now You Don't": The Temporality of the Cinema of Attractions', in *The Silent Cinema Reader*, ed. by Lee Grieveson and Peter Kramer (London: Routledge, 2004), pp. 41-50.

'Can You See?'

cinema (what Gunning calls the 'cinema of attractions') was a primitive cinema, one which had yet to develop the narrative strategies of later film-making. It was, in this reading, an 'immature' phase of development that cinema passed through on the way to 'mature' narrative form. The *spectacle* of the cinema (cinema as an experience or event, the primacy of wonder at what the spectator is seeing) was central to the early development of film, but the emphasis in film history on the narrative elements of film that developed later has led to a downgrading of the spectacular elements, particularly in film criticism and theory. Landon summarises thus:

> [Gunning] reminds us that the classical style codified by Bordwell, Staiger and Thompson in *The Classical Hollywood Cinema* was not just the development of primitive cinema, a refinement of its crude attempts at narrative, but the development of *one kind* of primitive cinema, while the non-narrative focus of what Gunning calls the 'cinema of attractions' represents another kind of primitive cinema, whose traditions continued even after the codification of the classical style.[32]

Gunning himself suggests that the 'cinema of attractions' finds a modern analogue in genres such as the musical, where semi-discrete elements of spectacle 'have become so important [that they] actually stop rather than advance the

---

[32] Brooks Landon, 'Diegetic or Digital? The Convergence of Science-Fiction Literature and Science Fiction Film in Hypermedia', in *Alien Zone II: the Spaces of Science-Fiction Cinema*, ed. by Annette Kuhn (London: Verso, 1999), pp. 31-49 (p. 33)

Textual Revisions

narrative.'[33] Landon goes on to suggest that this emphasis on *spectacle*, on wonder, has been inherited by the science fiction film, and particularly in science-fiction films' special effects sequences.[34] Michele Pierson, who has written extensively on special effects in cinema, continues this critical narrative, largely accepting the analogy between the 'cinema of attractions' and contemporary SF cinema. She writes:

> What becomes important in the counter-narrative represented by this "show-stopping" special effects imagery is not the power of special effects to represent the other-wordly technologies of future societies, but the power of special effects to present the awesome imaging capabilities of special-effects technologies themselves.[35]

---

[33] Landon, *Aesthetics of Ambivalence*, p. 69. An example of this narrative retardation would be in *Star Wars*, where Han Solo and Luke Skywalker escape the Death Star in the Millennium Falcon after Obi-Wan Kenobi's 'death'. They are chased by, and eventually 'shoot down', Imperial TIE fighters. This effects sequence has very little bearing upon the narrative; indeed, on reflection, Luke's elation seems inappropriately juxtaposed with his grief for the old Jedi. The purpose of this effects sequence is to present the effects themselves.

[34] Christine Cornea, in *Science Fiction Cinema*, has complicated this critical manoeuvre in suggesting that while 'it seemed to many critics that the form and style of Gunning's "cinema of attractions" had re-emerged to dominate popular cinema in the post-classical era', it is necessary to differentiate the special effects in the science fiction films of the 1960s and 1970s (especially Kubrick's *2001: A Space Odyssey* (1968)), which demanded a meditative response, to the kind of blockbuster spectacle films that followed Lucas's *Star Wars* (1977). See Christine Cornea, *Science Fiction Cinema: Between Fantasy and Reality* (Edinburgh: Edinburgh University Press, 2007), pp. 248-50.

[35] Michele Pierson, 'CGI Effects in Hollywood Science-Fiction Cinema 1989-95: The Wonder Years', *Screen*, 40 (1999), 158-76 (p. 165).

'Can You See?'

Pierson goes on to argue that the boom in CGI (Computer Generated Imagery) effects in the early-to-mid 1990s was so successful because it 'offered viewers the opportunity to participate in a popular cultural event that put the display of the digital artefact - or computer generated image - at the centre of the entertainment experience.' Pierson marks this as part of a wider cultural phenomenon, a 'popular, techno-futurist aesthetic that foregrounds the synthetic properties of electronic imagery.'[36] However, she also notes a tension in the use of CGI imagery:

> Pulled, on the one hand, towards photographic realism and, on the other, towards a synthetic hyperrealism, the computer-generated imagery in this cinema exhibits an aesthetic that plays across the two poles.[37]

This echoes what Landon explores (and what gives him the title of his book) in terms of the 'ambivalence': not only that SF cinema 'combines both narrative *and* spectacle, offers the pleasures of both art *and* trash, appeals to *both* the intellect *and* the emotions'; but also that there is a 'larger generic ambivalence as SF film is pulled between the antithetical poles of documentary realism and pure fantasy.'[38] The centrality of special effects to science fiction cinema produces a kind of ambiguity in terms of the formal organisation of the film itself. CGI and effects are designed to *represent* other worlds in as photorealistic a manner as possible, to create an immersive cinematic

---

[36] Pierson, p. 158.

[37] Pierson, p. 172.

[38] Landon, *Aesthetics of Ambivalence*, p. 64; p. 62.

environment for the viewer to engage with, while at the same time exceeding this sense of reality (becoming hyperreal) in the *presentation* of spectacle.

In her recent book *Science Fiction Cinema*, Christine Cornea also suggests that CGI in the 1990s and after develops in two directions: towards the 'bracketed off' 'wow'-producing spectacle, and also as a 'practical alternative to more traditional methods of creating both naturalistic and non-naturalistic effects', a tendency towards a photorealism that was increasingly indistinguishable from the 'real' world of the diegesis. The result, according to Cornea, is 'a move toward the total subjugation of this new technology to an already familiar aesthetic of filmic realism.'[39] In effect, Cornea suggests that special effects and CGI move from the realm of Christian Metz's 'invisible' cinematic tricks (which call attention to themselves) to the 'imperceptible', which we are not meant to notice. Metz, more widely known for his psychoanalytic criticism of film, published an early article on film effects and 'trick photography', called *'Trucage* and the Film', in 1977. Both Landon and Pierson cite Metz's article. *Trucages*, Metz's term for special effects, are created in two ways: firstly, 'profilmic' *trucages* (of theatrical origin); secondly, cinematographic' *trucages* (of filmic origin). Metz also differentiated between different types of *trucage*:

> Some *trucages* are imperceptible, while others are on the contrary meant to be discernible (accelerated motion, slow motion, etc.). *Imperceptible trucages*, moreover, are not to be confused with *invisible trucages*. Resorting to a stunt man is an imperceptible *trucage*.... Invisible *trucage* is another matter. The spectator could not explain

---

[39] Cornea, p. 258.

'Can You See?'

how it was produced nor exactly which point in the filmic text it intervenes.... They are *trucages* which everyone will agree are 'well made' by virtue of their perfect quality (whereas a sequence with a stunt man is successful only if we do not suspect his intervention). The spectator who is accustomed to cinema, and who knows the rules of the game, has at his disposal three apprehensible systems which correspond respectively, in the film, to imperceptible *trucages*, visible *trucages*, and to perceptible but invisible *trucages*.[40]

In the era of CGI, the boundaries between these definitions are perhaps less concrete than they might have been in the mid-1970s. What contemporary critics of science fiction cinema seem to agree upon is that, firstly, there is a specific use of special effects technologies in recent science fiction film (post-*Star Wars*, but more markedly in the time of CGI, the 1990s and after) which marks it out as a mode of cinema that offers itself as a spectacle, a 'cinema of attractions', although this can be understood as a return to a form of cinema that is as old as the technology itself (and which is in a tradition of visual spectacles that become increasingly prominent in modern culture);[41] secondly,

---

[40] Christian Metz, '*Trucage* and the Film', trans. by Françoise Meltzer *Critical Inquiry*, 3, (1977), 657-75 (pp. 663-4).

[41] Science fiction critic Scott Bukatman places spectacle cinema in a long tradition of visual technologies: 'The special effects of contemporary cinema are thus only a more recent manifestation of optical, spectacular technologies that created immersive, over-whelming and apparently immediate sensory experiences, such as "Renaissance" and elevated perspectives, panoramas, landscape paintings, kaleidoscopes, dioramas and cinema – a cinema, to borrow Eisenstein's phrase, of *attractions*.' Scott Bukatman, 'The Artificial Infinite: On Special Effects and the Sublime', in *Alien Zone II: The Spaces of Science-Fiction Cinema*, ed. by Annette Kuhn (London: Verso, 1999), pp. 249-75 (p. 254).

that the use of these technologies produces an inherent self-reflexivity; and thirdly, this self-reflexivity or self-consciousness about the status of the image produces a tension between the construction of an immersive and seamless 'real' (through CGI, for instance, in Lucas's second *Star Wars* trilogy) and the necessary visibility of these visual artefacts *as unreal* (designed, constructed, as spectacle). The 'imperceptible' and 'invisible' *trucages* are, at the same time, in a state of mutual antithesis while one blurs into the other.

Vision and choice in The Minority Report

As Garrett Stewart and Cornea note, the tension between representation of a 'real' world and the expressive possibilities of CGI imaging is often thematised in SF cinema through a narrative focus on the photographic image itself. Garrett Stewart also notes the connections between SF cinema and a self-consciousness about photographic and other representational or 'imaging' technologies[42]. He writes:

> How might recent cinema contrive to figure its strategic capitulation, through so-called special effects, to a generalized computer technology that threatens to swamp wholesale, even while locally enhancing in the meantime, the motion picture's representational privilege?

---

[42] Garrett Stewart, 'Body Snatching: Science Fiction's Photographic Trace', in *Alien Zone II: The Spaces of Science-Fiction Cinema*, ed. by Annette Kuhn (London: Verso, 1999), pp. 226-48 (p. 226).

'Can You See?'

Closing in on an answer serves to rehearse an abiding tendency of the genre. Science-fiction cinema, it can be shown, has always taken media as its subject. In particular, the genre often takes such mediation to task for its violations of the real. This directs us to an equally long-standing tradition within film science fiction, exacerbated lately under the reign of the electron: the tendency to take cinema itself back to its roots in the science of photography. Within broad parameters, we can delimit further the photographic object as subject.

Cornea concurs, specifically citing *Minority Report* as a science fiction film that foregrounds photographic or 'imaging' technology as part of the film diegesis. She writes:

> Like *Blade Runner* (dir. Ridley Scott, 1982), *Minority Report* was also based upon a Philip K. Dick story, and like its predecessor the truth of the photographic image is also placed in question in this later film. But here our detective is dealing with moving images created by the Precogs, rather than the still frame photographs of the replicants. The images are transmitted onto a flat transparent screen and Anderton is seen to carry out a kind [of] editing process in order to highlight the relevant information.... The supposedly real world that Anderton inhabits is actually juxtaposed with the literally flat and fluctuating photographic images that he handles throughout the course of the film... it is the photographic which is "bracketed off" in *Minority Report*.[43]

---

[43] Cornea, pp. 261, 262.

This 'bracketing off' is, Cornea suggests, a term used by Michele Pierson to suggest the way in which CGI becomes 'a distinguished element within the narrative of the film', foregrounded in the marketing and publicity of an effects-driven spectacle film, 'obviously graphic and designed'.[44] Cornea suggests that, in *Minority Report*, it is the photographic itself which becomes a kind of special effect, a spectacle placed in contradistinction to the 'real'. Of course, in the film, the photographs are not indices of the 'real', but of the possible future murders that Pre-Crime is instituted to prevent. Even the photographs of young children that John Anderton (Tom Cruise) discovers in the hotel room at the crucial narrative juncture (which we will return to later in this chapter), seemingly 'evidence' of wrongdoing, are fake. As we find out at the end of the film, the 'foresight' of the Pre-Cogs can itself be fabricated and falsified. Where, in *Blade Runner*, the replicants (and Deckard himself) cleave to photographic images because they represent a concrete 'real' past that compensates for their radical lack of memory (constitutive of subjectivity in the terms of the film), in *Minority Report* the photographs are fluid, manipulated, unstable.

Cornea notes that the photographic images aligned with the visions of the Pre-Cogs are themselves subject to a particular kind of cinematic technology: the 'squishy lens' (filming through a soft plate which contains liquid) which *precedes* digital imagining and manipulation. She writes: 'the flexibility of the lens allows for the peculiar distortion of filmed images, which in the case of *Minority Report* blurs and fans the outer edges of a central image or creates ripples of movement across the frame.'[45] It is noteworthy

---

[44] Cornea, p .258.

[45] Cornea, p. 261.

'Can You See?'

that the distortions the viewer sees in the 'Pre-Cog' visions are *prior to* digital processing and are instead produced by optical or mechanical effects. It is then Anderton (Tom Cruise), in the remarkable opening sequence of the film, who manipulates the images digitally. The film begins with a 'report', a report of 'murder', in a minute-long sequence of dislocated 'squishy lens' shots of a man returning home unexpectedly to find his wife with an adulterous lover, killing them both with scissors. After this sequence of shots, the camera holds on Samantha Morton's blue eye, and then zooms out. When the scene changes to the washed-out glass and chrome office of Pre-Crime, our attention is focused upon the kinetic form of Tom Cruise as he hurries into what seems to be some kind of AV suite. Here, the manipulation of the Pre-Cogs' images begins. Lester Friedman describes the sequence thus:

> Only after slowing down the rapid images, and then re-arranging them into a seemingly logical narrative configuration of cause and effect, does the government take action. But the apparently precise montages sutured together by Anderton prove inherently ambiguous, a series of actions open to competing interpretations despite their ostensible clarity.[46]

The images we see at the beginning of the film do not correspond to the structured time-space of Hollywood continuity cinema, and in fact what Anderton does is to

---

[46] Lester D. Friedman, '*Minority Report*: A Dystopic Vision', *Senses of Cinema: an online journal devoted to the serious and eclectic discussion of cinema*, 27, (2003)
<http://www.sensesofcinema.com/contents/03/27/minority_report.html> [accessed 13 August 2008] (para. 8 of 14)

reassemble these pieces into something which makes meaning as narrative. His digital manipulations, 'scrubbing the image', effected by the interaction of his datagloves and a transparent screen upon which (or in which) the images are displayed, are themselves a dense layering of images. The classical music, Schubert's *Unfinished Symphony*, that plays (one presumes) to aid the process of image recombination suggests that not only is Anderton a kind of 'director' or editor of a narrative, he also resembles the conductor of an orchestra. The interweaving and combination of image-tracks perhaps corresponds to the symphonic organisation of orchestral instruments, which without direction and notation would produce *noise*, rather than *music*: sound as informational nullity, resisting decoding, ultimately meaningless. Ironically, Anderton's reassembling of disparate images into causal narrative not only reinstitutes the narrative-time organisation of continuity cinema (visually, in the chase sequence which follows and supersedes the montage) but also locates it in *space*: Anderton's 'direction' of the images is oriented towards finding out *where* the murder would take place, rather than when, so it may be prevented.

Minority Report is everywhere suffused with images of seeing. As in *Blade Runner*, the insistent visual rhetoric of the film is introduced by an extreme close-up of an eye. In *Blade Runner*, the explosive bursts of flame from the cityscape are reflected in an unblinking (and unidentified) iris; in *Minority Report*, the camera swiftly zooms out from the eye of the Pre-Cog Agatha (Samantha Morton). In both, the image suggests that there is a presence watching over the city and the protagonists of the film. In both films, recurrent motifs suggest that these are surveillance societies. While Deckard uses the ESPER machine in *Blade Runner* to 'penetrate' one of the replicants' photographs

'Can You See?'

and reveal their identity, in *Minority Report* retinal scans flash as the fleeing Anderton enters a Gap store or subway train or the Pre-Crime facility, and are used by the mechanical 'spiders' that skitter through an apartment building in the search for Anderton, stopping even lovemaking couples to check their retinal patterns. The film therefore makes an interesting connection between the kind of surveillance technologies used by the state (in typical dystopian fashion) and those used by the instruments of commodity capitalism. The blurring of the two is also signified by the televisual advertisement for Pre-Crime (all too convincing, it must be admitted) which is interpolated near the beginning of the film. Running through a run-down part of the city, on his way to meet his drug connection, Anderton jogs past a wall-size screen that displays the emotive testimonies of the victims of crime, whose traumatic experiences would have been prevented by Pre-Crime. Spielberg inserts this advert not only into the world of *Minority Report*; it is also addressed directly to the viewer as part of the diegesis, attesting to its demagogical power.

The 'pusher' that Anderton visits to purchase the drug Clarity (presumably in order to see more clearly) is himself blind, two empty eye sockets revealed beneath his hooded, shadowed face. The film drives home the resonance of this image when the dealer intones, 'In the land of the blind, the one-eyed man is king': is partial sight better than no sight at all? Considering that the title of both short story and text refer to the 'minority report', the dissenting view offered in judicial review and by one of the Pre-Cogs, partiality or incompleteness of vision, is extremely troubling. Throughout the film, sight is distorted, and not only by the 'squishy lens' technology noted earlier. Vision blurred by water is a recurrent visual motif in the film. The Pre-Cogs float in a quasi-amniotic pool; Anderton loses his son when playing a 'holding-your-breath' game underwater at the crowded public swimming pool; Anderton attempts to hide from the surveillance spiders by immersing himself in a bathtub; and the originary murder that Lamar Burgess commits to provide the impetus towards instituting Pre-Crime, recurrently visioned by the Pre-Cogs, takes place in water. All of these images indicate distorted vision, blurred vision, the *inability* to see clearly. If, as Lester Friedman notes, Anderton's experience in the swimming pool is an inverted baptism, from which he arises a changed man (seeing differently), then the way that he sees, through grief and loss, is itself distorting. It prevents him from appreciating the ethical problems at work in the Pre-Crime system, that 'innocent' people are 'haloed' and placed in prison; he understands it as an intellectual argument, but it requires further traumatic experiences to change the way he sees the system.

If Anderton, at the beginning of the film, lacks ethical insight and requires the typical dystopian protagonist's trajectory of estrangement (displacement from his place in the system) to be able to see clearly, the idea of *foresight*, the subject as seer (able to predict the future), is also compromised in the film. The future, it is assumed by Pre-Crime operatives, is seen *clearly* by the Pre-Cogs; however, the existence of minority reports suggests that the future is undetermined, that choice is still a possibility. As Cynthia Weber states, 'previsions are not the same thing as predestination.'[47] In fact, the very idea of Pre-Crime intervention itself, to forestall a possible future, paradoxically signifies that future time is malleable and undetermined. If it were not, Pre-Crime would be

---

[47] Cynthia Weber, 'Securitising the Unconscious: the Bush Doctrine of Preemption and *Minority Report*', *Geopolitics*, 10 (2005), 482-99 (p. 492).

'Can You See?'

redundant: no matter what they did, the murder would occur. The Pre-Cogs therefore 'see' a future that never comes into being. What, then, is the status of their 'visions'? Are they completely unreal? The film's narrative works to undo the certainties about Pre-Crime offered in the emotive 'advertisement' for it that I referred to above; the film sets us up to partake of the Pre-Crime ideology before undermining the status of that mode of thinking.

Anderton undergoes a second, or even third 'rebirth' or baptism during the film. He arises from the bathtub with different eyes (literally a 'changed man'), having undergone an eye transplant to alter his identity; and he is also captured by Pre-Crime and 'haloed', only to be rescued by his wife in a narrative *non sequitur* in the final section of the film. It is this final transformation, perhaps more a resurrection than a rebirth, which completes his trajectory towards alienation from the system. The change from the Anderton who believes in Pre-Crime, that the future can be and should be forestalled because otherwise murder *will* occur, to the Anderton who believes that human free will or 'choice' renders the future indeterminate, is marked by two phrases repeatedly spoken by the Pre-Cog Agatha to Anderton: 'Can you see?' and 'You have a choice.' At the beginning of the film, and all the way through until he is 'haloed', Anderton cannot *see*; he believes he is being plotted against, that he is being 'set up', but he cannot penetrate beyond his own assumptions about Pre-Crime and his relationship with Lamar Burgess. Anderton is like the 'murderer' chased at the beginning of the film, who repeats his wife's phrase when confessing, 'I forgot my glasses.... You know how blind I am without them.' Anderton is ethically blind, blind to himself and his own motivations, blind to those around (including his 'lost' wife, one assumes); he needs a change of eyes. He also believes, one assumes, that he does *not* have a choice; once the 'red ball' with his name on it comes down the chute at Pre-Crime, he cannot decide *not* to murder the supposed victim. Agatha's repeated, 'You have a choice', signifies, of course, that he does.

It is this moment of choice that is crucial to Philip K. Dick's 'The Minority Report'. There, Anderton has to choose whether to kill General Kaplan, his intended victim, thereby condemning himself while sustaining Pre-Crime; or not to kill Kaplan, remaining 'innocent' of the crime but demolishing Pre-Crime in the process. Anderton arranges to be present at a rally conducted by Kaplan, at which Pre-Crime is to be 'exposed'. '"But there can be no valid knowledge about the future," says Kaplan. "As soon as the precognitive information is obtained, *it cancels itself out.* The very act of possessing this data is paradoxical."'[48] Kaplan has planned for Anderton's presence as a demonstration of the failure of Pre-Crime's principles, as the Head of Pre-Crime himself invalidates the report by refusing to murder Kaplan and fulfill the prediction of the crime. However, what Kaplan does not understand is that there is *no* 'minority report' in this narrative (in which one Pre-Cog delivers a dissenting report: so two Pre-Cogs 'see' Anderton murdering Kaplan, while one does not). The reports are sequential, out of phase: the first report indicates that Anderton *does* kill Kaplan; in the second, 'seeing' a future where Anderton has seen the first report, there is no murder; the third, the 'true' and final report, is where Anderton does kill Kaplan in order to preserve Pre-Crime. In the film, the moment of moral decision comes in the scene in the hotel room.

This is where the 'plot' against Anderton leads him. He discovers a room in which the photographic evidence of

---

[48] Dick, p. 136.

'Can You See?'

child abduction and probable murder has been arranged, and in which he finds a photograph of his son. This is designed to provoke him to kill the purported kidnapper, and thereby seal a constitutional change to institute Pre-Crime nationally and in perpetuity: even the Head of Pre-Crime is subject to its inviolable laws. When Anderton arrives at the hotel room, this, it seems, is the moment of moral choice relocated from the Dick short story: he must decide whether to kill, sacrificing himself, or not to kill, bringing Pre-Crime down. However, the film fudges and defers this decision. Anderton does not have to choose. He comes to realise that this moment has been set up, but in attempting to arrest the purported 'killer', the man commits suicide, making it seem as though the Pre-Cogs' vision has been fulfilled. How the film resolves this narrative dilemma, instead of turning on a moral choice, is related to the 'splitting' of Dick's Anderton into Cruise's Anderton and von Sydow's Burgess. In *Minority Report*, it is Burgess (much closer in age to Dick's character) who is determined to keep Pre-Crime intact, and has in fact murdered Agatha's mother in the past to ensure her continuing functioning as a Pre-Cog. In a sense, Burgess is Pre-Crime's 'father'. Rather than sacrificing himself, though, he would sacrifice his 'son', John Anderton. The film defers the moment of choice, then disposes of it altogether, by turning it into a father-son conflict between Anderton and Burgess, where the 'villain' is the betraying father.

In voiding the moment of choice, crucial to the narrative resolution of the Dick story, Spielberg betrays the generic transformation at work in the adaptation of 'The Minority Report' to the screen. Following the deferred/voided 'moment of choice' is a 30-minute coda, which seems to be from a different film entirely: Danny Witwer (Colin Farrell), the presumed architect of the plot, is revealed to be the 'good cop' and is then shot and killed by Burgess, who is revealed as the bad father. The film, in fact, itself splits into three distinct parts: the first is the Pre-Crime dystopia, shown in the opening sequences; the second is a chase movie, making full use of Tom Cruise as action star, which can be summed up in the marketing tagline, 'Everybody Runs'; the third, the coda, adheres to the conventions of the contemporary Hollywood thriller, where a deceiving father-figure is finally confronted by the son.[49] The narrative resolution of the film version of *Minority Report* turns the Dick story on its head: where Dick's Anderton sacrifices himself to maintain Pre-Crime, the revelation of the primacy of 'choice' (free will) to Spielberg's Anderton means that he brings Pre-Crime to an end. The final, sentimental shots of the Pre-Cogs, themselves released from the prison of their amniotic pool and relocated to an idyllic cottage in the wilderness, are signature Spielberg images. As Cynthia Weber tellingly notes, Agatha 'resembles an infant' throughout the film, and the final shots (played against images of the restored Anderton couple, complete with unborn child) returns the film to the typical Spielberg motifs of the child and of childhood innocence restored.[50] The change between source text and screen text irrevocably relocates the sensibility of the film: into Spielberg territory.

---

[49] I analyse such an Oedipal narrative, *LA Confidential*, in Brian Baker, *Masculinity in Fiction and Film: Representing Men in Popular Genres, 1945-2000* (London: Continuum, 2006), chap. 6, pp. 105-23. It might be noted that the third version of Ridley Scott's *Blade Runner*, 2007's *The Final Cut*, restores a line which makes clear the Oedipal conflict between the replicant Roy Baty and his 'maker', Eldon Tyrell: 'I want more *life*, Father.'

[50] Weber, p. 494.

'Can You See?'

Conclusion

Minority Report was released in 2002. Cynthia Weber's article, 'Securitising the Unconscious', notes the film's 'eerie allegory of the Bush Doctrine of Preemption', which

> ... holds that it is politically, legally and morally defensible for the United States to use force against a perceived foreign foe in order to prevent future harm against itself, even though that perceived foreign foe has not yet attacked the United States.[51]

The film's release in the USA, in June 2002, followed just weeks after President George W. Bush announced this doctrine in the wake of 9/11. Of course, this is an 'eerie' coincidence, as the film would have been in production for years before the 9/11 attacks, but Weber does suggest that the film keys into a debate about security that was current at the time. *Minority Report*, she argues, critiques the structures of thought (or 'moral geographies') that underpin the Bush Doctrine, in the shift from a judicial system or foreign policy which responds to *actions* to one which pre-emptively responds to presumed *intentions*. Although she does not mention it, the dystopian text that informs *Minority Report* here is Orwell's *Nineteen Eighty-Four*: Burgess, himself a splicing of Big Brother and O'Brien, oversees a system that punishes 'thoughtcrime' rather than criminal acts. The sentimentality that informs the final images of *Minority Report* are, I wrote above, an index of 'Spielberg territory'; but it must also be noted that this territory, or 'moral geography' in Weber's terms, is unmistakably a liberal one. The film bespeaks an anxiety

---

[51] Weber, 'Securitising the Unconscious', p. 483, p. 482.

about the erosion of civil liberties, the encroaching domination of surveillance technologies and fears of a 'police state' that have informed the left-liberal politics of dystopian fictions since the mid-twentieth century. The film's marked lack of fidelity to the ending of Dick's short story, in demolishing the system of Pre-Crime, exposes its political sensibilities. It also compromises assumptions that might be held about the operations of spectacle cinema or the questions about Spielberg's status as *auteur*: there is serious import to *Minority Report*, and its intentions, like 'serious' science fiction and dystopia itself, are to make *us* see *our* world a little more clearly.

Bibliography

Primary Works

Dick, Philip K., 'The Minority Report', in *The Collected Short Stories of Philip K. Dick, 4: The Days of Perky Pat*, new edn (London: HarperCollins, 1994), pp. 99-140

Minority Report, dir. by Steven Spielberg (Twentieth Century Fox, 2002)

Secondary Works

Always, dir. by Steven Spielberg (United Artists, 1989)

Amistad, dir. by Steven Spielberg (DreamWorks, 1997)

Artificial Intelligence: AI, dir. by Steven Spielberg (Warner Bros, 2001)

'Can You See?'

Baker, Brian, *Masculinity in Fiction and Film: Representing Men in Popular Genres, 1945-2000* (London: Continuum, 2006)

Blade Runner, dir. by Ridley Scott (Warner Bros, 1982)

Bukatman, Scott, 'The Artificial Infinite: On Special Effects and the Sublime', in *Alien Zone II: The Spaces of Science-Fiction Cinema*, ed. by Annette Kuhn (London: Verso, 1999), pp. 249-75

Bukatman, Scott, 'Zooming Out: the End of Offscreen Space', in *The New American Cinema*, ed. by Jon Lewis (Durham, NC: Duke University Press, 1998), pp. 248-72

Catch Me If You Can, dir. by Steven Spielberg (DreamWorks, 2002)

The Cinema Book, ed. by Pam Cook and Mieke Bernink, 2nd edn (London: British Film Institute, 1999)

Close Encounters of the Third Kind, dir. by Steven Spielberg (Columbia, 1977)

Cornea, Christine, *Science Fiction Cinema: Between Fantasy and Reality* (Edinburgh: Edinburgh University Press, 2007)

E.T.: The Extra-Terrestrial, dir. by Steven Spielberg (Universal, 1982)

Friedman, Lester D., '*Minority Report*: A Dystopic Vision', *Senses of Cinema: an online journal devoted to the serious and eclectic discussion of cinema*, 27 (2003) <http://www.sensesofcinema.com/contents/03/27/minority_report.html> [accessed 13 August 2008]

Gunning, Tom, '"Animated Pictures": Tales of Cinema's Forgotten Future, After 100 Years of Film', in *Reinventing Film Studies*, ed. by Christine Gledhill and Linda Williams (London: Arnold, 2000), pp. 316-31

Gunning, Tom, 'An Aesthetic of Astonishment: Early Film and The (In)Credulous Spectator', in *Film Theory and Criticism: Introductory Readings*, ed. by Leo Braudy and Marshall Cohen, 5th edn (New York: Oxford University Press, 1999), pp. 818-32 (first publ. in *Art and Text*, 34 (1989), 31-45)

Gunning, Tom, 'The Cinema of Attractions: Early Film, its Spectator and the Avant Garde', in *Early Cinema: Space, Frame, Narrative*, ed. by Thomas Elsaesser with Adam Barker (London: BFI, 1990), pp. 56-62

Gunning, Tom, '"Primitive Cinema": A Frame Up? Or, The Trick's on Us', in *Early Cinema: Space, Frame, Narrative*, ed. by Thomas Elsaesser with Adam Barker (London: BFI, 1990), pp. 86-94

'Can You See?'

Gunning, Tom, '"Now You See It, Now You Don't": The Temporality of the Cinema of Attractions', in *The Silent Cinema Reader*, ed. by Lee Grieveson and Peter Kramer (London: Routledge, 2004), pp. 41-50

Hook, dir. by Steven Spielberg (TriStar, 1991)

Indiana Jones and the Last Crusade, dir. by Steven Spielberg (Paramount, 1989)

Jaws, dir. by Steven Spielberg (Universal, 1975)

Jurassic Park, dir. by Steven Spielberg (Universal, 1993)

King, Geoff, 'Spectacle and Narrative in the Contemporary Blockbuster', *Contemporary American Cinema*, ed. by Linda Ruth Williams and Michael Hammond (Maidenhead: Open University Press, 2006), pp. 334-55

Landon, Brooks, *The Aesthetics of Ambivalence: Rethinking Science Fiction Film in the Age of Electronic (Re)production* (Westport, CT: Greenwood Press, 1992)

Landon, Brooks, 'Diegetic or Digital? The Convergence of Science Fiction Literature and Science Fiction Film in Hypermedia', in *Alien Zone II: the Spaces of Science-Fiction Cinema*, ed. by Annette Kuhn (London: Verso, 1999), pp. 31-49

Metz, Christian, '*Trucage* and the Film', trans. by Françoise Meltzer, *Critical Inquiry*, 3 (1977), 657-75

Munich, dir. by Steven Spielberg (Universal, 2005)

Pierson, Michele, 'CGI Effects in Hollywood Science-Fiction Cinema 1989-95: The Wonder Years', *Screen*, 40 (1999), 158-76

Poltergeist, dir. by Tobe Hooper (MGM/UA Entertainment, 1982)

Saving Private Ryan, dir. by Steven Spielberg (DreamWorks, 1998)

A Scanner Darkly, dir. by Richard Linklater (Warner Independent, 2006)

Schindler's List, dir. by Steven Spielberg (Universal, 1993)

Screamers, dir. by Christian Duguay (Columbia, 1995)

Slacker, dir. by Richard Linklater (Orion, 2001)

Stewart, Garrett, 'Body Snatching: Science Fiction's Photographic Trace', in *Alien Zone II: The Spaces of Science-Fiction Cinema*, ed. by Annette Kuhn (London: Verso, 1999), pp. 226-248

Total Recall, dir. by Paul Verhoeven (TriStar, 1990)

2001: A Space Odyssey, dir. by Stanley Kubrick (Metro-Goldwyn-Mayer, 1968)

Waking Life, dir. by Richard Linklater (Twentieth Century Fox, 2001)

'Can You See?'

War of the Worlds, dir. by Steven Spielberg (Paramount, 2005)

Weber, Cynthia, 'Securitising the Unconscious: the Bush Doctrine of Preemption and *Minority Report*', *Geopolitics,* 10 (2005), 482-99

'REFRACTED LIGHT': PETER JACKSON'S *THE LORD OF THE RINGS*

Chris Walsh

Peter Jackson's film of *The Lord of the Rings*[1] was released in three instalments in 2001, 2002 and 2003, nearly fifty years after J. R. R. Tolkien's book was published (in three volumes) in 1954-5.[2] The popularity of the film mirrored that of the book.[3] It is now commonplace to speak of 'the Tolkien industry'. Tolkien's books, translated into many languages, are worldwide bestsellers. What was in the 1960s something of a cult is now an international cultural phenomenon, only in part due to Jackson's dazzling, multiple-Oscar-winning[4] film, which broke so many box-

---

[1] References to the film throughout are *not* to the theatrical version (as screened in cinemas), but to the special extended edition on DVD, by abbreviated film title and scene number and title, where *FR* = *The Fellowship of the Ring*, *TT* = *The Two Towers*, and *RK* = *The Return of the King*. For example: *FR*, 27, 'The Council of Elrond'. Excluding credits, there are 188 scenes in the extended cut; the total running time is 10 hours, 54 minutes.

[2] All quotations from and references to J. R. R. Tolkien's *The Lord of the Rings* [*LR*] are by page number to the 50th anniversary one-volume paperback edition (London: HarperCollins, 2005) and are given in the body of the text.

[3] Tom Shippey's estimate – and, given that a single DVD or video can be seen by more than one person, it has to be a very rough estimate – is that there are 'hundreds of millions' of viewers of the film. See Appendix C, 'Peter Jackson's Film Versions', to the 3rd edition of Shippey's *The Road to Middle-earth* (London: HarperCollins, 2005), p. 409.

[4] In the long history of the Academy Awards, only *Ben-Hur* won as many Oscars as the third instalment, *The Return of the King*.

office records. The claim that *The Lord of the Rings* is *the* book of the twentieth century – and perhaps the most read book after the Bible – is not utterly absurd: its stratospheric sales figures, the fact that Tolkien continually ranks among the most borrowed classic authors in the UK's public libraries, and the work's repeated topping of numerous readers' polls underlines the lasting and widespread appeal of his *oeuvre*.

Perhaps the biggest such poll in recent years was the BBC's 'Big Read' of 2004, which attracted hundreds of thousands of votes. *The Lord of the Rings* beat Jane Austen's *Pride and Prejudice* into second place by a margin of some 40,000 votes. It is striking how often works of fantasy make it into the top twenty of polls of readers' favourite books. The next three of the 'Big Read' were Philip Pullman's *His Dark Materials*, J. K. Rowling's *Harry Potter and the Goblet of Fire*, and the late Douglas Adams's *The Hitchhiker's Guide to the Galaxy*. People enjoy, it seems, reading about intensely imagined alternative worlds. This enjoyment most obviously relates to a basic human need for narratives. Narratives clearly have a vital role to play in helping us to process experience. Indeed, as various thinkers including Fredric Jameson have argued,[5] narrative is the central function of the human mind. We think in stories. We learn and understand through stories. We communicate through stories. We all need good stories well-told. When we read a novel or watch a film, what we are trying to satisfy is our craving for those things which art supplies more readily than life: pattern, order, meaning – even (perhaps) beauty, or (more tendentiously) truth.

---

[5] Fredric Jameson, *The Political Unconscious: Narrative as a Socially Symbolic Act* (Ithaca, NY: Cornell University Press, 1981), p. 13.

Textual Revisions

But why do so many people read *The Lord of the Rings*? And why did they flock in such numbers to see the film-of-the-book (even when they had not read the book itself)? The most obvious explanation is that both book and film offer an escape route from 'the real world'. People read (so the argument runs) in order to escape from themselves and their pains and problems into another world where, for a while, they can forget their tribulations, or perhaps project and purge their personal preoccupations. And what an escape if *The Lord of the Rings* is the chosen route! A great escape, one might say. 'The Great Escape', even, in Tolkien's own words.[6] Has there ever been another world more intensely imagined, more comprehensively constructed? The stupendous inventiveness, the sheer wealth and precision of detail defy description. Alexandre Dumas *père* wittily (but reasonably) observed that, after God, Shakespeare had created most. But what would Dumas have made of Tolkien's plenitudinous creativity? Richard Hughes, previewing *The Lord of the Rings*, commented: 'one can't praise the book by comparisons – there is nothing to compare it with. What can I say, then? For *width* of imagination it almost beggars parallel ....'[7] Certainly, none of Tolkien's predecessors and none of his imitators (and he spawned, unwittingly and unwillingly, an entire industry) seriously rivals his unique *legendarium*.

Is not this explanation *too* obvious? If the escapist urge is so prevalent, then how do we explain what might be

---

[6] J. R. R. Tolkien, 'On Fairy-Stories', in *Tree and Leaf: Including the Poem 'Mythopoeia'; 'The Homecoming of Beorhtnoth, Beorhthelm's Son'*, ed. by Christopher Tolkien, new edn (London: HarperCollins, 2001), p. 68.

[7] Words quoted on the dust-jacket of the first edition and reprinted in Wayne G. Hammond and Christina Scull, *'The Lord of the Rings': A Reader's Companion* (London: HarperCollins, 2005), p. lii.

regarded as the countervailing urge in the equal and opposite direction – the realist urge (art not as a surrogate reality but as a critique of reality)? Austen's novel, after all, came second in the poll referred to above. Granted, Austen's novel offers a romantic story, complete with happy ending, and no doubt many readers do read her novels (and watch TV dramatisations and film versions of them) in order to enter a world so remote and different from ours that that constitutes part of its charm and appeal. But Austen hardly offers a consolatory picture of human behaviour. Her satire and comedy are deflationary, and sometimes merciless. And, Austen's fictions aside, every week several million UK television viewers tune in to the soaps. These, too, are far from other-worldly. Their representational realism is surely designed to evoke from viewers a pleasing shock of recognition. ('Yes, that is how life is. I can identify with that …'.)

In short, the escapist/realist dichotomy, however convenient, is false and self-deconstructs as soon as one starts to examine it closely. *The Lord of the Rings* demonstrably makes use of many of the conventions and techniques of fictional realism. Indeed, very arguably if somewhat paradoxically, *that* may account in no small part for its success, for Tolkien makes his imaginary world seem more recognisably real than the imaginary realities of many orthodox realists and naturalists whose subject-matter is the 'real' world in which they live(d). In Tolkien's phrase, his world has 'the inner consistency of reality'.[8] Moreover, *The Lord of the Rings* has a further authenticity

---

[8] Tolkien, 'On Fairy-Stories', p. 47. This is something very difficult to produce, and Tolkien's achievement in this regard is under-rated: critics often concede his imaginative fecundity, but ignore his organisational finesse and his exhaustive attention to detail.

that most realist novels lack: it not only has depth, but depths – a sense of other worlds and times receding into the distance – replete, more than fully three-dimensional. Time and again, casual allusions are made in a matter-of-fact manner to people, places, things, and events which, though of only tangential relevance to the main story-line of *The Lord of the Rings*, are important in helping to create a profound impression of overwhelming verisimilitude.

The same observation might justly be made of Jackson's film version. What Jackson has constructed is a celluloid fantasy with such an extraordinary degree of realism and such a thoroughgoing attention to minute detail (what Henry James memorably termed 'solidity of specification'[9]), with precisely that Tolkienian 'inner consistency of reality', that belief in another world is thereby compelled. But while that is, in itself, an astonishing achievement, it does not follow that either book or film is escapist. (Keats wrote about dreams, but that does not make him a dreamer.) On the contrary, it could be argued that both book and film force their readers and viewers to confront those aspects of reality which they would prefer not to confront. That is, essentially, Tom Shippey's position: 'When people say that this kind of fantasy fiction is escapist and evading the real world and so on … well, I think that's an evasion. It's actually trying to confront something that most people would rather not confront'. And what are the aspects of reality which Tolkien – and Jackson – refuse to evade? The answer may be thought by some to be surprising: war, evil, failure,

---

[9] The phrase is used by Henry James in his essay of 1884, 'The Art of Fiction', reprinted in *The House of Fiction: Essays on the Novel by Henry James*, ed. by Leon Edel, new edn (London: Mercury Books, 1962), pp. 23-45 (p. 33).

'Refracted Light'

suffering, and – especially – death. Shippey's phrase for Tolkien and other contemporaries who had experienced war and turned to fantasy as a way of dealing with their experiences (for example: William Golding, C. S. Lewis, George Orwell and T. H. White) is 'traumatised writers', for these writers

> ... needed a new explanation of evil, and they hadn't got one ... They have to write their own explanation and strangely, but pretty consistently, they cannot do it by writing realistic fiction.... They have to write something which is in some way or other fantastic.[10]

My argument in this paper is that, while Tolkien's *The Lord of the Rings* is indeed supremely concerned with death, the desire for death and the longing to escape from death, Jackson's film version develops and elaborates such concerns to a remarkable extent. Moreover, the death obsession – even more to the fore in the film (if possible) than in the book – may go some way towards explaining, paradoxically, the fascination of readers and viewers alike.

That death and deathlessness is the dominant theme of Tolkien's *The Lord of the Rings* is not a new claim. In the interview already cited, Tom Shippey observes succinctly: 'the major theme of his writing is death', while Patrick Grant commented as long ago as 1979: 'The central themes of *The Lord of the Rings* remain death and belief, and, within

---

[10] Shippey's comments are made in the course of an interview, excerpts from which are included in the appendices of the extended DVD edition. Shippey's line of thought is extrapolated in his paper, 'Tolkien as a Post-War Writer', in *Proceedings of the J. R. R. Tolkien Centenary Conference 1992*, ed. by Patricia Reynolds and Glen GoodKnight (Milton Keynes: Tolkien Society; Altadena, CA: Mythopoeic Press, 1995), pp. 84-93.

these, the problem itself of the mind's adjustment to reality in an increasingly disenchanted post-Renaissance world.'[11] But, oddly, there has yet to be a book-length study of Tolkien and death, even though Tolkien himself emphasised on several occasions how fundamental the theme was to his work in general and to *The Lord of the Rings* in particular. Here are just a few such statements from his letters on this subject:

> The real theme for me is about something much more permanent and difficult: Death and Immortality: the mystery of the love of the world in the hearts of a race 'doomed' to leave and seemingly lose it; the anguish in the hearts of a race 'doomed' not to leave it, until its whole evil-aroused story is complete.
>
> But I should say, if asked, the tale is not really about Power and Dominion: that only sets the wheels going; it is about Death and the desire for deathlessness. Which is hardly more than to say it is a tale written by a Man!
>
> It is mainly concerned with Death, and Immortality; and the 'escapes': serial longevity, and hoarding memory.[12]

Such an obsession with death is unsurprising. Even a cursory knowledge of Tolkien's early life might lead one to

---

[11] Patrick Grant, *Six Modern Authors and Problems of Belief* (London: Macmillan, 1979), p. 149.

[12] All the above quotations are taken from the *Letters of J. R. R. Tolkien: A Selection*, ed. by Humphrey Carpenter with Christopher Tolkien (London: Allen & Unwin, 1981), pp. 246, 262, 284.

expect as much. His father died when he was just four, and his mother when he was twelve. Tolkien himself was a combatant in the First World War and his experiences in the dug-outs of the Somme are plainly apparent in the Mordor episodes of *The Lord of the Rings*. Indeed, Tolkien's earliest tales, which he started to write during that war, all have strong death themes. John Garth's recent study, *Tolkien and the Great War*,[13] makes clear how Tolkien's grand mythology evolved out of his friendship with the three fellow-pupils who made up the 'Tea Club and Barrovian Society', two of whom were to be killed in that war. For when Rupert Brooke, Siegfried Sassoon, Wilfred Owen, Robert Graves *et al.* were writing their war poems, Tolkien was embarking on a very different project, while the luxury of detached experimentation that his modernist contemporaries (Yeats, Eliot, Joyce) enjoyed was not available to him. Tolkien was not so much meditating on the problem of evil and pain as caught up in it. Fortunately for him (and for us) he escaped relatively early, having been diagnosed with 'pyrexia of unknown origin' (trench fever) and so was invalided home. Some twenty years later, during the Second World War, while he was writing *The Lord of the Rings* and carrying out duties as an air-raid warden, his son Christopher was serving in the RAF in South Africa. That war, too, made its mark on Tolkien's work, though not as straightforwardly as some critics have imagined.

The essential *donnée* of *The Lord of the Rings*, of course, is that of the Rings of Power themselves. The epigraph, repeated in the second chapter, is worth quoting in full:

---

[13] John Garth, *Tolkien and the Great War: The Threshold of Middle-earth* (London: HarperCollins, 2004).

Textual Revisions

Three Rings for the Elven-kings under the sky,
  Seven for the Dwarf-lords in their halls of stone,
Nine for Mortal Men doomed to die,
  One for the Dark Lord on his dark throne
In the Land of Mordor where the Shadows lie.
  One Ring to rule them all, One Ring to find them,
  One Ring to bring them all and in the darkness bind them
In the Land of Mordor where the Shadows lie. (LR, p. v)

All the Rings of Power have one thing in common, as Tolkien explained in a letter: 'The chief power (of all the rings alike) was the prevention or slowing of *decay* (i.e. 'change' viewed as a regrettable thing), the preservation of what is desired or loved.'[14] But the Rings of Power fashioned by Sauron alone are doubly escapist. They confer both longevity and invisibility. Their anti-death powers, however, are not quite as they seem. As Gandalf points out to Frodo:

> A mortal, Frodo, who keeps one of the Great Rings, does not die, but he does not grow or obtain more life, he merely continues, until at last every minute is a weariness. And if he often uses the ring to make himself invisible, he *fades*: he becomes in the end invisible permanently, and walks in the twilight under the eye of the dark power that rules the Rings ...' (LR, p. 47)

And of supreme power and importance is the One Ring, the ruling ring. The central story of *The Lord of the Rings*

---

[14] *Letters of J. R. R. Tolkien*, p. 152.

'Refracted Light'

concerns the quest to destroy the One Ring, this ring that confers a spurious immortality, and the escapades of the Ring's bearer, Frodo, and his companions as they flee from deadly peril into deadly peril. Fundamentally, then, *The Lord of the Rings* confronts both the reality of death and what Tolkien calls the 'primordial' and uniquely human wish to escape from it.

The ending of *The Lord of the Rings* presents us with what one might describe as a 'Dover Beach' moment, with Sam listening to the sound of the sea at the Grey Havens as Frodo, Gandalf and the others sail (not into the sunset, but) to the 'Undying Lands'; though the book actually ends with Sam's return to the 'real' world of domesticity, at home in Hobbiton, the last words being: '"Well, I'm back," he said' (*LR*, p. 1031). However, hidden away in the appendices there is another ending – to 'The Tale of Aragorn and Arwen' (in Appendix A). The last words of Aragorn (an old Man of 210) are spoken to Arwen, who has sacrificed her Elven immortality to wed him, for 'now the time of payment draws near'. He speaks to encourage her, as he is on the point of relinquishing his life: '"In sorrow we must go, but not in despair. Behold! We are not bound for ever to the circles of the world, and beyond them is more than memory"' (*LR*, p. 1063). In a letter, Tolkien commented on the significance of both the ending and that appended tale thus:

> The passage over Sea is not Death.... I am only concerned with Death as part of the nature, physical and spiritual, of Man, and with Hope without guarantees. That is why I regard the tale of Arwen and Aragorn as the most important of the Appendices.[15]

---

[15] *Letters of J. R .R. Tolkien*, p. 237.

Textual Revisions

It is interesting that this 'most important' tale, which Tolkien had reluctantly relegated to an appendix, should have been incorporated into the main narrative of Jackson's film. Indeed, the climax of the tale – Aragorn's death – is strategically placed almost exactly half-way through the film trilogy, in its very centre. Earlier, we witness Elrond's attempt to persuade Aragorn to abandon his quest for Arwen's hand: 'Let her bear away her love for you to the Undying Lands.... I will not leave my daughter here to die'.[16] But in the critical scene there is a sudden flash forward as Elrond paints a premonitory vision for his daughter of her predicament as widow to the late King Elessar. ('There is nothing for you here: only death' – a phrase repeated in the following instalment.) We see Aragorn's corpse, and then his tomb, with a veiled Arwen nearby, grieving at her loss, and later wandering in the woods of Lothlórien immediately before her own death.[17] The point is that here, as elsewhere in the film where death (whether feared or desired, real or imagined) is the focus, Peter Jackson and his fellow scriptwriters, Fran Walsh and Philippa Boyens, force us to see and absorb what in the book is either briefly alluded to or only very sketchily narrated.

This is a consistent pattern in the film. Of course, films have to dramatise and make visual what is merely (and, inevitably, incompletely) described on the page. But, repeatedly, Jackson's film dramatises and elaborates what is at best only implied or minimally present in Tolkien's book. Thus, we are shown Boromir's corpse in his funeral boat *twice* in the film: his death scene is reprised; an

---

[16] *TT*, 33, 'The Evenstar'.

[17] *TT*, 38, 'Arwen's Fate'.

'Refracted Light'

extended flashback develops movingly Faramir's relationship with his dead brother; and their father Denethor, in his madness, is made to see a ghostly vision of his dead son. We are also made to see this all-too-visible 'bodying forth' (nowhere alluded to in the book), and we begin to appreciate the significance of this miniature *Hamlet* variant before our more than 'mind's eye'.[18]

Denethor's crazed distress at the death of his elder and favoured son finds a parallel in the belated realisation by Théoden of the death of his (only) son, Théodred. Again, the film develops and embellishes the little that the book tells us of this matter. In the book, Théodred's name is mentioned a mere six times, his death happens off-stage, and the only words his father says of him are: 'I have no child. Théodred my son is slain' (*LR*, p. 523). In the film, Théodred's death and its purport are very much in view: he is discovered, unconscious, on the battlefield; we see him dying from his wounds, attended by his cousins Éowyn and Éomer; we see his corpse as Éowyn mourns over it (before Wormtongue's entry); we see Théoden's stricken discovery that his son is dead; we see his corpse again at his funeral; and then we watch and listen to Théoden and Gandalf reflect, with tragic dignity, on Théodred's death and its aftermath.[19] Théoden's words and tears, as he reflects that 'no parent should have to bury

---

[18] See *FR*, 46, 'The Road Goes Ever On'; *TT*, 40, 'The Window on the West'; *RK*, 11, 'Minas Tirith'; *TT*, 41, 'Sons of the Steward'; *RK*, 22, 'The Wizard's Pupil'.

[19] *TT*, 7, 'Massacre at the Fords of Isen'; *TT*, 8, 'The Banishment of Éomer'; *TT*, 20, 'The King of the Golden Hall'; *TT*, 21, 'The Funeral of Théodred'; *TT*, 22, 'Simbelmynë on the Burial Mounds'.

their child', are among the most moving in the film.[20]

No opportunity is spurned by Jackson and his team to ventilate the death theme in the film. One of the film's many strengths is the way in which dialogue is effectively used, not merely to advance the plot and develop character, but for informative, expository purposes. This has the further merit of enriching the thematic freight of the film economically. Thus, in the course of a seemingly casual conversation between Aragorn and Théoden on the way to Helm's Deep, Éowyn's life story is unobtrusively adverted to: Théoden tells Aragorn of how orcs had killed her father and her mother had died of grief (information which readers of the book can only glean from an appendix: *LR*, p. 1070). Moments later, they themselves are attacked by orcs, in the course of which Aragorn appears to fall to his death.[21] This episode and its (apparent) upshot is certainly not in the book, and the film contains many such moments. Shippey argues that Aragorn's subsequent revival is there to show that 'there is always hope'[22] – an important Tolkienian emphasis (to which I shall return). Brian Rosebury, on the other hand, thinks that there are too many implied deaths, the cumulative effect of which is to 'flatten out the plot' (an excess of peripeteia).[23]

---

[20] The only textual basis for this remark is perhaps Théoden's earlier (*King Lear*-like) comment to Gandalf: 'Alas for Boromir the brave! The young perish and the old linger, withering' (*LR*, p. 517).

[21] *TT*, 34, 'The Wolves of Isengard'.

[22] Shippey, *The Road to Middle-earth*, p. 419.

[23] Brian Rosebury, *Tolkien: A Cultural Phenomenon*, 2nd edn (Basingstoke: Palgrave Macmillan, 2003), p. 219.

'Refracted Light'

Ubiquitous as death is in Tolkien's text, the film is still more relentless in this respect. Many characters are threatened with, or express their fear of, death at various points. Several important characters actually die (notably Boromir, Théoden, Denethor, Gollum and Saruman). Gandalf dies (reprised in the film), but returns to life. A few characters who do not die in the book are killed off in the film (Haldir and Damrod most graphically and lingeringly). But the list of characters who are (wrongly) thought to be dead or dying at some point or other includes Frodo, Merry, Pippin, Aragorn, Faramir, Éowyn and Arwen. Frodo, indeed, appears to be killed on three (if not four) occasions.[24] This cannot be satisfactorily explained by the film director's understandable wish to maximise dramatic tension in order to ensure an exciting movie, even though in an interview for the extended DVDs Peter Jackson sometimes gives the impression that such a motive is paramount: of the ending to *The Two Towers*, for example, he observes: 'we had to create an emotionally fulfilling climax … We had the disadvantage of not having anybody dying [at the end of] this film …' (unlike Boromir at the end of *The Fellowship of the Ring*). But elsewhere, Jackson stresses that he wished to be true to the spirit of Tolkien's work and to reflect Tolkien's major thematic concerns. Oddly, each successive draft of the screenplay took the writers closer to the book, Jackson insisted. In practice this sometimes meant that crucial passages in Tolkien's original had to be included in the film even if a

---

[24] Though, because of Jackson's 'interlacement' or chronological intercutting of the book's various strands, the Mouth of Sauron episode in the film, unlike in the book, cannot fool the *viewer* into believing that Frodo is captured and/or dead. Cf. *LR*, pp. 889-90 and *RK*, 64, 'The Mouth of Sauron'.

speech had to be relocated,[25] or given to another character.[26]

But the *invented* passages of dialogue are perhaps still more revealing of the screenwriters' purposes. Consider the following three instances. As Gandalf escapes from Orthanc, Saruman declares: 'So you have chosen death'.[27] When Frodo 'accidentally' puts on the Ring in Bree, the voice of the Eye of Sauron whispers menacingly to him (it is difficult to catch the words easily without subtitles): 'There is no life in the void: only death'.[28] And Arwen emphatically declares to Aragorn: 'I choose a mortal life'.[29] The instances could be multiplied, but the main point is clear enough. Death is more than a leitmotif running through Jackson's film. Nor is the emphasis on death a merely adventitious, unintended by-product. What the film actually presents is a complex rhetoric of death and

---

[25] As with Gandalf's key speech to Frodo about Gollum ('Many that live deserve death. And some that die deserve life …'), switched from the chapter 'The Shadow of the Past' (*LR*, p. 59) to Moria in the film (*FR*, 34, 'A Journey in the Dark').

[26] For example, Gandalf's splendidly Shakespearean speech about Éowyn ('But who knows what she spoke to the darkness, alone, in the bitter watches of the night, when all her life seemed shrinking, and the walls of her bower closing in about her, a hutch to trammel some wild thing in?': *LR*, p. 867), relocated *and* reallocated (surprisingly effectively) to Wormtongue who addresses Éowyn directly (*TT*, 20, 'The King of the Golden Hall'). As Philippa Boyens observed in one of the DVD interviews: 'what's crucial isn't who says it, but that *someone* says it'.

[27] *FR*, 22, 'Rivendell'.

[28] *FR*, 15, 'At the Sign of the Prancing Pony'.

[29] *FR*, 26, 'The Evenstar', repeated in Aragorn's dream: *RK*, 30, 'Andúril – Flame of the West'.

'Refracted Light'

the beyond, in which a Tolkienian argument is allowed subtly to unfold.

This becomes clear if one considers various revealing juxtapositions which Jackson and the editorial team contrive. Some of these are telling indeed, and are not simply the consequence of opting for a chronological reordering of the book's events. This is especially clear in *The Return of the King*, where contrast after contrast builds to create a sustained meditation on death and attitudes to death. In scene 43, 'The Choices of Master Samwise', Sam thinks Frodo is dead, then learns that he is not dead, but only drugged. Moments later we are back in Minas Tirith, listening to Pippin insisting to Denethor that his son Faramir is not dead. Denethor will not listen, for he wants a funeral pyre for himself and his son. Pippin looks for help from Gandalf, but before they can reach Denethor and Faramir, they encounter the Chief of the Nazgûl, who asks Gandalf: 'Do you not know death when you see it, old man?' But then we hear the horns of the Rohan army, and the camera pans to the battlefield where twelve times the Rohirrim chant their battle-cry of 'Death!' The Battle of the Pelennor Fields unfolds, and we witness the deaths of Théoden and the Witch-King, and Éomer's misapprehension that his sister Éowyn is dead. And so on. The film never lets up.

It is perhaps an understatement to point out that the film's perspective throughout is indeed mortal (as it is in the book).[30] A telling sequence, omitted from the theatrical version, can be seen in the extended version of *The Return*

---

[30] This is made clear from the outset when we look over Bilbo's shoulder as he writes the opening pages of what will turn out (self-consciously) to be *The Hobbit* and *The Lord of the Rings* (FR, 2, 'Concerning Hobbits'), a point emphasised again at the end as we see Frodo at the same desk concluding the work (RK, 75, 'Homeward Bound').

of the King, as Gandalf expatiates critically to Pippin upon Gondorian culture and history; he attributes Gondor's decline to an obsession with death and living in the past: 'Kings made tombs more splendid than the houses of the living', he comments.[31] But not only can a (mortal) culture be thus described, so too can individual characters define themselves by their attitude to death, and their behaviour in the face of it. While Aragorn is able to declare as he sets out on the Paths of the Dead: 'I do not fear death', Denethor embraces death precisely out of fear and cowardice: 'Better to die sooner than late. For die we must'.[32] Denethor's is the voice of despair and, solipsistically, he attempts to commit suicide and to cremate Faramir at the same time; from the latter deed he is prevented by the courage of Pippin and the power of Gandalf. In fact, nearly all the main characters are made to show courage in the face of death, and to display hope rather than despair. Jackson was evidently keen that Tolkien's distinctive amalgam of Northern heroic code and Catholic metaphysic should not merely inform, but shape, the film's dominant ethic.

As Patrick Curry points out in a DVD interview clip, despair is not only a sin, theologically (an unforgivable sin if persisted in), but (quite simply and starkly) a mistake. This essentially Catholic position finds corroboration in Gandalf's words to the Council of Elrond: 'despair is only for those who see the end beyond all doubt. We do not' (*LR*, p. 269). Hence Gandalf's counsel, not of despair but of

---

[31] *RK*, 12, 'The Decline of Gondor'. These are the words of Faramir in the book (*LR*, p. 678), but since he is Gandalf's 'pupil', the reattribution is apt.

[32] *RK*, 33, 'Dwimorberg – The Haunted Mountain'; *RK*, 41, 'The Tomb of the Stewards' (the book has 'burn' for 'die': *LR*, p. 825).

'Refracted Light'

hope, during the Last Debate: 'We must walk open-eyed into that trap, with courage, but small hope' (*LR*, p. 880), a sentiment given to Aragorn to express in the film. In that scene Gimli sums up the Northern theory of courage (almost) perfectly as he comments on Aragorn's plan: 'Certainty of death ... small chance of success ...what are we waiting for?'[33] Gimli's attitude contrasts vividly with Legolas's earlier in the film trilogy. Jackson occasionally ratchets up the tension in the film by contriving (or elaborating) a disagreement or conflict between characters which is not to be found in Tolkien. It is striking that the only heated exchange between Aragorn and Legolas in the film (there is no such disagreement in the book) is just before the Battle of the Hornburg, Legolas pointing out how overwhelming the odds are against them (ten thousand against three hundred), and Aragorn refusing to give in to despair, despite the seeming inevitability of defeat and death.[34]

If despair is anathema, courage is the *sine qua non* – for Jackson as much as, if not more than, Tolkien. That this is so can be seen from two of the most powerful and effective scenes in the film. The first shows Théoden in a sombre moment of self-questioning ('Who am I?') donning his armour before the battle of Helm's Deep. Jackson has Théoden chant a modified, abridged version of the poem recited by Aragorn in the original:

Where is the horse and the rider?

---

[33] *RK*, 59, 'The Last Debate'. *Almost* perfectly: '*no* chance of success' would have more accurately reflected the Northern theory of courage – fighting on when all *is* lost.

[34] *TT*, 45, 'The Glittering Caves'. Théoden takes a similar line ahead of the Battle of the Pelennor Fields: *RK*, 32, 'No More Despair'.

Textual Revisions

> Where is the horn that was blowing?
>
> They have passed like rain on the mountain, like a wind in the meadow.
>
> The days have gone down in the West behind the hills into shadow.

As he speaks, we are shown the desperately young boys being equipped for the battle. Théoden's final rhetorical question ('How did it come to this?') is unanswered. This resonant reworking of Tolkien's poem is a filmic triumph, undoubtedly one of the high points of the film, with Bernard Hill especially effective as the King of Rohan.[35] The second scene is similar and shows Faramir and his knights of Gondor riding towards Osgiliath – knowing that they are going to near-certain death – about to be bloodily slaughtered. The slow motion footage is finely done, intercut with shots of Faramir's father Denethor (who has sent his son and the knights of Gondor to their doom) portrayed as a Field Marshal Earl Haig figure from the First World War, greedily feasting, secure behind the battle lines. The juice of the tomato spurting down Denethor's chin as the volley of arrows whiz through the air is no cinematic cliché, not least because Pippin's song, 'Home is behind', is the voice-over, and this offers more than nostalgia, with its last word – 'fades' – fading before a bell is heard mournfully tolling.[36]

---

[35] *LR*, p. 508; *TT*, 46, 'Where is the Horse and the Rider?'. Tolkien's 'original' is itself a rendering of the *hwær cwom* (or *ubi sunt*) sequence from the Anglo-Saxon poem, 'The Wanderer'.

[36] *RK*, 28, 'The Sacrifice of Faramir'. Here, as elsewhere in the film (see, for example, the following scene, *RK*, 29, 'Marshalling at Dunharrow'), the sheer brutality of battle, and the very real fear it elicits, are made vivid.

'Refracted Light'

In the end – and all art, it might be said, is about death 'in the end' – death is treated with due seriousness in Jackson's film of *The Lord of the Rings*. Neither minimised nor sensationalised, neither glorified nor sentimentalised, its reality is confronted, faced up to, courageously, but (in the end) accepted. Twice Sam speaks to Frodo at the climactic moments in the Cracks of Doom. First, to urge him to destroy the Ring: 'Just let it go!' Second, to urge him not to give up clinging to the chasm's edge: 'Don't you let go! Don't let go!' and then 'Reach!' Inevitably, one is reminded of the dying Théoden's last words to Éowyn: 'You have to let me go'. When to let go: Gandalf, Aragorn, Frodo, Théoden and Boromir knew when to let go. Saruman, Denethor, Gollum and the Nazgûl did not know when to let go. And critical to knowing, it seems, is the overlooked theological virtue, hope, even though hope (by definition) has to be, in Tolkien's memorable tautology already quoted, 'Hope without guarantees'.[37] Hope: that movement of heart and head that reaches out to a beyond, somewhere, refusing to admit the finality (while conceding the reality) of death. The crucial dialogue is between Gandalf and Pippin. Gandalf, his mirth bubbling over despite the desperateness of their situation in the very midst of the Siege of Gondor, smilingly reassures Pippin:

> 'Death is just another path, one that we all must take. The grey rain curtain of this world rolls back and all turns to silver glass. And then you see it … white shores, and, beyond, a far green country under a swift sunrise.'[38]

---

[37] *Letters of J. R. R. Tolkien*, p. 237.

[38] *RK*, 49, '"A Far Green Country"'. Pippin, it must be admitted, does not look completely reassured! The words are adapted from the book's final

Shippey observes of this episode in the film: 'One feels that here the wise men, Tolkien or Gandalf or Jackson, are talking to everyone, and talking to them about death, a subject well beyond the range of most Hollywood rhetoric.'[39] Similarly, Charles Moseley makes the astute point that Tolkien somehow managed to 'hit some mysterious need' through his work; he continues: 'Tolkien seems to have spoken to this spiritual need. This mythology of and for England seems fundamentally religious, keeping the rumour of the Other alive in a materialist culture and mind-set'.[40] Tolkien himself could not have been clearer: '*The Lord of the Rings* is of course a fundamentally religious and Catholic work; unconsciously so at first, but consciously in the revision.'[41] Indeed, Tolkien's very method in *The Lord of the Rings* is one which goes beyond requiring of his readers a suspension of disbelief. So comprehensive and credible is the Middle-earth which Tolkien has 'created', so thoroughgoingly three-dimensional, that belief itself – belief in an other reality – is thereby invigorated. 'What if?' becomes 'Perhaps'. In fine, Tolkien's grapplings with this *ur*-theme throughout his writings – from his earliest tales which eventually found their way into the posthumously published *Silmarillion*, through his short stories, poems,

---

chapter (*LR*, p. 1030) and are included in the song, 'Into the West', sung hauntingly by Annie Lennox.

[39] Shippey, *The Road to Middle-earth*, p. 418.

[40] Charles Moseley, *J. R. R. Tolkien* (Plymouth: Northcote House, 1997), pp. 78-9.

[41] *Letters of J. R. R. Tolkien*, p. 172.

scholarly and critical works, and writings for children, and culminating in *The Lord of the Rings* – exert such a powerful fascination over his readers precisely because he is tapping into a deep spiritual hunger – a hunger that is insatiable and (if anything) growing. Tolkien's writings both whet this appetite and feed it – at least for anyone who has not completely lost the child's capacity to wonder. It is this strangely numinous quality, above all others, which Jackson has managed to evoke and capture, awesomely, in his filmic interpretation of *The Lord of the Rings*. And the success of the film – artistic and popular – is explained by that achievement.

Tolkien, in his poem 'Mythopoeia', writes of what he terms the 'sub-creative' process. Tolkien likens sub-creation to the refracting and transmuting of white light into the colours of the spectrum:

> the refracted light
> … splintered from a single White
> to many hues, and endlessly combined
> in living shapes that move from mind to mind.[42]

It is a metaphor not simply for artistic inspiration (sacred or profane), but for aesthetic communication from writer (and director) to reader (and viewer) – 'from mind to mind', indeed. In the case of *The Lord of the Rings* it may truly be said that, from Tolkien through Jackson to the many millions of viewers of the film, there was indeed

---

[42] J. R. R. Tolkien, 'Mythopoeia', in *Tree and Leaf: Including the Poem 'Mythopoeia'; 'The Homecoming of Beorhtnoth, Beorhthelm's Son'*, ed. by Christopher Tolkien, new edn (London: HarperCollins, 2001), pp. 85-90 (p. 87).

such a movement of minds, and that Tolkien's 'original' light was not broken in vain.

Bibliography

Primary Works

Tolkien

Tolkien, J. R. R., *Letters of J. R. R. Tolkien: A Selection*, ed. by Humphrey Carpenter with Christopher Tolkien (London: Allen & Unwin, 1981)

Tolkien, J. R. R., *The Lord of the Rings*, 50th anniversary edn (London: HarperCollins, 2005)

Tolkien, J. R. R., 'Mythopoeia', in *Tree and Leaf: Including the Poem 'Mythopoeia'; 'The Homecoming of Beorhtnoth, Beorhthelm's Son'*, ed. by Christopher Tolkien, new edn (London: HarperCollins, 2001)

Tolkien, J. R. R., 'On Fairy-Stories', in *Tree and Leaf: Including the Poem 'Mythopoeia'; 'The Homecoming of Beorhtnoth, Beorhthelm's Son'*, ed. by Christopher Tolkien, new edn (London: HarperCollins, 2001)

Jackson

The Lord of the Rings, dir. by Peter Jackson, special extended DVD edn (New Line Cinema, 2002-4)

Secondary Works

Carpenter, Humphrey, *J. R. R. Tolkien: A Biography* (London: Allen & Unwin, 1977)

Garth, John, *Tolkien and the Great War: The Threshold of Middle-earth* (London: HarperCollins, 2004)

Grant, Patrick, *Six Modern Authors and Problems of Belief* (London: Macmillan, 1979)

Hammond, Wayne G., and Christina Scull, *'The Lord of the Rings': A Reader's Companion* (London: HarperCollins, 2005)

James, Henry, 'The Art of Fiction', in *The House of Fiction: Essays on the Novel by Henry James,* ed. by Leon Edel, new edn (London: Mercury Books, 1962), 23-45

Jameson, Fredric, *The Political Unconscious: Narrative as a Socially Symbolic Act* (Ithaca, NY: Cornell University Press, 1981)

Moseley, Charles, *J. R. R. Tolkien* (Plymouth: Northcote House, 1997)

Rosebury, Brian, *Tolkien: A Cultural Phenomenon*, 2nd edn (Basingstoke: Palgrave Macmillan, 2003)

Shippey, Tom, *The Road to Middle-earth,* rev. and exp. edn (London: HarperCollins, 2005)

Textual Revisions

Shippey, Tom, 'Tolkien as a Post-War Writer', in *Proceedings of the J. R. R. Tolkien Centenary Conference 1992*, ed. by Patricia Reynolds and Glen GoodKnight (Milton Keynes: Tolkien Society; Altadena, CA: Mythopoeic Press, 1995), pp. 84-93